❖

Short Fiction in France
1800-1850

Short Fiction in France

1800-1850

✦ ✦ ✦ ✦ ✦ ✦ ✦ ✦ ✦ ✦ ✦

ALBERT J. GEORGE

✦ ✦ ✦ ✦ ✦

SYRACUSE UNIVERSITY PRESS 1964

Manufactured in the United States of America
by The Heffernan Press of Worcester, Massachusetts
and Vail-Ballou Press of Binghamton, New York

FOR PEGGY

Acknowledgments

FEW BOOKS are produced unaided, and this one is no exception. Unfortunately, I can only indicate the extent of my debt, for the ritual words of acknowledgment rarely convey the depths of gratitude. I should like to thank my colleagues, Professor Edwin Cady of Indiana, Professor Antonio Pace of Syracuse, and Professor Edward Sullivan of Princeton for their advice and patient work on the manuscript. After my daughter Martha proofread the drafts, Mrs. Helen Renske carefully typed them from battered pages. To all of them, my heartfelt thanks. But most of all, I wish to express my appreciation to Professor Jean-Albert Bédé of Columbia University, master and faithful friend, for the aid and comfort given me.

ALBERT J. GEORGE

Poitiers, France
Spring, 1964

Contents

Contents

Introduction

UNTIL RECENTLY, literary historians have paid scant heed to the development of the forms of short fiction in France. Poetry, the novel, the drama, have all received their share of monographs, learned essays, or scholarly congresses, but the brief narrative has been ignored except by a few dedicated writers.

In July, 1913, Mrs. A. Taylor published "The Short Story in France 1800-1900" in the *Edinburgh Review*. This was a quick survey of the characteristic traits of the major writers of the nineteenth century. Fifteen years later James B. Tharp prepared a dissertation on "The Fantastic Short Story, 1850-90" at the University of Illinois, but not until 1941 did the first half of the century receive any consideration, in Alfred Engstrom's thesis, "The Artistic Short Story before Maupassant" (Chapel Hill). Engstrom subsequently published "The Formal Short Story in France and Its Development before 1850" in *Studies in Language and Literature* (University of North Carolina Press, 1945). And in 1952 Robert Lewis investigated the brief fiction of the early period more broadly in his dissertation, "The Development of the French Short Story, 1745-1850" (Johns Hopkins, 1952).

Slightly more attention has been paid to specific varieties of the early nineteenth-century brief narrative, as in Edith Cumings' *The Literary Development of the Romantic Fairy Tale in France* (Bryn Mawr, 1934) or Pierre-Georges Castex's *Le Conte fantastique en France* (Corti, 1951). Most scholarly work, however, has centered on particular writers, as, for ex-

1

ample, Trahard's *Prosper Mérimée et l'art de la nouvelle* (Nizet, 1952), or Edward Sullivan's *Maupassant* (London, Arnold, 1962).

One of the obstacles to any history of the development of the short narrative is the abundance of material. The writer of such a history must read a multitude of tales that poured from an ever multiplying number of magazines and periodicals; he must scan a bewildering variety of collections, and search through the works of a vast number of writers, few still famous, most now forgotten. Jules Sandeau, Alphonse Karr, and Frédéric Soulié must be considered in company with Stendhal, Gautier, and Balzac. In addition there are always the prolific, if undistinguished, lady writers, the purveyors of popular tales, and the specialists in Pollyanna literature. From this cornucopia of riches a selection must be made which can be fashioned into a meaningful pattern.

A second circumstance poses difficulties of another order. Whereas American and British critics have long paid attention to the development of the various forms of brief fiction, the French have only recently framed a body of opinion on the subject. In the United States clear distinctions have traditionally been made between such varieties of the short narrative as the sketch, the tale, the formal short story, or the anecdote. In France, on the contrary, the designations *conte* and *nouvelle* had so little meaning during the first part of the nineteenth century that they were often used interchangeably or confused with the word *roman*. Most writers made length the principal criterion of distinction and, with scant heed paid to the potentialities of the genre, usually clung close to the tradition of the oral anecdote or the chronicle. Writers were just beginning to seek new techniques for a rapidly developing art form that could express radically different views of human behavior in the dynamic and uncertain world of post-Revolutionary France. In effect they were in the process of suggesting a definition of short fiction. The brief narrative boasted an ancestry that reached far back of the novel and the romance. As old as poetry, it had, however, long suffered from a lack of literary status because of its oral origins and plebeian associations. For historical reasons the short story did not "arrive" in England, the United States, or France until the nineteenth century, when it finally shouldered its way into a respectable place in the hierarchy of literary forms; hence it is almost impossible to pose any definitions *a priori*. The problem indicates the necessity of studying the undifferentiated older forms of the short tale, whatever we may choose to call them, in order to arrive at conclusions meaningful in modern terms. Furthermore, since no French writer of the romantic age ever bothered to theorize on short prose fiction, each author's work must be queried for his understanding of the genre.

The present work is concerned with changes in the conception of French short fiction which occurred between 1800 and 1850, and the modes of expression then developed. The dates are, of course, only approximate, intended merely to suggest the period from the French Revolution to the end of romanticism, or from Xavier de Maistre to Gérard de Nerval. The turn of the century represents the shift to the conditions that ultimately would produce romanticism but, fifty years later, many of the men important in the first development of French short fiction had died: Stendhal (1842), Nodier (1844), Chateaubriand (1848), Balzac (1850), Nerval (1855). Still others had completed their major work by then: Borel left for Africa in 1846, Mérimée stopped writing for publication by 1847, while Gautier had composed most of his stories by 1850. A great generation disappeared at mid-century and another, with new and different ideas, pushed forward to take its place.

So many men and women turned their hand to short fiction between 1800 and 1850 that it has not been possible to consider the work of all of them. This study is not intended to be exhaustive, but to include material illustrative of the problems encountered and solved, haphazardly at first, by the early practitioners of brief fiction. It hopes to relate the history of a form, the *new* short story rather than the medieval or classical one, from the time of its first clouded conception, through the travail of gestation, to the moment when it acquired distinct personality.

To have done otherwise would have resulted in a tedious catalogue of unknown names, much repetition, and so much incidental information that any general lines of development would have been obliterated. Even a strictly historical order is impossible, because most of the authors discussed were contemporaries. Therefore the presentation, while more or less chronological, groups the writers according to similarities of manner or of doctrine in tales which *they* considered short and most of which were initially published in periodicals. Thus Balzac, Stendhal, and Mérimée are encountered first, followed by the great romantics, then the second generation, Gautier included. The works of each are treated in separate essays, in order to indicate personal development as well as to show relationships both to contemporaries and to the genre as a whole. Individual writers are also measured against the brief fiction published in the mass media, to permit gauging the work of the better known writers against the norm of current taste and performance.

Two major difficulties were that none of the writers discussed the aesthetics of the short form and that many of the stories are unfamiliar to modern readers. It has been necessary to provide résumés of plots sufficiently ample to make the commentary intelligible. The discussions have had to consider, at least partly, how the author wrote, how he exploited his material, in order to allow reconstruction of each writer's concept of brief fiction. And because the terms *conte* and *nouvelle* had so little specific meaning for the age, they have deliberately been shunned to avoid implying distinctions that did not then exist. Instead, the phrases "brief fiction" or "short narrative" are employed and, where proper, the English distinctions of sketch, portrait, formal short story, or chronicle.

Few scholarly works stand for long, since every generation finds it necessary to view the literature of the past in its own terms. The purpose of this book is to suggest meaningful patterns in the development of French short fiction during the age of romanticism, to begin the task of winnowing a large number of facts for their kernels of meaning.

The problem is the old one of the forest and the trees, for certainly no literary generation prior to romanticism had ever felt the accumulated pressures of so much historical happenstance. A centuries-old political framework, apparently indestructibly fixed in the mores of a people, had suddenly disintegrated into the Revolution. Then for a quarter of a century France careened from one government to another, to land in the arms of Napoleon and to march proudly through the Imperial epic all the way back to the Bourbons. When Charles X stubbornly threw away a throne, Louis-Philippe became king of the French and the darling of the middle class. Political stability seemed to have left the country in the wake of the emigration at the end of the eighteenth century.

The whole world, in fact, appeared to be rearranging itself kaleidoscopically. Not only had the source of power shifted to the people, but the slow growth of education was insidiously enlarging the cultural horizons of the nation. By 1830 the first impact of the Industrial Revolution had brought disturbing symptoms of technological change as France moved ponderously into the modern world. Railroads and factories began to blight the cities; slums proliferated, to be jammed by refugees from recurrent agricultural depressions. Concomitantly, there appeared the scourges of alcoholism, crowded and substandard housing, a marked increase in illegitimacy and in the child death rate.

Yet this same socially destructive technology had a brighter side; it provided writers for the first time in history with the means to reach a mass audience. New presses, new methods of making paper and ink permitted publishers to dream happily of constantly expanding sales to every literate Frenchman. The number of large-circulation periodicals increased with the reader potential, and when the penny press burst on the scene about 1830 both these media provided an unexpected ready market for authors. No longer did writers need to beg for the humiliating support of patrons; they now stood as defiant entrepreneurs of their own brain children, dependent for economic security only on the tastes of a fickle reading public.

Superficially, the romantics seemed to have rejected the great literary tradition that was their heritage. At least they thought so. They loudly cried revolution and heaped scorn on a literary value system that had atrophied into neoclassicism. The bourgeoisie, which had inherited the political and social earth, reacted in scandalized fashion to brash young men who appeared to be threatening the stabilizing forces of French civilization. The result was a bitter wrangle over the purposes and functions of art, with strong political overtones, that continued through most of the nineteenth century.

However, the break with literary tradition had actually never occurred. By the time the young romantics began to write, roughly a third of a century had passed since the fall of the Ancien Régime, and they were grappling with an age startlingly different from the old monarchy. In reality, they had another universe to fathom, with problems peculiarly their own, and they rapidly discovered, as first they dutifully emulated their elders, that the old forms and attitudes no longer sufficed to express their concerns. They had to adapt the old genres, the theater, for instance, or develop new ones, like the novel, in order to speak of matters meaningful to their contemporaries. Hence, they objected violently to the tyranny of the unities and the Alexandrine, experimented with verse forms, and turned to prose, once anathema to the purists of the Ancien Régime. Yet, as modern scholarship has demonstrated, they were not nearly so radical as they claimed. In many ways their ideas and work reveal a strong kinship with the classical age.

In prose, however, they made a mark all their own. The era

of romanticism saw the appearance of the first giants of the French novel, Balzac and Stendhal. Hugo's group of poets considered prose to have connotations of the vulgar, but when technology opened a large market for it, with no corresponding increase in the sale of verse, they capitulated to the siren call of the cash register and produced memoirs, romances à la Scott, or novels. Short fiction appeared, too. When newspapers and periodicals began to compete for subscribers, the publishers discovered that literature had a commercial application of tremendous interest: readers could be induced to switch their journalistic allegiance for a good *feuilleton*. The brief narrative, once the ugly duckling of French literature, metamorphosed into an economic swan as editors encouraged writers to maintain the great output they needed. Between 1829 and 1832 so many *contes* and *nouvelles* appeared that the critics groaned in complaint.

The romantics began to create this short fiction in the only way they knew, by continuing a long tradition that still clung closely to its origins in oral anecdote. Because the genre had roots in the folk tale, it had difficulty overcoming its humble beginnings as pure entertainment. This lowly position in the hierarchy of a literature oriented to the worship of poetry had become almost legalized by the firm dicta of the classical critics. Given such a handicap, the short narrative initially had few illustrious practitioners. Consequently, the characteristic mode of storytelling followed that of the old chronicle, the history, in which the sole voice heard was that of an author interested in exposition. A writer stated the conditions of the story, then related events chronologically, often without any sense of climax and heavily dependent on social stereotypes. Many of these stories are only expanded anecdotes. To this legacy, the eighteenth century added the fairy tale, exotic *contes*, moralizing tales for readers of all ages, and the *conte philosophique*. For the older structure it increasingly substituted the technique of effectism, that is, moving a plot from one emotional crisis to another, but even after this innovation writers persisted in telling stories in the same old way.

Modern French short fiction was, in fact, born during the romantic period, not the least of the age's contributions to literature. Tentatively at first, then with increasing confidence and sophistication, the romantics turned their considerable talent to the brief narrative. Many of them treated it cavalierly, but from men like Nodier, Mérimée, and Gautier short fiction received its first serious attention. By mid-century, after a long struggle to change the genre from a vehicle for didacticism to an autonomous art form, it had attained sufficient respectability to warrant investigation by conscious artists.

However, most of the short tales of the first half of the century were written without any sense of a poetics. True, Chateaubriand, Constant, and Mérimée had added an intellectual dimension but, in general, the words *conte* and *nouvelle* had ceased to yield meaningful distinctions. Each was used indiscriminately, as with Nodier and Musset, to denote shortness, although they were sometimes interchanged with the word *roman*. But this vagueness did not prevent the appearance of such brilliant natural storytellers as Paul de Kock or Dumas *père*, who differed from their predecessors only in their sense of story.

Over a period of fifty years almost all the themes popular from the time of Chateaubriand to that of Nerval appeared in short fiction: primitivism in *René*, the cult of the uninhibited and unbounded personality in Stendhal, Dumas' young world of personal nobility, Nerval's private universe of the subconscious. The characters included every contemporary stereotype: the adolescent in search of himself, vampires, assorted ghouls, hot-blooded Corsicans, Italians, Spaniards, materialistic Philistines, frustrated *bousingos*, the *Jeunes-France*, and countless unhappy lovers. In addition, lady writers created a kind of agony column, ringing all the changes on the boy-meets-girl plot or, along with a few men, ground out a nauseatingly moral literature full of Pollyannas. And recent interest in historical subjects encouraged the primitivists and produced a spate of old legends and pseudohistorical tales.

Inevitably, the writing of so much short fiction led the romantics to seek new modes of expression, particularly when they found the old forms inadequate for expressing contemporary ideas. The age bubbled with experimentation and, since art is a way of thinking, some of these authors felt dissatisfied with the limitations of the genres they had inherited. The formal short story, as later defined by Poe, came into being with *Mateo Falcone*; the portrait reached its height in *René* and the *Curé de Tours*; Mérimée created the *nouvelle* and established the sketch with *L'Enlèvement de la redoute*. Slowly the words *conte* and *nouvelle* took on implied meaning: the *conte*, generally shorter in length, tended to focus on a single situation, while the longer *nouvelle* included a series of incidents for the analysis and development of character or motive.

Meanwhile, as they were arriving at these tentative definitions, the romantics were developing the art of brief fiction. At the end of the eighteenth century the short story remained a subsidiary of the *conte philosophique*, its techniques geared to creating exempla for some philosophical theorem, as in the case of *Atala*. Constant, however, took a long step forward with *Adolphe* by shedding this burden; preach he did, but not in connection with some *Etudes de la nature* or a *Génie du Christianisme*. In *Adolphe* the moralizing was no longer hung on the plot but made organic, implicit. Paradoxically, this shift made it difficult to strip short fiction of its didactic overlay. Then the brief narrative ran headlong into its more robust relative, the novel, particularly the romance à la Scott. But the simultaneous, if unconcerted, efforts of Mérimée, Gautier, and Musset, finally built the short story into an autonomous art form out from the shadow of its giant cousin. After them, after Baudelaire and Nerval, it became possible to work *within* the genre, to soften the rigidity of a Mérimée as the brief narrative became more malleable, more fitted to express the aspirations of a modern, industrial world. Thus, by 1850, French literature had accumulated the literary wisdom necessary to permit the birth of modern short fiction.

The Historical Background

SEEN in the long perspective of history, the changing fortunes of the brief prose narrative illuminate the manner in which literary tastes change. The transformations of short fiction reveal the slow and often circuitous approach of succeeding generations to fresh understandings of art. New genres arise to satisfy changing social, economic, and political concepts or psychological insights. The history of forms, those unified structures which writers discovered to furnish satisfactory modes of expression, indicates a close relationship between social circumstances and literary media; it suggests that comprehension of the function of form, the conscious practice of a literary type, and the exploitation of its potentiality, vary with each new audience or major social shift. Moreover, this perspective reveals the speed with which scales of values changed, since some genres achieved popularity slowly, others more rapidly, while a few maintained their vitality even when transposed from verse to prose. In many instances forms carried overtones of status, being elaborated variously for the people, for the middle class, or for the aristocracy.

In the general development of French literature, prose long stood in the relationship of poor cousin to poetry. What literary sophistication existed in the earliest days of the nation was limited primarily to the monasteries. The first indigenous narrative works developed around the church or rose from the people, many of them simple anecdotes that betrayed their source in a strong oral tradition. The apologues, the exempla, the *contes dévots*, and the fables generally lacked artistic merit, burdened as they were apt to be with moral precept. Later there emerged the courtly, aristocratic *lais*, the *contes courtois*, and *dits*—forms much shorter than the verse *romans* and generally constructed around a single scene. The *lais*, some of which showed brilliant technique, dealt largely with folk material, often Celtic in origin. In the *fabliaux*, droll tales of adultery and corruption, the medieval period reached, perhaps, its peak of concision, though these *contes à rire* reveal their lowly origin in sketchy development and an insistence on the treatment of certain social types.

Verse stories dominated short fiction until prose finally began to come into its own during the fifteenth century, when great lords like Philippe of Burgundy favored transposing the *chansons de geste* into prose. The *Cent Nouvelles Nouvelles*, salty stories based on familiar erotic themes—impudent monks, betrayed husbands, and faithless women—indicate an appreciation of the brief tale little different from that of the medieval period. The *nouvelle* had become a dramatic, concentrated narrative that culminated in a surprise ending, but it had not advanced technically much beyond the anecdote or scenario.

By the sixteenth century prose had gained a modicum of prestige, although its ascendancy was impeded by the appearance of a clutch of major poetic talents. The *Pléiade* not only established the social acceptability of the French language, it also maintained verse as the prevailing literary mode. So completely did the group dominate the age that short fiction, popular in origin and oral in tradition, never could attain status. Rabelais' work, in fact, emphasized the low repute of prose in general. Those few, such as Bonaventure des Périers, Marguerite de Navarre and Noël du Fail, who tried to imitate Boccaccio, actually had little influence on subsequent writers.

Malherbe came, but the literary value system of the previous age persisted. However well the French seventeenth century understood Aristotle, its interpretation of his doctrine tended to ossify some of the judgments of the Renaissance. The classicists, who arranged the various forms of poetry in a clearly delineated hierarchy, with verse tragedy at the summit, tolerated prose only in the peripatetic romance and the fairy tale. The long, meandering *romans à clef* were considered no more than ephemeral diversions which provided thinly disguised portraits of contemporaries as a kind of sophisticated puzzle. Otherwise they constituted undistinguished collections of strange occurrences, long discussions, and incredible love affairs. And when these *romans* showed evidence of gaining popularity, Boileau shredded their respectability in the *Dialogue des héros de romans* with an attack that momentarily slowed the development of all prose forms.

Nonetheless, toward the end of the century, the salons fostered a rage for fairy tales that inevitably led to publications. Perrault, Mlle de la Force, Mme de Murat, Mme d'Aulnoy, Mlle Bernard, Mlle L'Héritier, and Mme Durand became fascinated with the plight of beautiful princesses in never-never land. Since these stories were manifestly tainted by popular origin, their authors dismissed them as bagatelles for fear of being associated with the *Bibliothèque bleue*, a collection for the little folk these aristocrats despised. In many cases they even avoided admission of authorship: Perrault hid behind his son's name and the Chevalier de Mailly used only initials, while Mme de Murat and Mlle de la Force wrote anonymously. The vogue spread to the provinces, even invaded the convents, but these narratives never quite attained social acceptance, as Cotgrave noted when he defined a *conte* as "a story, relation, historie; tale, fib, fable"; a *nouvelle* was a "strange report . . . or tale unheard of before."

As France passed through the eighteenth century, the brief narrative gained wider popularity, if no more respectability. The age tended to curb the loquacity of its predecessors: the novels of ten of twelve volumes slimmed down to one or two and the *Mercure* published *histoires* of ten to fifty pages. The translation of Galland's *Mille et une nuits* dethroned the fairy tales and introduced the *conte oriental*, to which were added the *conte licencieux*, the *conte moral*, *conte grec*, *conte fantaisiste et galant*, *conte satirique*, and the *conte philosophique*. A steady, though small, flow of short stories appeared every year until the Revolution.

The eighteenth century, hypnotized by the doctrine of classicism, never seriously challenged the values of the golden age of the past. Verse tragedy still ranked highest, and the scale ran all the way down to the prose forms. Yet the *romans* managed to remain in vogue and along with them followed an increase in the production of the various *contes*. Coincidentally the century witnessed the expansion of a middle class that became the source of almost all contemporary authors. These men continued to grind out mediocre tragedies and verse but they used prose more naturally and in increasingly greater measure than ever before. It suited their propensity for philosophizing, for didacticism and witty observation.

After the success of *Manon* in 1731, writers reacted strongly to the way in which readers relished short tales. Florian, with his *nouvelles*, Duclos, Crébillon, the Chevalier de Mouny, all tried their hand at simple narratives, generally moral, with little or no character development. As Paul Morillot noted, the eighteenth century had its own notion of brief fiction: "C'est un roman auquel personne ne croit, ni auteur, ni lecteur. . . . Un conte nous intéresse ou par le mérite de la narration, ou par la drôlerie du sujet, ou par l'esprit, ou par les allusions, ou par la profondeur même de la pensée; mais voilà tout." Even as late as the publication of the *Encyclopédie*, a writer like Diderot could define the *conte* as "un récit fabuleux en prose ou en vers . . . une suite de comédies enchaînées les unes aux autres . . . . Conte se dit aussi des histoires plaisantes, vraies ou fausses, que l'on fait dans la conversation."

Only Marmontel considered the brief narrative an art form. Writing in 1776, he contended in the supplement to the *Encyclopédie* that "un récit qui ne serait qu'un enchaînement d'adventures, sans cette tendance commune qui les réunit en un point et les réduit à l'unité, ce récit serait un roman et ne serait pas un conte." This constitutes perhaps the first suggestion that short fiction differed from the *roman* in more than length. Yet even he described the conte as a "genre léger," built on *négligence* and *finesse.*

However, when the romances began to pall, and as the age sharpened its wits, the eighteenth century found the short narrative admirable for the political and social satire in which it reveled. Voltaire, for example, refashioned the tale for his conception of the *conte philosophique.* By no means an invention of the eighteenth century, this amusing and vitriolic genre provided a vehicle for pungent observations on human foibles. Setting the figure of the *picaro* amidst elements from the fairy tale, Voltaire presented his characters just fully enough to support his ideas, arranged episodes to create suspense, and seasoned everything with razor-edged irony. He understood the *conte* as utilitarian, a vehicle for intellectual debate, and extended no sympathy to a protagonist whom he dumped into an inconsistent fictional world. Only the ideas and the satire counted in this fusion of philosophy with the imaginary voyage.

Voltaire represented as conscious an approach to brief fiction as the century offered. Most other attempts flowed from the pens of the untalented, many from the lady writers who blossomed in considerable numbers. After 1760, especially, the century witnessed the rise of a literary feminism that signaled a determined revolt against a masculine world. Some, like Mme de Mazarin, Mme de Grammont, Mme de Tencin, were seeking solid educations, becoming active patronesses of the arts. As exclusively feminine periodicals like the *Bibliothèque des femmes* and the *Journal des Dames* made their appearance, the ladies inevitably succumbed to the urge to write. Gentlewomen like Mlle Gaillard rhymed quantities of bad verse, but it was the novelists who swamped the presses with *histoires galantes* and rambling, sentimental *contes.* Mme de Gomez even managed to inflate the *Cent Nouvelles* into thirty-five volumes. So enthusiastically did women turn to literature that, at the beginning of the nineteenth century, one fusty Sylvain Maréchal proposed *Un Projet de loi portant défense d'apprendre à lire aux femmes*.

Meanwhile the ever curious Diderot was inquiring into the nature of brief fiction. In the preface to the *Deux Amis de Bourbonne*, he divided the *conte* into three categories: *merveilleux*, *plaisant*, and *historique*. The first depended on exaggeration and hypothetical truth, the second demanded only gaiety, variety, even extravagance, while the third "a pour objet la vérité vigoureuse: il veut intéresser, toucher, entraîner." And yet, for all the freshness of his view, Diderot still thought in terms of an oral tradition. As he explained in the introduction to *Ceci n'est pas un conte*, "Lorsqu'on fait un conte, c'est à quelqu'un qui l'écoute: et pour peu que le conte dure, il est rare que le conteur ne soit pas interrompu quelquefois par son auditeur."

Bernardin de Saint-Pierre's *Chaumière indienne* (1791) indicates how little the tradition of the brief narrative had changed during a century which revamped so much else. Bernardin produced a minor variation on the philosophical tale, filled with exotic detail and complete with a weeping hero. He paid homage to primitivism in a story the major portion of which was a monologue. Full of clichés such as "la vérité est une perle fine," the *Chaumière* contained a diatribe against civilization. In the sentimental tradition of the end of the century, Bernardin used the framework structure, a story within a story, to have his wandering hero find truth in mystic India, but the result resembled a humanitarian sermon more than a tale. He paid little attention to the integrity of his fictional world, being primarily concerned with manipulating flat characters toward an edifying end consistent with his *Etudes de la nature*.

From 1798 to the beginning of the nineteenth century short fiction was completely eclipsed by the excitement of the day's events. Political man, long frustrated during the eighteenth century, burst forth to dominate the development of society for more than a decade. France suffered the travail of a new world a-borning, and the sentimental heroes of the immediate past found that they could not breathe in the epic atmosphere of current events. The Revolution, played to the staccato counterpoint of marching feet, made the creation of imaginary worlds revoltingly innocuous at a time when exciting dramas of life and death were acted out publicly for the highest stakes imaginable. The issues of personal existence and national survival rendered the petty concerns of petty lives anodyne and foolish. Not until France had solved a multitude of pressing problems could the writing of prose fiction resume its place in the national life.

II

Transition

Xavier de Maistre

AUTHORS caught astraddle of the Revolution found to their embarrassment that ancient bottles did not always suffice for new wine. The staid old forms of brief fiction, well shaped to hold the ideas and aspirations of an age preoccupied with other problems, proved too fragile to contain the explosive and unstable elements of a society riven by revolution and dissent. The writers of brief fiction struggled manfully, but at first unsuccessfully, to fashion the short story into an instrument capable of meaningful communication for an era of revolt.

The change from eighteenth-century techniques to the more sophisticated ones of the nineteenth century did not occur suddenly. By the time of the Revolution, when France was facing a moment of social truth, brief fiction had bogged down in the *conte philosophique*; it had become so entangled in philosophical debate that it was utilized primarily to propagandize some ethical or moral position. Its heavy burden of didacticism slowed down the development of the short narrative and made it of limited use for expressing the problems and concerns of the emergent nineteenth century. Since established techniques were geared to the presentation of moralizing, writers inevitably found themselves having to choose between accepting limited horizons for their fiction or changing these techniques.

The dilemma can be seen in the first attempts of nineteenth-century writers to work with the old form, in the tales of Xavier de Maistre, for example. Just before the new century burgeoned, the expatriate population of refugee aristocrats pro-

17

vided French literature with a new name when Maistre turned author in the safety of Saint Petersburg. As a sometime writer and literary dilettante, Maistre brought no new insights to the short narrative; but his work reveals the kinds of interests and emphases that would soon force renovation of the genre. His anecdotes follow the best eighteenth-century tradition but indicate how inadequate the old form would prove to express the conditions and emotions of an age of social turmoil.

In a burst of nostalgia Maistre recalled an episode from his service in the army of Piedmont, when he had been confined to quarters for fighting a duel. To amuse himself, during his arrest, he began a *Voyage autour de ma chambre* (1794). A product of the eighteenth-century passion for description, the *Voyage* contains a meticulously detailed catalogue of the prisoner's surroundings. The world of fiction was reduced to the minimum as the author presented a personal essay written for the "lecteur raisonnable." Imitating, as he thought, the "disorder" of *Tristram Shandy*, Maistre reflected on his furniture, the times, his dog Rosine, and his valet; he even included a dialogue between his body and soul. Often ironical, sometimes witty, the *Voyage* frequently revealed the boredom the author was trying to dispel.

In 1811, Maistre published another anecdote from his past, *Le Lépreux de la vallée d'Aoste*, an incident with which he had long amused Russian salons. In 1797 a French soldier entered the supposedly haunted Tour de la Frayeur in the town of Aoste to discover a disfigured occupant, a leprous orphan who had lived there with his sister for fifteen years. In the best sentimental practice, Maistre directed the tale at the reader's emotions. The plot was organized in framework fashion, as a story within a story, with the leper giving a first-person confession. Eighteenth-century *sensibilité* ran riot as the afflicted man reached the desperate conclusion that cultivating his garden and following the will of God made him happier than a king. However successful this tearful appeal, Maistre had obvious difficulty controlling his material. He conceived the story as a series of increasingly charged emotional experiences, with the leper portrayed as a latter-day Job, an object lesson to the worldly and ambitious. Consequently, incident took precedence over any sense of unified and economical form as he manipulated episodes to produce pathos.

Back in Paris after the Bourbon Restoration, Xavier de Maistre recalled another salon anecdote in *La Jeune Sibérienne* (1825). As sentimental as the *Lépreux*, this tale contained a picaresque element that permitted the author to indulge again in what has been called the visceral approach to literature as he described how the eighteen-year-old daughter of an exiled officer set out for the capital to seek her father's release from Siberia—alone, afoot, and with only her virtue to protect her. Maistre knew a great deal about Russia and, though he exposed the girl to the usual perils of peripatetic innocence, he surrounded her in believable local color. He worked with materials guaranteed to soften an age tempered in violence: a virginal maiden protecting old parents; a lone girl against the world; virtue surmounting all obstacles. Heaven did help this poor girl through incredible adventures as she crossed all Russia; hardened thieves pitied her, even an emperor was moved by her plight. Maistre seized the opportunity to describe various sections of Russia, and to portray the social hierarchy, all in the service of the moral that simple, virtuous people enjoy the special protection of a benign Providence. Although the conclusion seems inevitable, a modicum of dramatic tension arises from wonder over the length of Prascovie's plight. The tale took on form only from the meanders of the plot, each exploited for its emotional content, and the story ended not with the pardoning of the father but with the daughter hying herself to a convent.

This simple narrative was accompanied by *Les Prisonniers du Caucase*, an exotic tale of border life along the far reaches of the empire in which Ivan, the faithful orderly of Major Kascambo, used his native wit to rescue his master from the savage Tchetchengas of Wladi Caucase. Like Maistre's other tales, this one depends on the flow of episode as the plot follows a traditional line: capture, harsh treatment, the desperate plight of prisoners apparently abandoned by their friends, the flight complete with final rescue just when one of the escaped prisoners seems doomed to collapse from exhaustion. Basically another anecdote, it presents a case history in loyalty in which Major Kascambo and Ivan remain flat characters, the latter dominating the action in his allegorical representation of virtue. As resourceful as Figaro, Ivan charmed savage breasts with guitar music and, in a classic escape scene, supported his faltering master until the cavalry raced to the rescue.

Surprisingly, Maistre intervened only at the end of the story to create emotional effect by misdirection, implying monstrous ingratitude, then satisfied the reader's sense of justice by having Ivan join the officers as an equal. In this way, Xavier de Maistre combined two manners of storytelling. He related the anecdote from the point of view of the uncommitted observer, using local color and Russian words adeptly, with fewer digressions than contemporary practice permitted. But at the end he could not resist falling back on first-person narration, as he used emotional appeal in the epilogue to round off the tale. Thus, he lost tonal unity by his lack of consistency and his unwillingness to trust the structuring of his story to communicate meaning.

Mme de Staël

Despite the patronizing airs of male writers smug in the security of accepted superiority, the ladies were not to be denied their place in the history of literature, though none of them seems to have cared to depart from the traditional modes of expression. Women had published before the eighteenth century, but not in impressive numbers, although their ranks had increased during the Enlightenment. Whereas scant opportunity and limited education had restricted the ranks of lady poets, prose offered them broader opportunities. They first entered literature as patronesses, then metamorphosed into celebrity hunters, vying bitterly with each other for the status a distinguished guest list would bring. Inevitably some undertook to try their own wings, but they hesitated to enter the domain of poetry and did not even dream of invading the stage. Here the competition was keen and the critics were ruthless with the mediocre and the untalented, however beautiful their complexions. Understandably, they followed current fashions, writing long romances, fairy tales, or highly moralistic literature.

Paradoxically, as men like Voltaire and Diderot adapted current forms for their needs, the lady authors limited themselves to sentimental tales written according to the formulae currently in vogue, and this despite the fact that they diligently kept abreast of the latest literary developments. Even when so redoubtable a woman as Mme de Staël took up short fiction briefly, her youthful peccadillos showed astonishing mediocrity: *Zulma, Adelaide et Théodore, Mirza ou Lettre d'un voyageur,* and *L'Histoire de Pauline,* all propose in undistinguished fashion the thesis that a woman grows spiritually when warmed by true love.

Zulma, fragment d'un ouvrage (1794) had originally been planned as part of the *Influence des passions,* a "tableau du malheur le plus terrible, et du caractère le plus passionné." Mme de Staël actually employed the story as a kind of catharsis for her love affair with Narbonne as she described the fate of the fickle Ferdinand, stabbed for philandering by the faithful Zulma. *Pauline, Mirza,* and *Adelaide,* published in 1795, were likewise tales of love in distress. Adelaide committed suicide when husband Théodore wasted away because of unfounded jealousy. Pauline came from the same mold: an orphan, married at fourteen, widowed at fifteen, she pined away when her puritanical husband believed idle gossip about her seduction by the wicked Meltin. Mirza had no better luck; she killed herself when her beloved Ximéo was forced into an arranged marriage.

The four narratives indicate that Mme de Staël was more interested in fighting the battle for women's rights, into which she charged with characteristic fierceness, than in trying to renovate brief fiction. The moral tale served her purpose so well that she had undertaken in the *Essai sur les fictions* (1795) an apology for the calumniated romance. "C'est dans la peinture de quelques sentiments du coeur qu'est leur seul mérite." To help her case, she even quoted Mme Riccoboni, an authoress decidedly from the bottom shelf. The four narratives have as heroines women of great sensitivity and passion for whom love stands above all law, its own justification. Mme de Staël had read all too well the first part of Rousseau's *Nouvelle Héloïse*, as well as many other popular novels. Her heroines, three of them orphans, were all "belle comme le jour"; all died from an overdose of emotion; great passion, in Mme de Staël's experience, could never lead to happiness. These young creatures, innately decent and virtuous, held true to their affection at all cost. The heroes also demonstrate a kind of consistency. Brave, generally without friends, they were handsome, though less intelligent and imaginative than the women. Given to easy misunderstandings, they lived such high-strung, neurotic lives that both they and the heroines constantly punctuated the plot by fainting. The characters represent Madame's dream world, her conception of herself, her lovers, and how the world treated the kind of grand passion reserved for great natures like hers.

Mme de Staël's idea of short fiction came directly from the long romances of the eighteenth century. Incident was piled on incident for the sole purpose of wringing the last drop of anguish from a situation. Only death solved her heroines' problems in plots motivated by coincidence, misunderstanding, or stubborn pride. Mme de Staël's fictional universe had narrow boundaries and revolved around the single theme of the all-consuming power of feminine love. On this topic the loquacious authoress could not resist digressions or long descriptions of the sterling virtues of her faithful heroines. The result was an uncontrolled and lachrymose narrative that had been strung together only as a vehicle for her convictions on true love.

Chateaubriand

Chateaubriand, the contemporary of Xavier de Maistre and Mme de Staël, could boast of a higher order of talent, and he intended to remove *Atala* and *René* from the disrepute of popular short fiction by attaching them to the poetic forms of antiquity. However, he, too, struggled with the problem of a narrative heavily burdened by explicit sentimental moralizing. In the last analysis he did not, as he had hoped, create two fragments in the style of the *Iliad* and the *Odyssey* but, at least in *Atala,* produced a latter-day version of the sentimental *conte philosophique.*

At the turn of the century he had long been preparing the *Génie du christianisme,* a discourse which proved the truth of Christianity by demonstrating the artistic superiority of its rites and cathedrals. He had, however, hesitated over publication because of the bitter anticlericalism that accompanied the Revolution. But in April, 1801, at the insistence of his friend, Fontanes, he extracted *Atala* as a trial balloon for the larger work.

Essentially pagan in attitude, *Atala* recounts the unfortunate love of Chactas, sage of the Natchez, for a determinedly virtuous Muskogee princess. Chateaubriand fell back on the wellworn framework structure to authenticate an incident which the blind sage, Chactas, revealed to René as they hunted.

However fresh *Atala* seemed in 1801, it had many close ties with the past. In a letter published in the *Journal des Débats* and the *Publiciste* in 1800, and later reproduced as a preface to *Atala,* Chateaubriand remarked: "J'ai donné à ce petit ouvrage les formes les plus antiques; il est divisé en *prologue, récit* et *épilogue.* Les principales parties du récit prennent une dénomination, comme, les *chasseurs,* les *laboureurs* . . . et c'était ainsi que dans les premiers siècles de la Grèce les rapsodes chantaient sous divers titres les fragments de *l'Iliade* et de *l'Odyssée.*" *Atala* was to be "une sorte de poème, moitié descriptif, moitié dramatique." Yet, for all his explanations, Chateaubriand remained more French than neo-Greek. Following tradition, he fell back on the box-car structure so popular during the eighteenth century. The chronological arrangement, with peripatetic major characters in the fashion of the *conte philosophique*, permitted him to indulge a passion for painting exotic scenes. Since he grasped storytelling primarily in terms of *sensibilité*, he graduated the scenes according to what William Dean Howells called "effectism," a steadily increasing charge of emotion infused into successive episodes that came to a climax in Atala's funeral.

For this purpose Chateaubriand broke the story into two parts: the first centered around Chactas, his stay with the Spaniard Lopez, his capture and impending execution. Once the hero escaped, the focus shifted from the problem of his survival to the preservation of the maiden's virginity. Atala then dominated the action as her dilemma provided increasingly stronger sensations. Even the characters reacted to the constant stimulation as, in turn, Lopez, Chactas, Atala, all wept copiously at their predicament. Time has not treated parts of this story kindly, but the modern reader must remember that the wandering plot, the tearful Indians, and the coincidences did not constitute faults as Chateaubriand understood brief fiction. On the contrary, he needed them for the creation of scenes he could exploit. Since he conceived the story episodically, the transitions mattered little. Only slightly occupied with cause and effect, he intended to comment on human experience, not facts, and the structure he chose filled his requirements.

There is much in *Atala* that now seems to verge on the comic and the absurd. The logical-minded find it hard to accept Chateaubriand's determination to twist a pagan love story into a religious apology proving "les harmonies de la religion avec les scènes de la nature et les passions du coeur humain." The Indian lovers have the ardent temperament of the *fin du siècle*, with the vocabulary and delicacy of an age sophisticated in such matters. One may boggle at historical inaccuracies, wince at the "miracles" that occur opportunely, or balk at a conversion that takes place in the middle of a seduction. Father Aubrey's utopia comes from a long line of other paradises inhabited by "good savages" whose proximity to nature glorifies their primitiveness. The casual attitude toward probability, the ridiculous picture of the Mississippi, and the arranged ending all provide serious obstacles to the willing suspension of disbelief. Worst of all, the plight of the lovers helps little to understand the present; *Atala*, however delightful, exudes the odor of a faded past.

Yet, despite manifold objections, partisans of *Atala* can summon strong arguments in its defense. During Chactas' monologue, Chateaubriand painted word pictures powerful enough to conceal his inaccuracies. His mastery of the language, his brilliant descriptions, overshadow the plot. And if the narrative structure is understood in the author's terms, if *Atala* is accepted as a poem, the "faults" disappear and the work increases in stature. Certainly Chateaubriand dazzled his contemporaries, and few subsequent writers have been able to match the evocative rhythms of his prose.

Now a change became discernible. The eighteenth century had believed that it could grasp the world from the exterior, that it could apprehend events and people in a way that could be communicated logically to readers. The concepts of the descriptive scientist governed the classical and neoclassical approach to prose fiction. An author, standing apart from a fictional world, entered only to draw the obvious moral; he pictured events and personalities according to the tenets of Descartes and the philosophy of the universal man. A writer saw and related; he functioned like an omnipresent deity who explained people and their actions to an interested audience. As a result the characters tended to remain flat, to serve as allegorical figures in a kind of morality play. The notion of an individual, separate and unique, of an inner world that functioned according to its own dynamics, remained unknown in short fiction until Chateaubriand published *René*. Still greatly influenced by eighteenth-century custom, he nevertheless indicated new worlds to explore as he shifted the focus of his narrative from what his hero did to how he felt and reacted. The artist's vision moved from outside to inside as Chateaubriand related the story of a young man's reaction to the discovery of his sister's incestuous passion for him.

Chateaubriand narrated *René* in much the same manner as *Atala*, with the same pictorial use of wild storms, sad autumns, and brilliant setting suns, although the tale was more economically told, its elements better controlled, and the power more concentrated. Whereas *Atala* was a story of frustrated love, *René* dealt with the powerful turbulences that rend a human being. Emotion was no longer merely stated but described in its genesis, development, and explosive effect on a human being. To do this, Chateaubriand relied on the form that had proved so successful with *Atala*, reusing the framework device and the first-person narrator who confessed his spiritual torments. Once again he turned to description to convey mood, although this time he was attempting to relate reaction to an event as well as the event itself. The plot developed around the problem of incest, a common eighteenth-century theme, and *René*, like *Atala*, depended for dramatic tension on an unrevealed secret that precipitated the dénouement. Chactas remained the same noble savage, living in dignity and wisdom close to nature, but now reversed roles to become René's confidant.

In *René* the emphasis falls on a personality that sums up the temper of a France deep in the shock of revolution. In *Atala* Chateaubriand had narrated almost flatly, his painted descriptions lending themselves to a shallow, exterior form of writing. In *René* he moved inside the protagonist to recreate an emotional history, to explain the pressures that warp a man's psyche. Although the action was set earlier, the hero mirrored contemporary concerns. An aristocrat, René saw his world crumble with the Ancien Régime, leaving him disenchanted and conscious of impermanence. He felt alienated from society, lonely with the loneliness of the insecure, unable to act because he lacked motive and direction to give life meaning. He *felt* the *mal du siècle*, the ennui of the young born old, the confused yearning of those passed by. René suffered an exaggerated form of the despair that faces every hypersensitive adolescent and, in this case, his incapacity to struggle out of his spiritual bewilderment matched that of a culture beset with similar difficulties. Since the past offered no guidance, his search for certainty only proved once again the theme of Ecclesiastes. Nature alone remained secure. René repeated every man's pursuit of a personal Holy Grail, and his geographical wanderings were but the exteriorization of mental anguish.

The major difficulty facing Chateaubriand was how to co-ordinate mental states difficult to express with contemporary literary techniques. To do this, he reduced the story to three scenes: René's pursuit of stability; his momentary happiness; and the discovery of the terrible secret. His sister Amelia's passion for him served as the organizing principle for René's spiritual adventure; he symbolized the sensitive man who paraded his great suffering as a mark of genius. He reacted to some unknown original sin like the existential man lost in the void of his own being. His indecision was transformed into purpose by Amelia's acknowledgment of her illicit love. "Le moment étoit venu où j'allois expier toutes mes inconséquences. Dans mon délire, j'avois été jusqu'à désirer d'éprouver un malheur, pour avoir du moins un objet réel de souffrance: épouvantable souhait, que Dieu, dans sa colère, a trop exaucé!" He actually came to enjoy his suffering, to convert it into an occupation. Destiny could offer this great soul only the courtesy of a punishment for his humanity beyond that accorded ordinary mortals. *René* translates the theme of intellectual alienation into physical exile, a tragic atonement for the sin of a mysteriously imposed destiny.

In *Atala* the lush paintings had almost obscured the story, but in *René* Chateaubriand put his pictorial talent at the service of the plot. The usual scenes underline mood: ruins, stormy seas, the sadness of autumn—all hallmarks of the eighteenth century's enjoyment of grief and morbidity. The bells tolled to recall the message of Christianity and to speak of loneliness and salvation. In *Atala*, Chactas had confessed; now it was René's turn. At the end of the tale René, Chactas, and Father Souel returned to the village, the three figures symbolizing Chateaubriand's meaning: René as man's confusion and suffering; Chactas, blind wisdom; and the priest, the answer to the human predicament. René walked between the two older men, supported by unseeing faith.

In the conclusion, Father Souel gave René the answer: "Jeune présomptueux, qui avez cru que l'homme se peut suffire lui-même! La solitude est mauvaise à celui qui n'y vit pas avec Dieu; elle redouble les puissances de l'âme, en même temps qu'elle leur ôte tout sujet pour ses semblables: s'il les laisse inutiles, il en est d'abord puni par une secrète misère, et tôt ou tard le Ciel lui envoie un châtiment effroyable." Amelia had solved her dilemma by withdrawal, and René tried to adopt her solution after she restrained him from suicide. He even imitated her consecration to chastity since he never consummated the marriage required to make him a member of the tribe. René hoped to find salvation in primitivism and a life close to nature, lived beyond the snares and delusions of civilization. He imagined himself a compulsively driven Wandering Jew, cursed by Heaven to bring misfortune to all he touched. Hence he followed Atala and Amelia in the cult of virginity, a notion that made the irreverent Mme de Staël bellow with laughter.

Though Father Souel clearly expressed Chateaubriand's meaning, the nineteenth century ignored his message, preferring to have René remain intellectually unsatisfied. The romantics found him the perfect exemplar of their imagined predicament; he became the model for a public personality which they paraded as proof positive of their genius. René symbolized the major problem of these artists: how to find a self, given the hostility of society toward the different and the nonconforming. As a result, Father Souel's religion was watered down into religiosity; the introspection, the aversion to life, the mystery of a great destiny, served as patterns for Hernani and Antony. In the matter of form, Chateaubriand merely continued an eighteenth-century tradition, but his word-magic and the gigantic portrait of René greatly influenced a generation seeking the respectability of ancestry. Moreover, by his exploration of the private world of the mind, the insistence on what differentiated his hero from other people, he helped destroy the hitherto accepted conception of the universal man. The romantics would continue his exploration of the subconscious, developing new psychological understanding and constructing an image of man vastly different from that dear to the classicists. René thus achieved the ultimate compliment: later generations abstracted the hero from the tale, stripped him of his fictional world, then gave him the status of human being.

Charles Nodier

The changes in brief fiction visible in the work of Chateaubriand show clearly in the stories of Charles Nodier. The shift seems more evident because Nodier, unlike any other previous writer, dedicated his talent primarily to the brief narrative, winning popularity and a durable reputation for himself as a *conteur* of note. Contemporary with Xavier de Maistre, Chateaubriand, and innumerable lady practitioners of the form, he moved more naturally than they within its confines. Much of his work followed the standard recipe, but when he found himself unable to fit his thoughts into the accepted modes of expression, he moved beyond the strictures of the past to become perhaps the first author of his age to recognize short fiction as a form independent and valid in itself, not a dehydrated version of the novel or an episode foreshortened by unimaginative composition. When he laid down his pen, new areas of

subject matter had been opened up to the creative imagination
of later French writers.

To be sure, Nodier was little clearer than his predecessors
on the precise nature of the medium he was handling. The
words *conte, nouvelle, historiette, anecdote,* and *roman* were
carelessly attached to his stories without concern for sharp
theoretical distinction. In the preface to *Trilby,* Nodier called
his tale both a *conte* and a *nouvelle*; the same blithe indifference
toward nomenclature occurs in the preface of *Les Quatre
Talismans* and the dedication of *Inès de las Sierras.* Length
and subject matter seem the principal factors of differentiation.
Paul ou la Ressemblance was entitled an *historiette* or an
"histoire véritable et fantastique" while *Les Fiancés* was tagged
a *nouvelle.* He called *Piranèse* a *conte psychologique. M.
Cazotte* a fragment of a novel, and *Le Génie Bonhomme* a
conte fantastique.

As one might expect, little of Nodier's work departs
radically from previous practice. His roots lay too deeply in
the eighteenth century for that, and sorties into new territory
were as infrequent with him as with any of his contemporaries.
Most of his narratives, in fact, did not survive his death for
understandable reasons: the bulk of them belonged in an
already weary tradition. The plots are anodyne, simple structures on which Nodier draped moral dissertations. They are
peopled with flat characters who live emotionally superficial
lives, uninspiring as illuminations of human conduct or as
insights into the values of another age. And, unfortunately,
these stories constitute the major portion of Nodier's production, among them the *Souvenirs de jeunesse,* many of the
Contes de la veillée, and most of the so-called *romans.*

All are genial tales told in the tradition of the undisciplined
anecdote. Each follows a chronological development and recounts

the adventures of an innocent young couple whose love will be frustrated almost at the moment of fulfillment by parental fear of mésalliance, or by an illness that consumes one of the main characters, leaving the other a choice between suicide and life as a religious. Thus the *Neuvaine de la chandeleur* tells of a young man's worshiping a dream girl who died the day after he found her. In a like vein, *Les Aveugles de Chamouny* concerns the thwarted love of the heiress Eulalie and orphaned Gervais, both blind.

Even more emotional are the *Souvenirs de jeunesse*, a collection of lachrymose accounts of ill-fated love taken purportedly from a manuscript which fell into Nodier's hands. The reader is led from Séraphine to Thérèse, Clémentine to Amélie, Lucrèce, and Jeannette, while the author minutely examines his ego. The book catalogues the unknown writer's tragic love life: Thérèse and her young husband succumbed as victims of revolutionary justice; Clémentine refused to marry for fear of a mésalliance; when she died, the author entered a monastery. Later he persuaded Protestant Amélie to change her religion and marry him but almost immediately she succumbed to an unknown illness.

At first glance these stories show little variance from the trite practices of the past. This kind of expanded, formless anecdote had been the specialty of ladies like Mme Cottin. But a second look reveals a primitive kind of pattern. Each is constructed to permit Nodier to arrange the incidents in a succession of sentimental peaks that culminate in the final catastrophe of young love betrayed by death. The story wanders along a path predetermined by the author's need to manipulate episode for the production of increasingly stronger emotion.

The plots meander as mood dictates, some of them complex, with incidents strung bead-fashion, since Nodier had no use for cause-effect relationships. There is almost a complete lack of tension, for the suspense he sought was not of the kind that would induce tightness of plot. The insoluble predicament of characters trapped by a hostile life provided him with far more interesting material. Thus, the *Fée aux miettes* made a direct emotional appeal to the reader; the *Proscrits* was "l'effusion d'un coeur vivement ému, qui se répond dans le coeur des autres." *Thérèse Aubert* made even its author weep while he wrote of Adolphe, a wounded Vendéen hiding from Republican pursuers, who fell in love with his rescuer, Thérèse, only to watch her die slowly of smallpox.

Pathetic stories and naïve plots, to be sure, but many of them provided Nodier with a vehicle for more serious purposes. He was attempting to reverse literary history and return the brief narrative to what it once had been: a literature for the people. Since he considered his tales an arm of morality, he often used situation to provide ethical dilemmas on which he could comment. The preface of *Hélène Gillet* asserted that all *contes* had to convey a message, a dictum to which Nodier willingly conformed. In the *Peintre de Saltzbourg* or the "diary of the emotions of a suffering heart," Nodier concluded with a discourse on the evils of suicide. *Paul ou la Ressemblance* contained a sermon on overcoming disappointment and sorrow; *Mademoiselle de Marsan*, a tale of secret societies, furnished opportunity for a lecture on tyranny, republicanism, and clandestine organizations. In *Jean Sbogar*, the most popular of Nodier's works, Antonia found the diary of her beloved Lothario to consist of a series of gloomy meditations. Lothario-Nodier resented the use of money, was convinced that cities were the curse of civilization, that murder constituted a sin, and capital punishment a still greater one. He had reason for the last, for Jean was executed for banditry by the French and Antonia dropped dead from shock. So keen was Nodier's interest in moralizing that on occasion he passed from the usual enlarged anecdote to the apologue, or moral fable, to satisfy his compulsive didacticism.

Because these stories carried a meager ideological burden, the means of expression were not particularly inspired. Most of them followed the oral tradition recommended by Diderot, according to which the author claimed the right to interpose.

Since Nodier aimed at pure exposition rather than revelation or illumination, there is little conversation. He constantly interjected himself between reader and story because he considered his function that of directing attention to the implications of each situation. Hence digression and comment became important and intrinsic to his manner of storytelling. The characters assumed simple allegorical meanings, but were never trusted to carry the whole burden of the writer's intent.

This passion for preaching made Nodier vulnerable to critical attacks on the realism of his fiction. Consequently, he generally fell back on the story-within-a-story and the first person singular for verisimilitude. To bolster the meager probability of his work, Nodier relied on such clichés as the lost manuscript, the journal left by the hero, or the account taken from an old hagiographer. He assumed that these devices would protect him from charges of fantasy since he was dealing with "real" life. Thus *Thérèse Aubert* purportedly came from a manuscript discovered in a prison; *Adèle* was based on the correspondence between two young men; the *Peintre de Saltzbourg* appeared in diary form; *Soeur Béatrix* was drawn from Bzovius, an old historian. One entire collection appeared as *Souvenirs de jeunesse,* another manuscript entrusted to him. Often Nodier digressed to reassure readers that nothing had been invented, as in *Mademoiselle de Marsan,* or to insist that his stories could be taken literally since the author's natural bent was for "le vrai."

Naïve pretensions, perhaps, as hostile critics sneered, but necessary from Nodier's point of view. As he admitted in a footnote to *Les Quatre Talismans,* the workers and peasants— the only class which understood the obligations of life—formed his audience. For these readers of scant education, he made his characters of modest station, generally from rural areas. He hoped to replace the literary fare usually available to them and to pitch his didacticism at a level they could reach. His characters were types, familiar to ordinary folk in personality, if not in the tenor of their more exciting lives.

This kind of story, although it forms the major portion of Nodier's work, gives an inexact measure of the man. His talent offered more than moral dissertations on the sad fate of young lovers, for his mind contained the vision of a universe larger than the painful stories of Paul, Hélène, or Adèle. These originated in his experience with life, but so would the fairy tales, a reaction to the same circumstances, which constituted his greater claim to literary recognition.

The relationship of these fairy stories to Nodier is more apparent that that of the weepy tales he authored. Even his beloved daughter recognized in the author of *La Fée aux miettes* and *Le Trésor des fèves* a child who had lost contact with reality and become hostile to the world around him. He himself admitted in the *Souvenirs de la Révolution* that his most pleasant memories dated from early youth. Crippled with debts, he had arrived at maturity with the tragic knowledge that he had missed his goal. As secretary to Sir Herbert Croft, he had wasted precious time in hack work. He had never known the security of good position and certain income; improvisation and makeshift had been the order of his day. His talent had gone into bibliographies, the preparation of a dictionary, and entomological studies, as well as into the creation of fiction not far removed from the potboiler. By nature gentle, he loved study and the amiable pursuit of hobbies, but destiny chained him to a desk to pay off nagging and ever-mounting debts. "What did we gain by growing old?" he asked his friend Weiss in 1825. And so in his sentimental stories he painted human existence as pitiless and escaped its vengeance in the gentle safety of the fairy tale and the uncomplicated tenor of once-upon-a-time.

His refuge into make-believe stemmed in part from a resentment of the conditions of modern life. Nodier had always felt deracinated in Paris. The intimate life of the provinces and the close friendships known in Besançon seemed impossible in the bustle of the capital. His emotional life suffered from lack of an established frame of reference. As highly strung as any of his characters, he resented the "forte éducation des évène-ments" that had suddenly thrown him out of his childhood. Nodier felt old-fashioned in his dislike of cities, in his complaint that supercilious youth no longer respected its elders. Melancholy and chronically ill, he scorned the theory of the perfectibility of man. Modern writers, as he wrote in *Le Bibliomane,* merely ground out fashionable poetry and academic prose; printing and the alphabet spread their woes to the most sheltered cottage, until the "enfants de la nature" became as stupidly wicked as their masters.

And so Nodier fled reality in search of an inner equilibrium. He wanted to move among his own kind in a world his mind could encompass and direct. It became all the more necessary to fill this need when his daughter married. As the center of his existence Marie had given meaning to his life, but once she became engaged he felt himself alone in a hostile environment. He began to address himself "to the reader who reads prefaces" and to fashion a universe in which suffering could be controlled, money had no meaning, and a benign Providence ensured the triumph of virtue.

The fairy tale gave Nodier the perfect form for combining his urge to teach and his desire to move beyond the restrictions of reality. "Once upon a time there were fairies," he began the *Génie Bonhomme* and in a humorous introduction he presented Bonhomme, a djinn of modest pretensions who gave Saphir and Améthyste, the grandchildren of Tropbonne, the secret of freedom from boredom: useful labor. This story, like *Trésor des fèves et Fleur des pois,* represents a tradition old in French literature when Nodier wrote. Writers like Madame d'Aulnoy, Mlle Lhéritier, and Perrault had accepted from folk art the general outline and assumptions of this kind of tale and their literary posterity had found no reason to challenge the custom.

With them the genre received the sanction of the sophisticated and made its way into literature as a conscious art form. Just before the Revolution, in 1785, the fairy tale had experienced a resurgence of popularity with the publication of the *Cabinet des fées,* a collection of practically all these narratives written in French. Then, during the Empire, the fairy tale flourished again, partly because of the censorship of contemporary materials, partly because of the general stagnation in art. At this time the fairy tale turned into something close to the love story, with unhappy endings and melancholy characters.

Nodier was well acquainted with his distinguished predecessors, but he chose to speak to the same audience toward which he had directed his other work. Consequently, he kept his plots on an elementary level and continued the bad literary habit of digressing on any topic that caught his fancy. The exigencies of a tightly controlled art bothered him not at all; his audience reacted only to plot, caring little for niceties of structure or fine points of characterization.

Trilby (1882) provided just the kind of narrative he liked. Nodier recounted in an intimate, folksy manner the love of a sprite for the Scottish lass Jeannie, using many of the ingredients traditionally involved in the concoction of a fairy tale. The story begins with a bit of local color, a short disquisition on the prevalence of elves and sprites in Scotland. There is the usual sage, the centenarian monk Ronald, who summons Trilby thrice, and thrice reads the litany of the Virgin. The elf uses the hoary device of disguising himself as an old man, deceiving nobody but Jeannie, and his end is foreshadowed by the interpolation of a legend of how a monk overpowered a giant through prayer. The tale ends in a cemetery, at which point Nodier falls back on the genie-in-a-box idea and multiplies the emotional impact by having Trilby sealed away for a thousand years.

The plot, however, contains divergences from the old recipe. There is no villain, no wicked giant or nasty ogre, and a priest brings about Trilby's downfall. Trilby is mischievous but never malicious; he prefers the company of the poor and disdains the rich. Those he favors prosper and are never threatened by sudden reversals of fortune. And Trilby loves Jeannie with a mundane passion surprising in a fairy tale. The streak of sensualism that runs through Nodier's work has often been noted, but here it is almost painfully evident. At night Trilby dances through Jeannie's hair, whispering endearments, and she dreams of him in what Nodier blandly calls her "rêves innocemment voluptueux." But no such statement can keep the dullest reader from recognizing Trilby's meaning when he begs Jeannie to recall him because he loves her. The words are seductive, for here Nodier could not disguise the fact that his plot revolves around the sprite's attempt to steal Jeannie from her husband, even though Nodier insisted on the other-worldly quality of his affection.

Basically, the story departs little from Nodier's customary manner. *Trilby* is an intimate but wandering tale that winds from one strong emotion to another. The lovers never surmount the difficulties which the author hurls in their path; their predicament is resolved by death and the intimation that their reward will come in the hereafter. Jeannie's tomb lies conveniently near the tree and her headstone carries a message for the young at heart: "Mille ans ne sont qu'un moment sur la terre pour ceux qui ne doivent se quitter jamais."

It would be easy to carp at Nodier, to titter at his description of how the wind sobbed a requiem for Jeannie. Even though he never succeeded in controlling his plot, some of his descriptions, particularly those of the loch and its surrounding mountains, should earn him a measure of forgiveness. He believed that the fairy tale suited his talents, and when critics disagreed he paraphrased Luke 18:16: "Permettez aux petits de venir, car il n'y a point de danger pour eux à écouter mes récits, et vous me connoissez assez pour me croire."

In 1831, he returned to the fairy tale with *La Fée aux miettes*, his most ambitious project, and in some ways his most significant contribution. In terms of length, the *Fée* falls outside any consideration of brief prose fiction, but actually it differs from Nodier's shorter works only in that it was expanded to volume size by multiplying the number of obstacles set before the hero. The story seems, in fact, an attempt to marry the structure of the romance to the fairy tale plot. Nodier utilized the framework technique to capture the attention of his readers, beginning near the end of his tale by having young Michel, a carpenter, recount the saga of his star-crossed love for the fairy queen Belkiss in a lunatic asylum.

Nodier called the *Fée aux miettes* a "bluette de peu de valeur," but obviously he had poured a great deal of himself into it. Michel's story dispensed with even that small bit of logic on which the element of the fantastic is usually superimposed. Nodier ignored cause and effect; the story moves along in an atmosphere of unreality, with the plot resting entirely on coincidence and arbitrary movement. Fantastic event piles on fantastic event in a weird mixture of dream sequences, strange metamorphoses, and irrational situations to produce an almost surrealistic effect. Poor Michel falls into bloody and terrible nightmares which foreshadow tragic events in a manner customary in fairy tales, kaleidoscopes of horror that hint at evil. Similarly, when the boy is to be tried for the murder of a bailiff who suddenly revives, he appears before a jury composed of animals. In *La Fée aux miettes,* as in Kafka's *Der Prozess,* there is a complete lack of communication between Michel and the judge, and his lawyer offers a defense so absurd as to seem ludicrous. Nodier, in fact, was indicting the legal profession for inconsistency, pedantry, and lack of concern with justice.

The book represents an excursion into what Nodier had come to accept as the "real" world, beyond time, where death was not really death, nor misfortunes endless. Michel, the dreamer, learned to his sorrow that the world of human prejudice and pragmatism refused to understand him. Therefore, Nodier created a better universe for the type of simple young man he thought himself and for whom he acted as benevolent Providence. Only in this kind of fantasy, Nodier argued in the preface, could happiness really be found.

In *La Fée aux miettes,* as in *Trilby,* Nodier used the basic ingredients of the fairy tale, liberally spiced with criticism. Michel loved Belkiss in all his adolescent innocence, but soon the affair took a more adult turn as Nodier described the worldly aspect of their love. Belkiss, or the Queen of Sheba, was the traditional good fairy who tested the fidelity of the mortal she favored. Following custom, she placed him in jeopardy three times, borrowed money three times, then required him to accomplish the impossible to save their love. Yet the reader follows the boy's adventures with the comfortable assurance that all will end well to the tune of the mandrake's song.

Because Nodier was expanding the fairy tale, approximating the structure normally used for the romance, the central themes are almost buried. As in *Trilby,* he intended to involve the reader emotionally with Michel's plight by moving from crisis to crisis. Nodier had inherited this method from the eighteenth century and it would have constituted a revolution of the first magnitude for him suddenly to have rejected it. In all fairness, he can be understood only in these terms.

The *Fée aux miettes* is difficult to read not just because of the complexity of episode and the author's propensity for slipping from "realism" to a conventional fairyland and thence to nightmares of Freudian proportions, but also because of the extremely heavy overlay of didacticism. In this respect Nodier was following the major precept of seventeenth- and eighteenth-century prose fiction: to teach morality, either by lecture or by horrible example. Michel is a naïve country boy who successfully resists the world's temptations. Some classified him as a fool, or an epileptic, a fact which enhanced his value in Nodier's eyes, since he thereby became a better medium for expressing the subjective experiences that form an essential part of the plot. Nodier felt a special affection for this kind of protagonist, in his mind more in tune with things spiritual. Jean-François-les-Bas-Bleus, who lost his reason because he pursued the study of the occult too far, had a vision of the death of his beloved and died at the exact moment she was guillotined. The hero of *Une Heure ou la Vision* is an epileptic who mourns over his fiancée's grave and dies in a madhouse on the second anniversary of her death, just after seeing her rise to heaven on a cloud.

The loose structure of *La Fée aux miettes* permitted interpolations either in the form of direct explanation or long sermons by the fairy and the uncle. Michel receives a goodly share of advice on matters as disparate as personal conduct and the gathering of cockles. He leads the good life of simple tastes, shares his wealth with friends, and remains true to his word and his love. Even under great pressure he shuns temptation. It is no accident that the central figure is a carpenter, a Christ figure, perhaps, who carried Nodier's message, "pour les gens qui ont l'inappréciable bonheur de croire, les honnêtes paysans de mon village, les aimables et sages enfants qui n'ont pas profité de l'enseignement mutuel, et les poètes de pensée et de coeur qui ne sont pas de l'Académie." For them he indulged his love of childlike minds.

The didacticism, however, stands alongside biting irony. Beyond the pastiches of Fénelon, Cyrano de Bergerac, and Perrault, in addition to the essays on natural history, are indications of the lessons Nodier had learned from the master satirist Laurence Sterne. Nodier teases the reader with apparently serious remarks, or gives such facetious headings to his chapters as: "Le dernier et le plus court de la narration de Michel, qui est par conséquent le meilleur du livre." Like Sterne he breaks off the story to address the reader, comments on his characters, or tosses barbs at unbelievers. Nodier mocked the critics with Uncle Toby's refrain, or called attention to a conclusion "which explains nothing and can be dispensed with." He whimsically named his characters Folly Girlface, the other woman; Master Finewood, the builder; or Jap Muzzleburn, the canine bailiff of the Isle of Man.

No doubt he enjoyed this kind of humor, but he also used it to strike back at those who objected to his work as the maundering of an unsophisticated mind. *L'Histoire du roi de*

Bohème et de ses sept châteux (1830) recalls a story mentioned in *Tristram Shandy* but never related. Nodier, in like manner, did not get around to discussing the king of Bohemia. He turned the full power of his tremendous erudition on critics who accused him of producing only pastiches; he burlesqued Cervantes, Rabelais, Swift, Goethe, and even his teacher, Sterne. He indulged his keen sense of humor with the kind of typographical experimentations that later would amuse Xavier Forneret: the use of various type sizes, arrangements of sentences on the page, chapters of two lines, or lapidary formation such as:

en

descendant

les

sept

marches

de

l'escalier

Nodier the scholar played with words, tossed off literary allusions to a variety of famous writers, and inserted asides to Victor Hugo, Tony Johannot, and his own wife and daughter. Occasionally he made long lists of interesting or nonsense words; some pages were even printed upside down. Although the tale purportedly concerned the king of Bohemia, it was Popocambou-le-brèche-dent the 42, the 633rd autocrat of Timbuctoo, who received more attention.

Of plot there is none. Nodier wandered from topic to topic as interest dictated. Supposedly, he was talking to three people: Théodore, Don Pic de Fanferluchio, and Breloque, characters representing aspects of his mind, each of whom commented on his narrative technique. Instead of traveling to Bohemia, the reader finds, amidst the digressions and bursts of pure fantasy, the tale of two blind youngsters, Paul and Eulalie, which Nodier had already recounted in *Les Aveugles de Chamouny* (*Contes de la veillée*), and the pathetic anecdote of Bichonne, the woodcutter's brave dog, who died saving two children from the wolves. When he finally came to the king of Bohemia he regretfully stopped for lack of paper and ink. Nodier was amusing himself, but the story, if such it can be called, also contains a bitterness that stirs pity for this gentle and misunderstood writer.

Over the course of his career Nodier had slowly elaborated a theory of the fantastic that was to color most of his work. By fantastic he meant something very different from Hoffmann, whose work he came to know after he had already learned his art. He preferred to exploit what is normally termed the marvelous, utilizing fables, legends, fairy tales, and dreams. His was a "true fantasy"; "it was the relation of fact considered materially impossible which, however, happened to everybody's knowledge." In November, 1830, he published an apology for his writing which denied the doctrine of social perfectibility. Only in the marvelous, he claimed, could the imagination find perfect freedom. "Quelle autre compensation," he demanded of the critics, "promettrez-vous à une âme profondément navrée de l'expérience de la vie?"

With this essay Nodier could, as Montégut admitted, claim the title of "chef du parti légitimiste des fées." Certainly he took himself seriously for, as he wrote to Weiss, his boyhood friend, on July 21, 1832, he had been privileged to perceive the truth. For him, rational man was the lowest of God's creatures. As he confessed in the preface of *Les Quatre Talismans*, he believed in the ability to foresee the future, in legends and superstitions, and in the science of higher things. "Les *Nouvelles* que je me raconte avant de les raconter aux autres, ont pour mon esprit un charme qui les console. Elles détournent ma pensée des faits réels pour l'exercer sur des chimères de

mon choix; . . . elles me font vivre d'une vie qui n'a rien de
commun avec la vie positive des hommes. . . . C'est pour
cela que j'ai fait des contes."

Although Nodier dabbled in many aspects of the fantastic, he
made his greatest contribution to literature through his exploitation of the dream. Jules Janin recalled that Nodier was much
given to dreaming, and Nodier corroborated in the second
preface to *Smarra* (1832) that sleep permitted him to enter
a life beyond the reach of the conscious. The essay, *Le Pays des
rêves,* noted that "le sommeil est non-seulement l'état le plus
puissant, mais encore le plus lucide de la pensée." An interesting
idea, but Nodier was actually expressing his disapproval of
reality by fleeing into the more pleasant climate of an imaginary
universe.

Dreams or visions occur repeatedly in his narratives, used
primarily for foreshadowing an ending, or as escape to a
better life. The hero of *Une Heure ou la Vision* sees Octavie,
his dead fiancée, float off on a cloud; Jean-François-les-Bas-
Bleus reads the death of Marie Antoinette in the sky. The
priest in *Franciscus Columna* writes a book on his lost love in
the form of a dream; and in *La Neuvaine de la Chandeleur,* the
protagonist envisions a beautiful girl whom he later meets. The
mother in *Paul ou la Ressemblance* sees the Virgin Mary,
as does the nun in the *Légende de soeur Béatrix.*

Inevitably Nodier passed from the story in which the dream
was simply one of the several ingredients of his art, to *Smarra,*
in which the dream constituted the whole story, a nightmare of
human sacrifices, succubi, ghouls, and sorceresses. The basic plot
came from the first book of the *Golden Ass,* with the addition
of the element of vampirism. As with his fairy tales, Nodier
offered *Smarra* as a serious venture into the unknown, "true"
fantasy from which he hoped to draw important conclusions
on the nature of man. Nodier insisted that *Smarra* (1821) was a
"study" translated by an Illyrian writing under the pseudonym
of Count Maxime Odin, apparently the same Maxime respon-

sible for his *Souvenirs de jeunesse*. The book recounts in pseudo-Greek form the nightmare of Lorenzo, a recent bridegroom who had dallied overlong with the poetry of the ancients.

The experiment brought out the worst in the critics, who branded Nodier a romantic, a title he resented because it lumped him in with Hugo's group. Most of them attacked the lack of a traditional story line or snapped angrily because he had dispensed with chronology and cause-to-effect. With their classical background, their dedication to "reason" as an esthetic touchstone, they could not comprehend a world where time had no meaning, in which content shaped its own form and the subconscious followed its own inexplicable laws. In his second preface to *Smarra* Nodier patiently explained that digressions, the absence of transitions, and the lack of a rational plan were all intentional. He had moved into the world of the mind, where the time and space of history ceased to function as coordinates.

Actually the critics need not have fussed so much, for the general outline of *Smarra* does follow the clearly discernible plan of a framework story with the nightmare as the inner section. Lucius' dream recalls that of Michel in the *Fée aux miettes* just before the murder of Sir Jap Muzzleburn, but here Nodier built the nightmare on the guilt Lucius harbored for the death of his friend Polémon and of his fiancée, Myrthé. Consequently Lucius dreamed of a punishment visited upon Polémon by a sorceress, and saw himself decapitated as Myrthé's assassin. The horror rises from the introduction of succubi and ghouls, from the unreality of scenes that fade one into the other without rhyme or reason. The work is another *pastiche*, of course—this time of Apuleius, Theocritus, Virgil, Dante, Shakespeare, and many another illustrious predecessor; but Nodier made it peculiarly his own—purposely unclear, full of the fleeting dread of nameless things. The *Episodes* play on human superstitions and fear of the dark, rising to a crescendo in the climactic decapitation scene.

In the development of the forms of short prose fiction, Nodier's is a name to be reckoned with, historically, as one of the first to dedicate a major part of his literary life to the brief narrative. Much of his work, written under pressure, did not extend beyond tales of thwarted love, arranged as stories-within-stories. Generally these narratives were only long anecdotes of the woes of frustrated young folk, which he attempted to justify as "true" or "historical." Occasionally he flirted with the apologue, or resuscitated the pseudo-diary and epistolary forms so fashionable in the previous century. Most of all he preferred the fairy tale, in which he could arrange incident to satisfy his outraged sense of justice. In this way he solved the dilemma facing him as an artist: how to be in a hostile world, yet not of it. He ventured into make-believe, folk stories, or dreams, always giving free hand to an incurable didacticism. Thus he performed what he considered the function of art when he acted as moral guide to his readers, whom he considered lesser beings. To the public he presented a grandfatherly personality, hiding the private one that cringed from life.

In these instances Nodier added little to the technique of brief fiction. Structurally he followed eighteenth-century usage by building his plot in terms of emotional crises. He showed little sense of the capabilities of the form, no willingness to depart from ancient tradition. As he answered his critics in *Dioclétien*:

> Je suis parleur, dit-on, mais qu'importe le temps?
> Je tiens qu'en cet objet c'est la dernière clause,
> Pourvu que le lecteur prenne goût à la chose.
> Et qui vous dit que je prétends
> A conter avec art? Il n'en est rien, je cause!

Perhaps he was misled by the audience he aimed at, the little people in the villages, for whom he pioneered a literature far in advance of George Sand and Lamartine. For the unsophisticated and the newly literate he used highly sensitive characters in stories full of pathos to teach a code of behavior. Consequently, he had no need of a story line that culminated in a crisis reached by the constant interaction of personality and incident. Successful as he may have been in his time, this insistence on emotional content has dated this part of his work. The increase of literacy and the changes which industrialization brought to France left him an author with a decreasing public and stole the freshness from his work.

It would not be fair, however, to dismiss Nodier cavalierly as only of historical importance. Parts of his writing still sparkle: the descriptions of Trilby and Jeannie on the lake, the unexpected flashes of wit. A fine vein of irony runs through his tales, sometimes directed at his own art, as though he sensed its thinness, sometimes aimed at readers silly enough to take him seriously. With a measure of good will and some historical imagination, one can still read him with pleasure.

More importantly, however, Nodier indicated to later writers the treasures they could find by exploiting the world of the subconscious. In *Smarra* he moved away from the comfortable exterior world which had satisfied previous generations into the untracked, illogical, and frightening reaches of the human mind. In so doing, he departed from the fictional universe of causality, chronology, and incident. With *Smarra* he opened up new and unexplored lands, indicating, like Chateaubriand, the possibility of depicting inner conflicts, reaction rather than action, suggestion in preference to exposition. A writer could then step away from his reader and move into the minds of his characters.

Benjamin Constant

Nodier's suggestions appealed to later writers, some as far distant as the surrealists. It would take long practice in brief

fiction for subsequent authors to recognize the nuggets em-
bedded in the huge pile of tailings. But with what he called
an "anecdote" Benjamin Constant made an immediate contribution to the art of the short narrative. Paradoxically, it
would also impose another kind of strait jacket on a form
struggling to shed its burden of didacticism.

Adolphe (1816), one of the most distinguished pieces of
nineteenth-century short fiction, came from a writer who seemed
least likely to father it. A contradictory, enigmatic personality,
Benjamin Constant lived the life of a political chameleon.
When he came to write *Adolphe*, he poured into it the considerable sum of his emotional experiences, all the uncertainties,
the betrayals, and the weaknesses he felt impelled to review, if
only for himself.

Since Constant felt himself a victim of uncontrollable
circumstances, he conceived the tale as an indictment of the
age. "J'ai voulu peindre dans Adolphe une des principales
maladies de notre siècle, cette fatigue, cette incertitude, cette
absence de force, cette analyse perpétuelle, qui place une
arrière-pensée à côté de tous les sentiments, et qui par là les
corrompt dès leur naissance." He did not wish to offer an
apology for his life, Adolphe claimed; and the narrative bears
him out as it details his attempt to rid himself of a mistress he
had seduced from sheer vanity.

Constant used the old pattern Prévost had adopted for
Manon, with slight reminiscences of Boccaccio. The *éditeur,*
trapped in a Calabrian town by floods, met a melancholy
stranger whom he nursed through a sudden illness. Several
months afterwards the innkeeper sent him the "anecdote,"
and ten years later he published it.

Basically a monologue, *Adolphe* was another in a long line
of confessional works stretching from *Manon Lescaut* to *René.*
Constant had plenty of literary precedent for the hoary device
of the lost manuscript that revealed a tormented hero's inner-
most thoughts at a moment of crisis. The framework structure
permitted him to repudiate responsibility for the facts yet

comment on the meaning of the events. A first-person narrator indicated a chronological story line: he could use a relatively simple plot without concern for causality and concentrate on the ravaging effects of an unfortunate love affair on two people.

The form of the tale recalls Constant's knowledge of German literary forms, particularly the *novelle*, a prose narrative dealing with a specific situation or a single aspect of a personality. *Adophe* contains a goodly share of moralizing elements, but the action develops ethical significance as it exposes the hero's life in relation to a central situation, with interest focused on Adophe's reactions. The incidents are starkly outlined in restricted fashion, illuminating the latent qualities of the person investigated. As Bourget pointed out, the technique called for concentrating all elements upon one dominant theme, with stress on the nature of the content rather than on form.

Founded in autobiography, the story reveals Constant's wish to understand himself and to take revenge on Mme de Staël. *Adolphe* stands as his answer to her portrait of him as Oswald in *Corinne*. More important, however, is his appreciation of his role in a series of love affairs: with Mme Lindsay, Mme Trévor, Julie Talma, Mme de Charrière, and Wilhelmina von Cramm. In the process he applied a major talent for penetrating analysis with devastating effect. He dissected himself so pitilessly, seeking motives and understanding, that often the book makes painful reading.

Adolphe dominates the story; all the other characters lack clear definition. Only two are called by given names; the others are the Ambassador, the Comte de P . . . , or the Baron de T . . . . Even Ellénore remains a shadow for, since events are seen only through Adolphe's eyes, she can function solely as the cause of his emotional upheavals. Similarly, the settings remain vague: Caden, a small city in Bohemia, D . . . , or an estate a short distance from Warsaw. In this manner Constant could focus attention on the only matter of real interest, the protagonist's behavior.

Adolphe's father stands as an indistinct but powerful force

behind his son. Indulgent, he made it possible for his son to escape to Caden with Ellénore and follow her to Poland. His constant reminders of the career Adolphe had abandoned made the boy feel he was sacrificing his youth and success to an older woman. Even the solution of the painful dilemma was provided by the father, whose interference through the French ambassador directly caused Ellénore's death. It was he who originally sent Adolphe to D . . . , where he met Ellénore. The boy left carrying false parental hopes but later understood how ill-prepared he was to repay his father with any measure of success. Insecure, an introvert, he irritated people with his reserve, concealing his basic timidity behind a sharp tongue. He felt "un désir ardent d'indépendance, une grande impatience des liens dont j'étais environné, une terreur invincible d'en former de nouveaux." And yet he sensed a deep "besoin de sensibilité dont je ne m'apercevais pas, mais qui, ne trouvant point à se satisfaire, me détachait successivement de tous les objets qui tour à tour attiraient ma curiosité."

Constant was less interested in the seduction of Ellénore than in its results, for which the initial three sections set the stage. Of these, the first sketched a psychological portrait of the hero, the next described his growing uneasiness and boredom, the last told of her surrender. Constant prepared it in five pages; the event occurred in six words: "Elle se donna enfin tout entière." The subsequent seven sections develop the major themes, and the plot ebbs and flows around Adolphe's indecisions. For a brief moment he sipped the heady wine of new love, but from then on his lucid mind, in terror of entanglement, began to reject any attachment. With quick intuition Ellénore foreshadowed the end: "Je ne sais quel pressentiment me dit, Adolphe, que je mourrai dans vos bras."

The suspicions of the count and a letter from Adolphe's father precipitated the first crisis. At Ellénore's insistence the boy requested a six month's delay before his return home; she broke with her first lover, abandoned her children, and offered Adolphe this sacrifice. But the more she clung, the more he struggled to break away. The first argument made him regret a youth dribbled away in sloth. She bound him with tears, "mais un premier coup était porté." Ostracized by society when her flight from the count roused public opinion, Ellénore turned to Adolphe for security, but he rejected her: "J'avais pris en horreur l'empire des femmes." Yet he fought a duel when a man insulted her. He ran away, yet he took her to Caden when his father threatened to intervene. His final attempt at evasion was blocked by the sudden death of her father. For a short spell some measure of intimacy returned but, as Adolphe noted in a haunting line of bleak vision, "nous vivions . . . d'une espèce de mémoire de coeur."

The last two parts concern the frantic struggle to escape that culminated in Ellénore's death. The lovers alternated between silence and sharp recrimination until the ambassador broke Ellénore's heart by revealing Adolphe's treachery. When she died, Adolphe reaped his reward. "J'étais déjà seul sur la terre . . . j'étais libre en effet; je n'étais plus aimé; j'étais étranger pour tout le monde."

Despite the fact that the story covers a four-year span, it is stated rather than conceived as action. The events are organized by the narrator, as in *René,* with his mind controlling the shape and content of the events that form the plot. Constant, the analyst, uses a clear, direct language, with little imagery; only towards the end, when Adolphe walks through the night in an agony of indecision, does he introduce the mournfulness of autumn. Then Ellénore dies in the dreary gloom of a Polish winter. The starkness of the style, however, adds power to the story. The consistent tone, though sometimes verging on monotony, pulls the rambling anecdotal structure into a unified whole.

Despite Constant's reliance on the conventional handling of plot, the concentrated story has always affected readers powerfully, most of them unpleasantly. Constant used the coincidence of two law suits to keep the story moving as he developed the theme of a conflict of interest between career and obligation to a woman. Ellénore's father recovered his fortune most opportunely and the ambassador's decision to forward Adolphe's letters caused Ellénore to perish of the mysterious fever that has carried away so many French heroines. But these ancient devices do not mar the effect of the slowly developed full-length portrait of a sensitive man clinically assessing himself. His vacillations, his incapacity to act, his unintentional cruelty, the sense of waste and humiliation that pervades the story—these revolt the reader because, perhaps, he may himself have known Adolphe's difficulties. Or he may be appalled by the thought of honestly exposing the true contours of a mind. Adolphe reveals the awful fact that man lives alone and is incapable of communicating his thoughts, especially in moments of emotional stress. Adolphe's honesty and lack of gentleness remind the reader that each man kills the thing he loves. His incurable misery seems a part of the human condition, in itself a nauseating thought.

Yet Constant indicted his contemporaries even more than himself: "Il faut du temps pour s'accoutumer à l'espèce humaine." The mediocrity of ideas, the hypocrisy, and the conformism of his time disgusted him. In Ellénore's salon Adolphe discovered that "les maris étaient dépourvus de sentiments aussi bien que d'idées; les femmes ne différaient de leurs maris que par une médiocrité plus inquiète et plus agitée." For him the society of his day was shot full of stupidity and jealousy. He found it emotionally bankrupt and confused in values, but he remained trapped in a dilemma: "La société m'importune, la solitude m'accable."

Constant wrote only one story but his sober confession marks a major advance in French short fiction. Previously writers had imposed moralizing on their stories by regulating incident to permit the interjection of comments and digressions for the edification of the reader. They interposed themselves between the plot and their audience as omniscient and pious prophets of the good life. There is, of course, a heavy content of moralizing in *Adolphe* but now it was no longer imposed but made integral to the structure, almost organic. Constant was not restricted by the thesis of an *Etudes de la nature* or a *Génie du Christianisme*. By stripping his "anecdote" to its essential ingredients, he could permit the actions of his hero to speak for themselves. Since Constant was speaking to a sophisticated audience, he could assume sufficient intelligence to grasp his meaning without authorial interference with the flow of events. He invited the reader, in effect, to stand beside the hero, not the author. And so successfully did he demonstrate the power of this technique that for a long time French short fiction would struggle to divest itself of its moral burden.

III

1828: Short Fiction Becomes Fashionable

Despite Chateaubriand's prestige, the success of Constant's *Adolphe*, and Nodier's dedication to the form, short fiction continued relatively unimportant in French literature until just before the Revolution of 1830. A new cluster of literary lights was appearing, the romantics, but they were struggling against the traditionalists for their right to experiment in the two traditionally important genres of the past, poetry and the theater. Since the brief narrative had as yet no literary standing, it failed to attract their attention. In effect, it would take another revolution, this one technological, to create more interest in the genre, but once this occurred brief fiction would accumulate a rapidly increasing number of devotees. The more artistically conscious of these would then produce the techniques on which the writers of the second half of the century would build the "modern" short story.

The literacy level of the nation had not been impressive before the cataclysm that buried the Ancien Régime. The monarchy had made only dilatory efforts to spread elementary education, with the institutions of higher learning reserved for the privileged. After the Revolution the Constituent Assembly fumed over the fact that only 72,000 students attended the *collèges*, but it did nothing to remedy the situation. Later the Convention voted the establishment of free public instruction, then sold off the property of all endowed schools. In his turn, Napoleon paid so little attention to education for the lower classes that in 1808 only some 25,500 students attended the *lycées* and the communal *collèges*. The Restoration, with Bourbon hostility toward the people, moved so slowly to correct the situation that in 1819 an estimated 15,000,000 adults could neither read nor write. And yet, with all the governmental bumbling, elementary education spread by means of mutual schooling carried on in *auberges académiques, athénées, musées,* or popular institutes. One taught one, in a desperate attempt to attain the freedom of the mind that literacy promised. But not until 1833 did the government produce the school system which, by 1848, gave some 3,500,000 children, or one-tenth of the population, at least a basic education.

As France was thus collecting with painful slowness a comparatively large number of literates, technological advances were providing writers with the means of reaching this audience with a literature it could comprehend. The facilities for producing books and periodicals had been limited prior to the Revolution. Not until 1808, for instance, did the nation boast a factory for the industrial production of printer's ink. January, 1812, saw the first results of Robert's paper-making machine, which replaced the old tedious method of hand production. By 1827 there were four in operation, twelve by 1833. And, finally, the single-stroke press and the inking of type by roller speeded up all printing processes. By about 1826 France had all the essential tools for manufacturing a mass literature as well as newspapers and periodicals in greater volume and for a lower price than ever.

The book publishers were not the only ones to appreciate the significance of the change. Newspapers fashioned in imitation of the English penny press revolutionized not only the exchange of news but the production of short fiction. Up to about 1830 journalism had scarcely existed. Prior to 1789, France could

muster only three papers but, with the Revolution and the subsequent constitutional guarantee of freedom of the press, it
became the inalienable, if momentary, right of every citizen to
air his opinions in a "newspaper." In 1789 some 500 journals
stridently advocated special points of view, while between 1789
and 1800 as many as 1,800 of them lived an ephemeral existence. Not surprisingly, Napoleon took the matter firmly in
hand: the number of such publications suddenly decreased to
thirteen, a kind of control which the Bourbons imitated. In
1824, seven papers spoke for the government, six for the opposition, but together they could claim only 55,600 subscribers.

The incredible *loi de justice et d'amour* of 1827 placed all
news media at the mercy of the ruler, although, when Louis-
Philippe came to power, he had to guarantee a measure of
latitude which allowed Emile de Girardin to introduce the
penny press. During the Restoration few had been able to afford
the annual subscription of 80 francs for papers which were
mailed out, rarely hawked on the streets. Consequently they
aimed their contents at a wealthy clientele, the same group that
espoused neoclassical literary values. No one had dreamed of
using a daily for advertising until Girardin put British ideas to
the test. In 1830 he launched a *Journal des connaissances utiles*
priced at half the usual cost and financed by advertisements.
Others stampeded to imitate him when, in 1832, he could boast
130,000 readers, but Girardin methodically built an empire
based on *La Mode*, *Le Voleur*, and *Le Panthéon littéraire*. In
1836, two years after the introduction of the cylindrical press,
Le Siècle and *La Presse* signaled a new day for journalism.

The shortage of readers, however, soon forced the papers into
a circulation war. *Le Siècle* and *La Presse*, *Le Constitutionnel*,
and their competitors ran into a new economic fact: if adver-
tisers were to pay printing costs, they had to be guaranteed
larger subscriber lists. Hopefully the publishers enlarged for-
mats, promised greater coverage, but soon discovered that the
feuilleton, short story, or serialized novel, lured more readers
than any other device. The same held true for the many maga-

zines that were simultaneously flooding the market. Thus the writer was handed a new outlet for his talent and, although editors preferred the serialized works of Dumas, Sue, or Soulié, the heavy demand for *feuilletons* provided a ready market for every variety of short fiction. Since papers like *La Presse* paid 300 francs for the slightest tale, the situation made it possible for Dumas *père* to bargain with Véron and Girardin for a contract guaranteeing 64,000 francs, then to write 100,000 lines a year for *Le Siècle* at one franc 50 a line. Writers like Balzac and Gautier were delighted to find such a relatively easy way to make money fast. One by one, even fanatically minded poets like Musset succumbed to the lure of the fast franc.

The sudden demand for brief fiction in large quantities made the medium highly attractive. Beginning in 1828, collections of short tales appeared with such monotonous regularity that they dismayed the critics, provoking bitter complaints from *La Revue de Paris* of June, 1832. And as the number of newspapers and magazines kept multiplying, more writers tried their pen at what seemed a simple genre, though few considered it within the province of serious literature. Even though illustrious predecessors could vouch for the short narrative, it would still take a literary generation to raise a minor art form, ephemeral in character and closely related to the anecdote, to a more respectable status.

As they considered the normal fare of contemporary readers, the disdainful knew they were right. A great many short tales had come from the diligent literary ladies of the eighteenth century, and their feminine successors continued the tradition. Most of them considered their writing a means of propagating the homely virtues; they preached adherence to the moral code of the middle class and set the pattern for the youth literature of the next century.

Madame Sophie Gay, for example, in the *Souvenirs d'une*

vieille fille (1843), raised the familiar cry of the embattled feminine defender of a public morality destined for the "lower classes." In a bristling preface she flayed the current literary taste of women, so low that it constituted a new social problem for men: "Comment baiser sans dégoût la main d'une jolie femme qui vient de tourner les feuillets gras et flétris d'un livre de M. de Balzac ou de M. Eugène Sue?" She found a crying need for cheap and amusing books for the workers and modestly proposed a series of episodes drawn from her own experiences. This new kind of "memoir" consisted of six stories: *Mystère et Leçon*, *La Providence de famille*, *Anaïs*, *Le Téléscope*, *Le Châle et le Chien*, and *La Princesse de Conti*. Admittedly feminine literature, it relied for success on tugging at the heart strings of lady readers while the heroines all suffered prodigiously in tales involving complicated love problems.

Despite the righteousness and indignation of the preface, Madame Gay did not produce any tales for the working classes. She aimed her titillating discussions of passion at the ladies of the upper bourgeoisie. And far from being impeccably pure, she indulged in the *volupté décente* so characteristic of the age. In *Mystère et Leçon* Madame openly espoused the cause of an adulterous couple, herself escaping a similar role only because she never met Alphonse. Nevertheless she wrung from the situation every particle of vicarious pleasure. In *Anaïs* she asked her readers to mourn the plight of a regenerated prostitute who missed true love only because malicious gossip drove her to a hasty suicide. Madame stood four square for love, with or without benefit of clergy. Even in *Le Châle et le Chien*, she approved the frustrated yearning of the fair Odille for Frédéric and raised the emotional temperature of her lady readers by ending in ghost-story style.

Madame Gay's stories unfortunately represent the level of a good share of the short narratives fed to the public. Casuistic discussions of passion became the patented product of the early lady writers who were, in fact, the predecessors of the twentieth-century agony column. To this domain they added children's stories of the variety favored by Mme Guizot in *Contes à l'usage de la jeunesse*. These contained a complete course in manners, morals, and the proper attitudes for well-raised boys and girls. In *Le Chapeau, ou Sachez mériter l'estime, L'Arbre et la Forêt, ou les Oeuvres de Dieu, La Bonne Conscience,* or *Le Présent du jour de naissance, ou la Véritable Bienfaisance,* Madame Guizot in syrupy tones lectured the youngsters on behavior. *Le Jeune Précepteur* taught adolescents of the lower classes their proper place in a bourgeois society. Little girls also needed advice. In *Ah! si j'étais fée,* little Angélina fussed because she had to finish her chores before playing, for which she received a tart lesson from her mother. Often the moral tale revolved around timeworn but still popular Horatio Alger situations. In *La Bonne Conscience,* Benoît, a carpenter, used his probity and skill to vindicate himself when he was wrongly accused of theft.

This saccharine moralizing even passed into periodicals proud of their high literary standards. In 1835 the *Revue de Paris* published Mlle Clémence Bailleul's *Une Grand'mère d'aujourd'hui.* Poor Emmeline adored the handsome Maurice de Tersy, but her worldly grandmother married him and palmed Emmeline off on an old man, at which the girl promptly went mad.

Since readers seemed to prefer this fare, the number of lady practitioners of the moral tale or stories concerned with the mysteries and intricacies of true affection increased steadily as the century aged. Mesdames had staked out a fertile, if monotonous, field. Few men cared to challenge their supremacy as guardians of youthful propriety and etiquette, although the good ladies brought to their task more zeal than talent. Because, for them, emotional impact counted for more than artistic unity, they jumped from one interesting episode to another with cavalier disdain for logic; they showed deep lachrymose concern for adultery or the fine points of an affair. In effect, they brought no professional concern to the form they abused, preferring to steal scenes and plots from each other with happy abandon.

Of the women, Delphine Gay, the daughter of Mme Sophie Gay and the future Mme de Girardin, demonstrated a talent well above that of her competitors. Her best-known effort, *La Canne de M. Balzac*, permitted her to use the old war-horse form for social criticism. The story, as she later wrote, was intended for herself, for those who did *not* analyze, to "passer une heure d'attente entre une affaire et un plaisir, entre un adieu et un retour." Subtitled *Un Don fatal*, it related the adventures of Tancrède Dorimont, a young man too handsome for employers with impressionable wives, who finally, with the aid of a magic cane, married a poetess from Limoges.

Delphine stands out from her sorority but she rambled as much as any of her sisters through a plot arranged to permit a variety of acid comments. The title invoked the prestige of Balzac, then the center of bitter critical debate, and Mlle Gay even used one of his favorite themes: how to succeed in Paris. After the cane had provided the hero with material success, Delphine shifted to a standard love story. Tancrède sought solace from the fair, though married, Malvina, but finally discovered the girl of his dreams. As Mlle Gay recounted his earnest quest, she satirized a husband's antagonism toward handsome bachelors and exploited current interest in the fantastic. The hero, of course, lost the cane, providing opportunity for broad comic relief. When Tancrède decided on seduction, he ended up spending the night in an antechamber and being bitten by the family dog. Clarisse turned out to be a protégée of Lamartine, a fact which gave Delphine the opportunity for unfavorable comment on lady poets. But she did manage to curb her tongue long enough to insure love's triumph.

Mlle Gay's work suffered from the same defects as that of her feminine counterparts. Her garrulity prevented economy of style, and she wove plots in helter-skelter design to accommodate ill-matched mixtures of social commentary and emotional casuistry. Virtue conquered vice, but only after an interestingly desperate struggle which allowed the author to conclude with a proverb. She heaped character upon character as she dissected society, her satire spiced with calculated doses of *la volupté décente*. Thus, in *Il ne faut pas jouer avec la douleur*, Delphine explained the psychology of seduction in detail, reluctantly rescuing Mme la Comtesse at the last possible moment.

Hard as they labored, these "damned scribbling females," as Hawthorne called them, received little credit for their work. Nevertheless, since they made this brand of short fiction an integral part of French literature, despite the mediocrity of their writing, they had the last word. By 1850, with the appearance of periodicals like *Modes parisiennes*, ladies' home journalism was enshrined as a national institution that specialized in such weary bromides as *Ce que vaut un faux diamant*, *Un Homme indispensable*, and *Une Larme d'enfant*. Mesdames fared better than most writers because they fossilized their conception of prose fiction in the nineteenth-century magazines.

The provincial journals contributed even less to the advancement of the cause of short fiction, although they added considerably to the statistics of production. Like the Paris magazines and dailies, they needed the brief narrative to intermingle with their articles and to sweeten their didacticism. As literacy spread and printing possibilities grew, each provincial capital hastened to create a review modeled on the important Paris periodicals. The *Revue de Bretagne*, for example, depended mostly on local talent but on occasion used the work of E. Souvestre and Marceline Desbordes-Valmore.

In general, however, the literary level of the offerings ran about the same as that published in the metropolis. Charles Sigoyer, for instance, published (*La Créole*; I, I, 1833) a first-person narrative of a young Creole who ran afoul of Coelia, a crafty and ungrateful prostitute. Again, in September, 1834, Edouard Corbière of Brest described in *Le Négrier Le Fantôme* a fight between a slaver and a British corvette, with the latter losing, of course. Valéry, in *Un Dénoûment, conte artistique* (March, 1833), told how an artist raised a girl foundling. When she grew up he lost his talent, to recover it only after he had fed on her virginity. Folk tales, Breton legends, stories of the fantastic such as *Une Nuit d'opium, rêve fantastique,* all these rubbed elbows with Sigoyer's tearful tales of misunderstood maidens in a periodical that provided reading matter for every taste.

La Gironde repeated the same recipe, a mixture essential for monetary success in the provinces. It mingled appeals to local patriotism with *La Chanson d'amour, légende des côtes basques,* by Auguste Bouet, *capitaine au long cours,* or *Le Château del Piombo, conte fantastique* (1835). *Léontine* (May, 1836) recounted the regeneration of a fallen woman by a poet who was exiled to Guiana for his probity. "Léontine était chaste et pure, sinon de corps, au moins de l'âme . . . comme je la purifiai du feu de mes enivrantes caresses."

Even the children's stories, hitherto dominated almost exclusively by women, began to attract the attention of professional writers when old hands like Ducray-Duminil assessed the fertility of the field. His *Fête des enfans ou Recueil de petits contes moraux* aimed at helping parents form "le coeur et l'esprit de petits êtres destinés à fonder la postérité." Consequently, *Le Jour de l'an, la leçon du grand'père,* described the lesson learned by Auguste and Julie, who hoarded their Christmas money rather than share with the poor. *Nancy* told a sorrowful tale of a penniless child cast out by a wicked stepfather who later became a nun famous for pious works. Or again, *La Distribution des prix* revealed how Félix, bright but erratic, cheated on an examination. "M. Delaville fit mettre le méchant Félix dans les prisons de Saint Lazare, où il resta trois semaines au pain et à l'eau, recevant, deux fois par jour, vingt coups de nerfs de boeuf. Cette correction le changea totalement, et il fit, par la suite, la consolation de son respectable père."

The giants of the magazine field, the *Revue de Paris* and the *Revue des Deux Mondes*, also had to depend on the recipe forms of short fiction for the bulk of their material since, as usual, exceptional talent and high quality literature were in short supply. Frédéric Soulié, a regular contributor to the *Revue de Paris*, offered the standard fare in *Message* (XIV, 1835): Rodolphe, a French tutor in Russia, had fallen in love with the princess Douchkina, thus breaking the heart of her mother, who coveted the boy's affection. Moral: if one loves contrary to duty, "on en meurt, et on n'est pas aimée." Soulié specialized in the unusual: *Une Nuit en diligence, extrait des mémoires du diable* (XXXIII, 1836), was an exemplum which proved a friend's stupidity about women with the tale of a young officer shot by a faithful wife he tried to seduce.

All the standard themes and conventions that had accumulated so rapidly during the short but vigorous practice of brief fiction appeared in the pages of the *Revue de Paris*. Eugène Guinot, in *La Relique* (VIII, 1834), repeated an anecdote about the retreat from Moscow during which a dragoon deliberately got himself killed to permit his twin brother to deliver a love letter from their dead colonel to a bored young lady. Méry, in *Antonio Gasperoni* (XIV, 1835), humorously sketched a group of bandits who preferred the comfort of a papal jail to the uncertain liberty of the mountains. Méry's *L'Ame transmise* (XV, 1835) related the undying love of Léonti and Stellina. On the other hand, Léon Gozlan sobbed over the plight of a dog whose child mistress was abducted by a wicked father (*Rog*, Sept. 28, 1834). In his turn, Roger de Beauvoir sketched the fate of a poor groom who, harrassed by another servant, poisoned his beloved horse after he had been unfairly discharged (*David Dick*, VI, 1834).

The general level ran higher in the *Revue des Deux Mondes*, though many of the narratives were undistinguished. *Le Lasso, ou la Vengeance corse* revealed the revenge of Tonino Guitera on the noble relative who had raped his betrothed, prompting her to jump into a chasm. Léon de Wailly offered *L'Autre Chambre, conte fantastique* (III-IV, 1831), supposedly an incident from the life of the young Hoffmann. To be sure, the *Revue des Deux Mondes* also carried stories by Balzac, Vigny, or Dumas, but sandwiched between them were gems like *Le Nécromancien*, the story of an old magician who proved that a nobleman had murdered his brother to marry his fiancée.

The normal provender found in magazines ran to much fictionalized history, with settings laid in Italy or in Russia. Translations increased rapidly, particularly from the English, and imitations of German *contes fantastiques*. The output, as is to be expected, followed the general literary interests of the period. In addition to the horror tales, the moral instructions for children, and fairy stories, plots ran heavily to the tribulations of the young. In most cases their love was obstructed by the elders or by society, providing authors with an opportunity to display their marked predilection for *la volupté décente*. Except for the few who gained more than ephemeral reputation, writers did not depart from the basic anecdotal structure. For almost all, the word *short* had only a linear connotation; they gave the reader a straightforward story without concern for economy or concentration. Episode was cultivated for its own sake to exploit the exotic, the unusual, or the bizarre, but always with a large dose of moralizing. Most authors calculated the sequence of events in terms of the mounting emotional tension, reaching the climax at a moment of tearful desperation. A few drew sketches, the bread and butter of magazines like *La Caricature*, where Balzac learned part of his trade, short portraits, biting in irony, of stereotyped characters like the National Guardsman, the Lawyer, the Merchant, among them Balzac's *Fragment d'une nouvelle satire ménippée*, or *La Dernière Revue de Napoléon*. This type of

satire formed a large part of the humor of the age, with under-
currents of sharp social criticism, similar to the drawings
Daumier produced to needle the bourgeois regnant.

These stories scarcely advanced the cause of short narrative
as an art form, but they do constitute a norm against which the
works of the major authors can be measured. They furnish an
excellent index of the public taste with which any author had
to contend, as well as some notion of the contemporary knowledge of a well-told tale. The sudden popularity of brief fiction had caught writers prepared only to rely on trusted recipes
and the conscious artists would have to contend with this leth-
argy as they tried to fashion the form into an instrument usable
for their needs. To do so, they would have to overcome an
inbred penchant for moralizing which threatened to keep short
fiction merely an instrument for didacticism.

Stendhal, Balzac, and Mérimée

UNFORTUNATELY, just as concentrated practice of the short forms seemed to promise further investigation of the nature and possibilities of short fiction, the genre ran head on into its giant cousin, the novel, particularly the type inherited from Walter Scott. Ever since 1826, this longer prose form, known now as the romance and its derivatives, had dominated French literature; it had even succeeded in attracting the attention of major writers who were willing to grant it comparable status with poetry and the theater. In this developing age of prose, when writers learned to apply the democratic average of taste to literature for the benefit of an increasing mass market, the novel or romance promised the widest audience and the greatest economic benefits. Moreover, the genre promised to provide nineteenth-century authors with a mode of expression suitable for handling the problems of post-Revolutionary France and a nascent industrial age. Given such competition, short fiction either languished within the confines of the eighteenth-century recipe or was turned into a dehydrated version of the novel by men like Stendhal and Balzac.

Stendhal

With the exception of the *Chroniques italiennes*, Stendhal's ventures into short prose have received scant attention. The creator of *Le Rouge et le Noir* and *La Chartreuse de Parme* has so dazzled scholars that they pass lightly over the author of the

Souvenirs d'un gentilhomme italien, Le Coffre et le Revenant, Le Philtre, and *Ernestine ou la Naissance de l'amour.* Nowhere are they treated as representatives of a genre long practiced in the national literature.

Stendhal himself helped foster this opinion since he considered the short tale a quick solution to his constant need for money. Only seven of his shorter pieces were published during his lifetime; the rest appeared posthumously, exhumed by Romain Colomb or by inquisitive and properly respectful professors. Of these, four, including the *Abbesse de Castro,* have far overshadowed the rest.

The fact remains that Beyle's brief narratives need the charity that only a convinced Stendhalian can bring them. Written primarily in two bursts of interest, between 1830-31 and 1837-38, most were conceived with the rapidity and carelessness given to the production of illegitimate children. Stendhal never pretended to understand the intricacies of the short narrative, on which he did not expect his fame to rest. Only the *Chroniques* earned the compliment of close attention; the others served their purpose by providing the few francs needed to steady a shaky budget.

Stendhal's first sally into short fiction came in 1826, when the *Souvenirs d'un gentilhomme italien* were published in the *Revue britannique* (IV, 250-83). The basic plot had been borrowed from *The life and adventures of an Italian gentleman, containing his travels in Italy, Greece, France &c,* which appeared in the *London Magazine,* October 1, 1825, through April 1, 1826. Only the first part, which concerns travel in Italy, seems to have interested Stendhal.

The *Souvenirs* consist of a series of anecdotes and portraits tied together only by the fact that they are recorded by an Italian commentator. In portraying Rome during the two French occupations between 1797 and 1814, Stendhal intended to satirize the church that had sapped the nation's strength, and to contrast with sketches of conforming, enervated believers, portraits of such energetic individuals as the free thinker, Burner, and Spatolino, the honest brigand.

"Je suis né à Rome . . . ," the gentleman began. He had received the usual education, poor Latin instruction and the threat of hellfire, but had risen to a position in the administration of the military occupation which permitted him a wide range of comment. Though inferior to most of Stendhal's work, the *Souvenirs* reveal many of his difficulties with short fiction. He unabashedly used the memoir structure for a bitter denunciation of the Church's record in Italy. Because the pseudoautobiographical form permitted him to wander as fancy dictated, he could skip from one topic to another, from religious education in the papal states to bandits, to the abduction of the Pope, and miracles. The "gentleman" served only as a reporter whose peripatetic existence allowed the loose picaresque form by which Beyle could pass from portrait to portrait without transition.

This mode of storytelling suited Beyle's temperament admirably. Because he understood his material as chronicle, a kind of "history," he contentedly followed the pattern of historical narration. Yet, even in this loose arrangement, Stendhal found it impossible to compress or direct his story. Whenever an association of ideas suggested fresh detail, he happily strayed from the plot. The detail, the portrait, or the anecdote were dearer to his heart than the production of a unified whole.

In 1830 Stendhal completed a number of tales, most of which appeared after his death, though two, *Le Coffre et le Revenant* and *Le Philtre*, were published in the *Revue de Paris* that same year. The first of these has no known source, a fact unusual in the history of this genial literary bandit. Subtitled a "Spanish adventure," it pictures a Spain remarkably similar to that popular in terror novels or the industrial literature of the day. Beyle allied love and danger in the manner approved by contemporary Byronism; villains diligently pursued virgins, but here virtue did not conquer.

Le Coffre et le Revenant consists primarily of a portrait of one of Stendhal's favorite characters, the arrogant despot who vied with young Don Fernando for the love of the unfortunate Inès. It provided Stendhal with an unusual chance to indulge his taste for the bizarre and the macabre. In actuality a study of jealousy, more particularly the portrait of a suspicious husband, it allowed him to direct the plot toward incidents revelatory of the character of Don Bustos. The police chief had spent eight years on the galleys, had fought as a guerilla chief against the French; somber, cruel, and arrogant, he brooked no rivals. Like the powerful family heads of Renaissance Italy, this man of action held his honor dear; what he wanted, he seized. Thus Doña Inès could only bend to his will and marry him—or die; Don Fernando could only flee. From the moment the youngsters dared trifle with Don Bustos, they were doomed, since Stendhal never could force himself to contrive a popular happy ending. The husband dominated the episodes, all of which were strung together to provide a black and white portrait of an overbearing and possessive personality.

Yet the story does not lack an ironic, albeit macabre, humor. Stendhal delighted in making the young lover pop in and out of a coffer to avoid the terrible husband, with enough presence of mind to jam the lock when the police chief tried to open the chest. Even the love scene had its tongue-in-cheek moments: Inès recoiled at finding Fernando in her bedroom, but a moment later she cried "Ah! nous sommes damnés, irrémissiblement damnés, Fernando!" and fell into his arms. The sense of sin lent spice to the affair, as Stendhal commented.

However successful the portrait of Don Bustos, Stendhal found himself succumbing to a penchant for the unusual. He had to invent a bandit menace to provide reason for the coffer, and use coincidence to place Don Fernando on the scene at the right moment; complicated alibis were constantly contrived to disguise the affair. Stendhal was obviously using the wrong medium for what he had in mind as he tried to create the image of a strong personality in a short tale by juggling the plot from one emotional crisis to another. The resultant tangled web of events lacked credibility or any sense of dynamism.

He failed to solve this technical difficulty in *Le Philtre* where, once again, he borrowed the plot, a "plaisanterie," a "plagiat dont j'ai averti la Revue." Though he blithely wrote "imité de l'italien de Silvia Lalaperta," he plundered Scarron's *L'Adultère innocent*, the first half of which he followed closely, while the second, full of derring-do and duels, he transposed in terms of his own age.

The story is as unusual as *Le Coffre*: a runaway wife who rejected her savior, Lieutenant Liéven, for the circus rider who seduced her. But the portraiture comes through less successfully because Stendhal failed to make Liéven as vivid as the jealous husband. Dazed by his adventure, the lieutenant fell in love unbelievably fast, thus contradicting Beyle's own theories. By using the framework device, Stendhal tried to tell of two fated loves that worked at cross-purposes, but he faced the impossible task of making the incredible seem likely: a naked lady falling from a doorway; beaten and robbed, she still adored her betrayer; a young officer who offered marriage to an adulterous woman he had just met. As a consequence, Liéven has tinges of caricature. He was afraid to rescue Léonor because she might be ugly. And the irrepressible Stendhal could not help repeating the incident of the returned husband. The seducer had hopped eagerly into Léonor's room only to find her spouse there. Hidden in the attic, he spent two days dodging the master of the house as he frantically tried to escape.

Fascinating because of its very incredibility, the tale is only momentarily amusing. Neither character stands out, both buried in a welter of peculiar events that prevented a plausible ending. To finish the story, Stendhal had to have Liéven make an incredible proposal and, when refused, commit suicide.

Le Coffre and *Le Philtre* were, for Stendhal, attempts to find a mode for describing strong personalities in action. He abandoned this type of narrative when he found a more comfortable manner of story telling in *Vanina Vanini*. *Vanina* is usually printed along with the *Chroniques italiennes* (1837) because it resembles them in technique and subject matter but, actually, the story had been written in December, 1829, and published that same year in the *Revue de Paris*. Here Stendhal was moving toward the chronicle, in which, like a historian, he trusted the facts to illuminate his fictional world. He wrote of events as they happened, haphazardly, full of coincidences, cruelties, and ironies; he did not compress or direct, since life does not. As the biographer of people interesting to himself, he treated events chronologically. His characters lived out their appointed days, heroic or cowardly, as history revealed the meaning of their existence.

In *Vanina Vanini* Stendhal plunged directly into the plot, introducing immediately the main characters, with a bizarre account of a wealthy Roman girl who gave her own kind of aid and comfort to a carbonaro until he rejected her for the security of religion. The recipe was taking shape, albeit awkwardly. Though Pietro's conversion and Vanina's marriage were hastily prepared, Stendhal obviously enjoyed a form which let him introduce his characters in the simplest terms: a bored and wealthy aristocrat and a poor, simple patriot. The episodes were then arranged to provoke a reaction from the characters, particularly Vanina. In this way the portrait filled out, with the personalities summed up in a few major moments. Vanina found in Pietro a revolutionary who could release her from boredom but, paradoxically, his patriotism incited a possessive woman to betray his band in order to keep him for herself. And when Pietro proposed a life without her, she exploded in dangerous anger.

In this second study of jealousy, events conspired to infuse a sheltered aristocrat with the violent energy of her Renaissance ancestors. Vanina became obsessed with a dream, for which she would lie, betray, and suborn. She reduced life to holding a lover who persisted in choosing his own fate. Of common clay, he acted in counterpoint to her, beginning as hero, ending as pious fraud. Here Stendhal reverted to the theme of the *Souvenirs*: organized religion sapped a man's energy, perverted his drive to action. Vanina shared Beyle's worship of the un-reconstructed rebel, but the more pliant Pietro could not live up to her expectations. The story was manipulated to afford the boy a choice of rejecting either Vanina or the carbonari. Hence, the plot slid from crisis to crisis, illuminating her strengths or disclosing his weaknesses until Pietro finally refused her sacrifice, when he found the price of patriotism too high. The tale forms a pendant to the *Souvenirs* as a commentary on contemporary Italy; in the one case the Church hounded a man who dared expose it, and in the other it smothered individuality in favor of conformism and abject acceptance.

When, in 1837, Stendhal felt pressed for funds, he extracted from his notes the material for the *Chroniques italiennes*. From a set of twelve old chronicles purchased in Italy, he drew *Vittoria Accoramboni, duchesse de Bracciano*, a blood and thunder tale of Renaissance vengeance. It was published anonymously in the *Revue des Deux Mondes* (March 1, 1837), and earned for the author Buloz' promise to buy six or seven more stories at a thousand francs apiece. Only three others followed: *Les Cenci*, July 1, 1837, signed F. de Logenevais, a pseudonym also favored by Blaze de Bury and Pontmartin; *La Duchesse de Palliano*, April 15, 1838; and *L'Abbesse de Castro*, February 1, and March 1, 1839. Two more, *Suora Scolastica* and *Trop de faveur tue*, were begun in 1839 but never finished.

The first, *Vittoria Accoramboni,* began with a warning: "Malheureusement pour moi comme pour le lecteur, ceci n'est point un roman, mais la traduction fidèle d'un récit fort grave écrit à Padoue en décembre 1585." It concerned Vittoria, the beautiful daughter of a wealthy family of Agubio who was stabbed by her relatives for going to live with the suspected murderer of her husband. Stendhal had actually transcribed the original into French as accurately as possible, with only a few minor changes, because he liked reporting incidents in chronological fashion. In Renaissance Italy he discovered personalities like Vittoria, surrounded by men like the Orsini, who knew no law but their own whim, or the killer who drove a knife into Vittoria's breast, moved the point around, and politely asked if he had touched her heart. This attitude, however barbarous, satisfied Stendhal's streak of sadism.

When he published *Les Cenci* (1837), he continued adapting more of the same extraordinary material. The story was a contemporary favorite, having been used by Shelley and Adolphe de Custine, among others. Monsters like Francesco Cenci, Stendhal wrote, could appear only during ages of hypocrisy, better than his own age of cant, which he considered too "collet monté." Cenci, an arrogant aristocrat without tenderness or trust, had tried to solve a personal problem common to the mass culture of the nineteenth century: "Comment pourrai-je me donner le plaisir si vif de me sentir différent de tout ce vulgaire?" His "solution" spawned a creature that even his own callous age rejected. Francesco Cenci, an atheist fond of esoteric sensations, had announced his intention to bury all his children, then burn the palace in celebration. As Francesco aged, he attempted to rape 14-year-old Béatrix in front of his wife. So repulsive did he become that his children hired two assassins who, whipped on by Béatrix, drove a nail into the eye of the drugged Prince. When a judge ordered the family questioned, all but Béatrix confessed under torture.

The adaptation was arranged to produce two major portraits

according to the mode Stendhal had worked out in *Le Coffre* and *Vanina Vanini*. In *Vittoria Accoramboni*, the princes Paul and Louis Orsini stood out as gigantic Renaissance despots who bowed only to superior force. In *Les Cenci* Beyle created the figures of the strong-minded Béatrix and the self-indulgent Don Francesco. The father dominated the first part of the chronicle, but once the family decided to kill him, Béatrix grew in stature. She it was who secured her brother's permission for the murder, she who encouraged the reluctant assassins to stab a drugged man. For the execution of her mother and herself, the girl calmly ordered simple dresses. "Madame ma mère est-elle bien morte?" she queried the headsman, and arranged herself skillfully for the beheading so the crowd might not see her breasts. Stendhal managed to give the impression that Béatrix directed her own fate as she instructed the executioner how to perform his function.

The unity of the story lies in the two portraits. Stendhal passed rapidly over some events, lingered lovingly on others, particularly the murder and the execution. The details which often slowed his plots now helped define the characters as he studied the anatomy of perversion. Here his love of violence served to maintain the tone of horror. By carefully delineating Francesco, he made Béatrix more plausible, and by emphasizing the arrest and execution he turned her from a poised parricide into an object of pity. As her personality began to develop, she became the complement of her victim, not so cruel, but as proud, as determined, and as courageous. And with the discovery of this manner of using incident to round out character, Stendhal's search for a satisfactory way to handle short fiction came to an end. He could now plunder history, exploit a wealth of detail, even wander, yet still hope to produce a unified tale.

He settled into this method with *La Duchesse de Palliano* (April 15, 1838), an adaptation of several manuscripts which contained Stendhal's study of Renaissance capital sins. This time he investigated aristocratic iniquity and its punishment, apologizing tongue-in-cheek for the shocking incident he was about to unfold: the strangling of the Duchess Palliano for an adultery never committed.

La Duchesse de Palliano contained such a complicated plot that Stendhal floundered in detail. Since the story came from several manuscripts, he did more adapting than in the other chronicles, occasionally interjecting parenthetical comments. But his faith in the revelatory power of historical fact betrayed him because the adaptation produced no portraits like those of Béatrix and her father. The necessity of following chronology left him with only two major scenes: the lover's death and the Duchess's assassination, which did not produce full characterizations. The complexity of plot, the multiplicity of incident, keep the reader's attention shifting to a series of minor characters. As a result the episodes do not cluster to reveal a single major personality and the effects are dispersed rather than centralized. The consequent lack of unity reveals the origins of the *Duchesse* in a series of records that yielded only the interest of a scandalous news story.

In view of this, Stendhal decided to add more of himself to the chronicles. When he published *L'Abbesse de Castro* (1839), he claimed the narrative came from two manuscripts. But only the first actually existed; the second was a long pastiche in which he abandoned his historian's principles long enough to change the conclusion by inventing an escape tunnel and returning the hero from exile.

Because he resented the restrictions of short fiction, Stendhal wrote this tale of frustrated love in a more leisurely way. Almost lyrically, he praised the bandits that infested Italy, in whom he saw the true Robin Hoods of the golden age of Western civilization. He admired their fierce spirit, their religion of the given word, their fine sense of honor. Though such men probably never existed, Stendhal made them the heroes of his primitivistic dream world. Along with the despots, they represented his version of the "natural" man as they indulged in ambush and dared perilous loves for a moment of happiness.

Once again Stendhal used all his favorite themes to create portraits from the raw material of history. He moved slowly, since he had learned from *La Duchesse de Palliano* that compression proved unsatisfactory, relating in detail the story of Hélène de Campireali's spectacular love affair with Jules Branciforte, a poor and passably handsome boy. Stendhal was fascinated by the destruction caused when the affections of two youngsters foundered on a local feud. After Hélène entered the convent at Castro, Jules reacted with Renaissance vigor by trying unsuccessfully to abduct her. "Nous allons, en effet, assister à la longue dégradation d'une âme noble et généreuse." For ten years Hélène lived in the convent while her mother forged letters showing Jules' progressively cooling love, simultaneously convincing the absent boy that Hélène had married. After Hélène gave herself contemptuously to the young Bishop Cittadini, she was condemned to a special convent. Her mother hired miners to tunnel into the prison but, when they reached her cell, Hélène refused to be saved. She wrote Jules of her love, then stabbed herself.

In *L'Abbesse de Castro*, Stendhal proved to his own satisfaction that his forte really lay in the novel. Beyle could create strongly delineated portraits, but he had to double the size of his chronicle, multiply episode, and compound complexity to illuminate the major characters properly. Thus, Hélène appears out of a welter of detail: clever enough to check the dust on the arquebuses and, not finding any, to suspect her father's ambush; courageous enough to walk disguised as a monk right by her brother; feminine enough to love Jules for his attack on the convent; and too proud to run away after an affair with the bishop.

The minor characters benefited from the leisurely pace. The mother silently watched her daughter fall in love, but it was she who forged the letters and spread the rumor of Jules' death, who bribed the clergy to have Hélène made abbess, and who engineered the escape tunnel. Beside these women, the men pale, particularly the foppish bishop who accepted Hélène's contempt, then turned coward at the investigation. Even Jules is almost too much of a cliché; he is Stendhal's bandit ideal, courageous to the point of rashness, daring in love, and loyal, but he is always overshadowed by the giant figure of the abbess.

As usual, Stendhal counted on presenting the story as history to overcome disbelief. Since he insisted on describing the rich fullness of Renaissance life, he did not feel bound by the logic of a closed fictional world, nor required to develop the characters from a set of premises. His personages could display all the unpredictable, contradictory facets of real personalities, move as haltingly and in as complex a manner as life itself. His tale of a love that brought only suffering moved in terms of emotional decisions: Jules' refusal to seduce Hélène; his attack on the convent; and the abbess's casual abandonment of herself to the bishop. This was how Stendhal's imagination worked, for he grasped the narrative as a report rather than as an unfolding, self-generated drama.

L'Abbesse de Castro represents Stendhal's farewell to the short narrative. He had struggled to condense his beloved portraits, to reproduce in brief the vigor of an age that demanded full satisfaction of life, but he recognized the obstacles he faced. The chronicles might earn quick money, but for his artistic purposes he required more room than they provided. In a sense *Les Chroniques italiennes* were only rehearsals for *La Chartreuse de Parme.* As he candidly admitted to Balzac, it had not occurred to him that there were *rules* for art. He achieved a kind of unity from the power of his portraits, but often had difficulty making the pictorial dramatic within a short narrative and apparently never understood the advantage of a shifting point of view. Lacking a capacity for invention, he preferred to rearrange the fictions of others, although the borrowings were often inadequate for his purpose. Since monsters fascinated him, he fell victim to his own special image of the Renaissance. His "natural man" no longer existed, if he ever had, which prompted him to satirize the flabbiness of his age, repugnant in its odor of piety. He was, as Victor Jacquemont noted, "crédule au point de croire à tous les contes ridicules." Sadistic, fond of bloody scenes and complicated plots, he reveled in strong, single-minded characters but had difficulty finding other things to say. The restrictions of brief fiction hampered him so much that he abandoned the genre; in his case the novel won out over the short story.

Balzac

Balzac's reputation rests so solidly on his contribution to the novel and the technique of realism that it is sometimes forgotten that he also wrote a large number of short tales. But from 1829 to 1847 he produced an impressive number of brief narratives, partly because the form interested him, partly for financial reasons. Since the newspapers and magazines were prepared to pay substantial sums for the work of popular authors, Balzac was glad to oblige, particularly since his ever-growing list of creditors made profitable work essential. However, like Stendhal, he had difficulty understanding the nature of brief stories. His talent lay in the field of the novel and the scope of his imagination was such that when he attempted a short narrative he could not concentrate effect or control incident.

Balzac's major contribution to the writing of fiction lay in his acceptance of contemporary society as the source of his material. Of all the major writers of the first part of the nineteenth century, he alone seems to have recognized the full implications of the crisis in France at the end of the Empire: the consequences of the Revolution, the first impact of the Industrial Revolution, and more particularly the dramatic rise of the middle class to power and responsibility. From a society based on birth, the country had shifted to one founded on money, and the modern world appeared. The greed for wealth and the control it represented, the acquisition of the symbols representative of success, these seemed to him the hallmark of the age. An orderly and ordered society had been transformed into a jungle; men and women lived by the law of the survival of the fittest. The meek would not inherit the earth but would be gobbled up by men like Vautrin and Rastignac who, each in his own sphere, would write the rules for the new order of gamesmanship. Balzac's vision was clear because, unlike Vigny, Musset, and Lamartine, he had had to fight his way to the top, learning the new facts the hard way. He knew no other world, and he felt compelled to etch the portrait of this one in acid of its own making.

Since he had the talent to satisfy his drive to become the historian of the new order, he organized this perception for expression in the various prose forms: the essay, novel, short fiction, and newspaper articles, both serious and humorous. By preference he chose to communicate his vision primarily in the novel, which offered sufficient space and time to satisfy his stylistic propensity to inflation. He could fit his world into its ample frame because his mind operated according to the optics of magnification. Balzac turned to the short narrative only as a professional who recognized a popular and marketable new genre.

Because Balzac's understanding of people was sociological, the short story forced him to squeeze his fictional universe into an uncomfortably small space. Like other writers of the early nineteenth century, he had to develop his own type of brief narrative, since the simple anecdote structure then available did not meet his requirements. Consequently, between 1830 and 1835 Balzac arrived at a structure for brief fiction that unfortunately hardened into a handy prescription. He began abruptly with a short opening scene calculated to hold attention, then proceeded via a flashback to sketch the antecedent facts. The rest of the plot was conceived in two or three segments, the first generally a major portrait of the leading character, the second the action resulting from the conditions previously established by the portrait. A short epilogue, moral in tone, clarified the author's intent and the allegory.

Since the portraits presupposed a special concept of man in society, the beginning of the narrative outlined the premises from which the action was deduced almost deterministically. A long preparation set up the simple plot like a syllogism. This kind of structure, fleshed out by Balzac's pictorial imagination, tended to make the work seem static, which consequently faced him with the problem of conveying a sense of the passage of time. This he did by repeated time references until he reached the last scene, where the principal action unfolded.

Most of the tales revolved around tragic themes, apart from the sex-centered *Contes drolatiques.* A fault committed by a major character in either the flashback or the first scene culminated in a crisis, at which point society claimed its payment. Yesterday's reality led to today's fall. Actually, Balzac was developing a modern conception of tragedy consistent with his view of society. Rastignac and Vautrin represent an amoral power loose in a world where human lions devour the lambs and doves of mankind. To be sure, Balzac understood the Aristotelian notion of tragedy as stemming from a personality fault that led to destruction, but he introduced another element: given the conditions of a modern, industrialized world, the very constitution of an increasingly complex society provided new sources of neuroses. Failure was conceived in other terms, with the petty and the degrading accompanying catastrophes that soiled more often than they destroyed. Man was denied the privilege of being overwhelmed in grand and courageous defiance of the gods.

Because the plots were generally inconsequential, the characters themselves had to carry the brunt of Balzac's message. These figures constitute a major contribution to modern mythology because so many of them verge on the stereotype. He emptied the world in his head onto his pages, peopling them with representations of the age in a perception of what the twentieth century would call the human condition. Through the courtesan, the status-hungry, the ambitious, the lawyer, the artist, and the speculator, he caught the features of many of his contemporaries. Basically he used them to formulate moral judgments but, as often happens, he succeeded better in picturing the rogue and the amorality of the cynic than in making credible the naïve and the innocent.

Balzac had drifted toward the short forms after his disastrous adventure as a poet and his production of such dubious novels as *Annette et le Criminel, Le Centenaire, ou les Deux Béringheld,* and *Clotilde de Lusignan ou le Beau Juif.* When he emerged from the shelter of pseudonyms like Lord R'hoone and Horace de Saint Aubin, he moved into the world of journalism. He made his debut as a chronicler for *La Silhouette* and *La Mode,* where he learned to draw the sketches that form an important part of his art, particularly in 1830, when he wrote pseudosociological studies of such assorted stereotypes as *L'Epicier, Le Charlatan,* and *Le Ministre.* He reproduced with heavy, obvious humor the personalities of the grocer, "the most Christian of all merchants," the very backbone of contemporary society, or the tricky charlatan, always with an eye on the main chance. In these sketches, Balzac concentrated on creating typical representatives of the various social categories that interested him.

Simultaneously Balzac was taking a fling at brief fiction, following the lead of a considerable number of his colleagues. Encouraged by the success of *Les Chouans,* he decided to exploit his new reputation by taking advantage of the rage for *contes* that had begun during the Restoration. The sales of *Les Soirées de Neuilly,* the favorable reception of such literary lights as Mme de Genlis and Pauline de Meulan, the renown of the Bibliophile Jacob, Lady Morgan, and Saintine, all encouraged him. In 1829 Mérimée had begun a career with *L'Enlèvement de la redoute,* and in 1830 Delphine Gay, Jules Janin, and a host of others joined him. The businessman in Balzac could not resist the temptation.

In October, 1829, he tried his hand with *El Verdugo,* a dramatic episode concerning the revolt of a Spanish town during the French occupation. The brief tale takes shape around the dilemma in which the recapture of Menda placed the marquis who led the rebellion. The story rests basically on the horror of the situation: the villagers and servants are hanged; the noble family is to be shot. At this point the marquis faced a dilemma: how to avoid the obliteration of his family name. Therefore, the focus shifted to the son, who might refuse to pay the price for his life, then to daughter Clara.

Balzac assumed that his readers would recall the guerrilla warfare that virtually imprisoned the French army in Spain and provoked a savage repression. He founded his narrative on the logic of the conqueror who finds himself outnumbered in a hostile land, and on the universal cliché of Spanish honor. French readers who remembered the glory of the Napoleonic epic could resent, yet sympathize with, the fate of the rebels; they could hope that a plebeian French lieutenant might wed a grandee's daughter, but they surely read with fascination the fate of the rebellious nobles. The characters derive their personality from their names, their positions, and their problems. They are stereotypes in familiar situations: a grocer's son moonstruck over an aristocratic girl, a marquis hypersensitive about family honor, an inflexible general, a son who does his ghastly duty. Told chronologically, the story moves fast because Balzac had not yet begun to amass detail and descriptions. Its form lies close to the oral anecdote, polished for literary usage.

Balzac's particular manner of conceiving short fiction is apparent in *La Maison du chat-qui-pelote,* dated October, 1829, and published in *Les Scènes de la vie privée.* Here the sociologist came to the fore in a tale of the love of Augustine, the younger daughter of a draper, for Thomas de Sommervieux, a painter. Balzac fashioned the story according to the pattern that became his most consistent method of organization. A detailed portrait of the draper's shop as seen by Thomas established Augustine's world and set the conditions that would ruin her marriage. The description moved over the face of the old house, disclosing M. and Mme Guillaume and the functioning of the staid establishment. The premises of the action were merely stated: the family resembled "ces débris antédiluviens retrouvés par Cuvier." The old draper ran his business shrewdly, bargained sharply, and trusted in safe investments. Life was slow, highly moral, and dedicated to the profits of commerce.

Having set the basis for his thesis, Balzac had to explain the relationship of the long introduction to subsequent events. Hence, he used a flashback to establish the plot, then distributed the story between two major scenes: the courtship and subsequent married life. In the first, when Guillaume offered his senior clerk, Joseph, a share of the business and his elder daughter's hand, the clerk listened to the clear call of reason; but sentimental Augustine persisted in following her heart over her parents' objections. By the end of a year, Augustine found that Thomas had begun to stray, whereas Virginie had settled into a "bonheur égal, sans exaltation." A short conclusion pictured a disillusioned Augustine who crept home to die in shame.

The epilogue contended that living with a genius required strong character and deep understanding in a woman. No girl, however beautiful, could be transplanted from the simple life of a shop to the hostile climate of high society and great art. Along with his portrayal of a mésalliance based on the unstable grounds of passion, Balzac could not resist moralizing as he indicated the relationship of the house to its inhabitants: "ces vieilles maisons étaient des écoles de moeurs et de probité"; he commented on interclass marriage, and discoursed on how to hold a husband. He had difficulty restraining an urge to inflate his descriptions beyond the needs of the story.

The structure enabled Balzac to juxtapose the major scenes for maximum effect: Augustine happy and Augustine heartbroken permitted even the simplest-minded to grasp his meaning. Moreover, the long preface made an essential point: that the girl's fate was inevitable, given her background. Hence Balzac wrung all possible meanings from the old house, and related the personalities of the characters to their background, station in life, and residence. Augustine's fate was the logical outcome of the opening scene, and she walked a predetermined path to catastrophe.

To clarify this intent, Balzac arranged the characters so that Joseph and Virginie acted in counterpoint to Thomas and Augustine. The clerk and his wife accepted the conditions of their *mariage de convenance* with understanding yet attained prosperity and a reasonable happiness, while Augustine met tragedy by marrying for love. Youth and inexperience foundered where age and logic prospered.

Balzac, however, paid a price for choosing so simple a scheme. The use of two scenes faced him with the problem of introducing a sense of temporal fluidity, since he had sacrificed any sense of action to pictorial composition. To overcome this handicap, he had to rely on such phrases as "three years later" and frequent references to the aging of the protagonists. Similarly, he could only state the characters in this kind of structure. Because Augustine's behavior was deduced from her social stratum, Balzac sketched her as the innocent product of a half-century of merchant tyranny, born to be a shopkeeper's wife. Thomas, Joseph, and Virginie also acted out stock parts, struck stock attitudes, each almost a caricature. Since the nature of Balzac's thesis demanded social types, he presented easily recognized faces and manipulated the plot in these terms.

The two volumes of *Scènes de la vie privée* published by Mame in April, 1830, contained—in addition to *Le Chat-qui-pelote, La Vendetta, and Une Double Famille*—a short portrait entitled *Gobseck.* Balzac had arrived at a basic conception of his art, but in this tale he utilized a variation on the method of contrasting scenes.

The portrait of the usurer forms a story within a story told to solve a problem set in the introduction. For his major characters Balzec employed a combination of two social types common to the satires written during 1827 and 1828: Derville, the lawyer, and Gobseck, the money lender. In order to recommend the young Count de Restaud as a proper husband for the daughter of a friend, Derville tells of two calls made by Gobseck—one on the poor but honest Fanny, the other on the adulterous Countess Restaud. To thwart the countess, Gobseck had agreed to help her dying husband by becoming administrator of his estate, a position he used to teach the young Count de Restaud respect for money.

The structure of the double scene used in the *Chat-qui-pelote* is repeated here. The introduction to Derville's story delineates in detail the personality of Gobseck, later enlarged in his antithetical meetings with Mme de Restaud and Fanny. The major episodes expose the countess ruining herself, and the countess ruined. Money, one of Balzac's favorite themes, motivates the struggle between Gobseck and the unfaithful wife, one seeking power, the other struggling to hold a lover. Gobseck wins because money has no real meaning for him and he can avoid the mistakes engendered by desperation.

Balzac carried the principle of antithesis into other details of the plot. Wealthy Gobseck chose to live simply, avoiding waste even in motion and emotion, while the wastrel countess threshed about in frantic scheming. Honest Fanny was juxtaposed to Goriot's frivolous daughter, and the moral husband helped highlight the despicable Maxime, the lover who sponged on his mistress. Even the description of Gobseck's bare apartment clashed with that of the luxurious Restaud home, in which the miser read the foreshadowing of her doom.

In a manner that later became his trademark, Balzac spent pages describing Gobseck as the necessary condition of the story, establishing those aspects of Maxime, the count and countess, upon which he based his moralizing. After the relationships were fixed, Gobseck's second sight permitted him to give the advice that motivated the tale. Since Balzac then had to avoid the jerkiness of a series of disconnected anecdotes, Derville stressed his student days, his purchase of a practice, and the long repayment of a loan. The count had to die, but slowly. The dramatic tension originated from the questions raised in the first introduction. Could Derville convince Camille's mother of M. de Restaud's respectability? In the second major scene, would Derville and Gobseck outwit the countess? Thus Balzac approached the main incidents in a leisurely way; the premises were explicitly stated and the characters well sketched before the action exploded in the last few pages.

Since the formula was still new, the elements of the narrative occasionally escaped Balzac's control. Gobseck dominated the action at first, but once the count agreed to follow his advice, Derville and the countess elbowed him from sight. He reappeared at the end, consistent with his portrait as a harsh and honest man, but the events concerned only Mme de Restaud. Recalling the melodramatic techniques of the Restoration novel, Balzac presented her as the hardhearted wife who could search a dead man's room while the corpse was still warm. Gobseck functioned both as *deus ex machina* and avenging angel; he represented the author's moral indignation in operation.

In March, 1830, Balzac introduced in *Adieu* a new theme, "le foudroiement de l'être humain," which would become the principal topic of the *Contes philosophiques*. He went back to the epic retreat from Moscow to explain how Philippe de Guez lost his beloved Stéphanie in the chaos of the Beresina retreat. He found her in a madhouse eight years later, and recreated the battle scene to shock her into sanity. She revived momentarily, then died muttering "Adieu."

In *Adieu*, time played a major role in the development of the story. Philippe found Stéphanie in 1819; then the action turned back to the Empire and returned to run into 1820. Balzac's literary prescription helped him highlight the drama and prevent the action from concluding too rapidly. Since the disappearance of Stéphanie, her long travels, and the many attempts at cures could only seem probable over an extended period of time, Balzac introduced a long digression on the history of a mad peasant girl who also lived at the asylum.

The distribution of incidents called for the usual arrangement of scenes, the most dramatic of which is the flashback. Under the Imperial spell like his generation, Balzac painted a stirring portrait of the rear-guard action at the Beresina retreat which caused Stéphanie's madness. Young Philippe, on the far side of the bridge, was trying to save a wagon carrying old General de Vaudières and his young wife. In the shambles of the rout, Philippe and his men built a raft for the general and Stéphanie. "Mourir avec toi!" she cried as she saw him crowded off. Left to the dubious mercies of the Russians, Philippe watched the general fall into the river and drown. Balzac deduced her behavior from this experience instead of from the usual sociological facts. Because of her breakdown and loss of identity, she was dragged along in the wake of the retreat; because of her madness, she could only be saved by shock treatment. But she died because the cure required more strength than she possessed. Recognition of the reality she had fled years before killed her.

With such a sensational plot, Balzac could not resist catering to his taste for the romanesque. Taking a page from the romantics' book, he set one of the scenes in a picturesque ruined abbey. Stephanie's cure took the form of an antithesis: Philippe failing and Philippe successful, with an ironic twist added to defeat the hero at the very moment of triumph. His picture of the retreat emphasized its ghastly aspects: men eating horses, sabering their comrades in hysterical panic; their mad rush to scramble aboard the raft; and the burning of the bridge, which left the stragglers to the avenging Cossacks. He described the scene on the grand scale, infusing it with an epic quality.

Balzac, however, was so concerned with incident that he paid little attention to the characters. Stéphanie, the beautiful wife, then the pathetic madwoman, remains a name and a condition. Philippe functions as the man who rescues his beloved at the cost of his own freedom and remains faithful forever after. A hardened officer who can cut down his own troops to save a girl, he nonetheless faints from strong emotion. Quite properly, he commits suicide after her death, after suffering quietly for years. The other characters, even the peasant girl, only help people the story.

With *Une Passion dans le désert*, Balzac moved to the very

short tale, well suited, as many of his contemporaries had discovered, for the new periodicals. On December 24, 1830, the
Revue de Paris published his anecdote of a minor episode in
the Egyptian campaign: A French soldier, captured by the
Arabs, escaped to a desert oasis where he found a female
panther whom he made into a pet. "Elle a une âme." All went
well until one day he stabbed the panther in panic after it had
nipped him.

Balzac fitted the narrative into a framework to emphasize
his point: "Vous croyez donc les bêtes entièrement dépourvues
de passions?" lui demandai-je. "Apprenez que nous pouvons
leur donner tous les vices dus à notre état de civilisation."
The soldier, now trainer at a circus, had been expiating the
murder of the panther ever since he found true religion in the
desert, "Dieu sans les hommes." Only the framework remained
of his usual formula for the short narrative, the central anecdote
of which was related chronologically. Suspense came from the
soldier's concern over the cat's behavior, and a mildly dramatic
ending was achieved when he killed it after its affection had
been well demonstrated. Balzac thus reduced storytelling to
its bare essentials by restricting his characters to a panther and a
trooper of the Old Guard, a popular figure in the mythology
of 1830.

What he called a *conte* intrigued him. In January, 1831, he
returned to it with *Un Episode sous la Terreur,* a tale first used
to introduce *Les Mémoires de Sanson sur la révolution fran-
çaise*: On a January evening in 1793, a mysterious stranger
followed an old lady to the hideout of a priest in order to beg
a mass for the repose of the soul of Louis XVI. A year later
the man reappeared with the same request. One day, after
Thermidor, the priest recognized the unknown on a tumbril:
he was the executioner.

The story reveals Balzac's manner of constructing in sections:
a scene in a pastry shop when the stranger first appeared, a
forbidden ceremony, a surprise ending. Events were arranged
to lend an aura of mystery and gloom: midnight mass in a

dingy slum, in the middle of the Terror, when fear walked the streets. The first part developed like a mystery story and this tension was maintained by withholding the identity of the "spy" to the very end. Except in the last few lines, Balzac stayed out of the plot, although he gave free rein to an overdeveloped taste for bizarre reminiscences of the Restoration and the terror novel. Unexplained boxes changed hands in mysterious trans-actions; a benevolent unknown watched over the fugitive priest; a midnight mass assuaged an uneasy conscience. He indulged current taste by returning to a well-established mode of storytelling: straightforward, chronological, with a surprise ending. In this he took a tip from the Gothic novel and the melodrama.

Balzac maintained his affection for mystifying the reader but reverted to his own manner in *Le Réquisitionnaire*. Printed in the *Revue de Paris* on February 23, 1831, the story revolved around the principle of extrasensory perception. In the pro-logue, Balzac described an unusual event in the small town of Carentan in November, 1793. Mme de Dey, at whose salon the principal revolutionary officials of the town gathered every evening, suddenly closed her doors. "Il est nécessaire d'ex-pliquer le rôle qu'elle jouait à Carentan . . . ," Balzac began his flashback to explain how Mme de Dey was trying to preserve her fortune for an émigré son. Scene II focused on a draftee who arrived at Mme de Dey's as her guests were leaving—but he was not her son. The conclusion gave the narrative the philosophical tinge for which Balzac included it in the *Romans et contes philosophiques*. The maid found Mme de Dey was dead in the morning, "sans doute par quelque vision terrible," since her death had come at the moment her son was shot in Morbihan. Balzac claimed not only that he had docu-ments to verify this story but that similar cases had been authenticated; the science of extrasensory perception awaited only some genius to found it.

Though the tale followed Balzac's usual pattern, it did not depend on sociological explanation, nor was the action deduced from a series of premises. Instead, the plot moved in response to a series of questions: Why did Madame de Dey close her salon? Would the boy escape? Who was the draftee? Why did she die? As each was answered, another cropped up to maintain the tension.

Le Réquisitionnaire is free from many of the romanesque elements that clutter most of Balzac's tales. Instead of seeking to intrigue the reader with the unusual, he attained the same end by misdirecting him about the identity of the draftee. Mme de Dey's death, a tour de force, was linked to that of her son and, since nothing had been done to prepare for such an ending, Balzac felt compelled to defend it on the grounds of extrasensory perception. However, he moved closer to the technique used in some of his great novels: the handling of small town atmosphere, and the intrigue and suspicion that underlie its superficial placidity. Madame de Dey's personality was briefly stated, mother love faced with danger to an only son, then the excitement of the plot took over until, once again, love killed a woman. Balzac rarely had as much opportunity to create character in his short fiction as he did in the novel and, in this case, the action depended on a stereotype, not on a developed personality.

In his insatiable quest for material, Balzac inevitably turned to the supernatural. The vogue for Hoffmann's tales, for the mysterious and the fantastic, offered a promising field for exploitation. He found in *Jésus-Christ en Flandre* (1831) a subject both to his and to the popular taste. "A une époque assez indéterminée de l'histoire brabançonne . . . ," a ferry was sailing from Cadzant to Ostend with a divided group of passengers: a bishop, a young knight, a noble demoiselle, a rich bourgeois, and, in the rear of the boat, a huddle of poor people. When a storm threatened to swamp the boat, the rich promised candles; the bishop blessed the waves while thinking of his mistress; the young knight felt certain his class-conscious God would not let him die with peasants. The ferry split open in sight of land but a golden-haired passenger walked on the water. "Ceux qui ont la foi seront sauvés; qu'ils me suivent." The plain folk followed him to safety; one, Thomas, doubted and sank, then repented and walked. The miser was dragged down by his gold, drowned along with the servant, the knight, and the bishop. Jesus walked away, leaving on the sand footprints over which a church was built.

Balzac's understanding of his stories as a series of building blocks led him to append to the *Romans et contes philosophiques* an epilogue originally entitled *L'Eglise*. A first-person account related the visit of a melancholy man to a church just after the revolution of 1830. As he stared at white-robed nuns, a huge Christ smiled maliciously, the columns danced, and he accused a woman freshly out of the cemetery of prostituting herself. Suddenly transformed, the woman showed the man thousands of cathedrals rising, hordes of men serving the poor or copying manuscripts. "On ne croit plus," the old lady cried, and Balzac closed with a profession of faith, "Je viens de voir passer le convoi d'une Monarchie, il faut défendre L'Eglise."

The opening of the story gave it a tone of fantasy, almost in Mérimée's tongue-in-cheek manner. Long ago and far away it happened. "Le narrateur y croit, comme tous les esprits superstitieux de la Flandre y ont cru." The anecdote was based on Matthew's account of the miracle of walking on water, and on the medieval legend of the divine stranger come to test a group of people. Balzac contrasted the poor to the rich, who were of little faith. With poetic license, he decided that not Peter but a doubting Thomas had to face drowning before he could believe. Resting shakily on Biblical authority, the plot combined appeal to the religious and interest in folklore, a pairing popular during the Restoration. Balzac, however, ruined the unity of the tale when he related the plot to his own religious views. The vision, reminiscent of legends like that of the Bloody Nun, formed an epitaph for a monarchy which had lost the confidence of the French. The epilogue pleaded for Catholicism on the grounds that it had fulfilled its social and cultural obligations. "Croire . . . c'est vivre." This was the miracle that could save a France which he symbolized as a sinking ship.

The added section allowed Balzac to give *Jésus-Christ et Flandre* a contemporary meaning at the cost of artistic integrity. The focus shifted from the figure of Christ to *I*, with no transition. The plot had little relation to the moral Balzac hung onto it; perhaps he envisioned himself as the new Messiah but, at any rate, his sorrow at the decline of monarchy did literature no favor. By turning the story into an exemplum he ruined an excellent tale enlivened by a highly active intelligence.

Balzac soon dropped fantasy for the more comfortable portrayal of historical or contemporary scenes; tales of the unusual were rapidly falling from fashion. In *Le Chef-d'oeuvre inconnu* he found a more congenial subject that permitted the use of a historical figure to support his ideas on art. Divided into two sections, *Gillette* and *Catherine Lescault*, the story concerns an experience of young Nicolas Poussin with the monomaniac Maître Frenhofer. For ten years Frenhofer had slaved over a mysterious unfinished painting, "La Belle Noiseuse," or Catherine Lescault. Frenhofer agreed to let Poussin see the portrait if Gillette, his mistress, would pose for him, but the finished painting turned out to be a mass of bizarre lines and colors from which stood out a beautifully executed foot. That night Frenhofer died of a broken heart after burning his picture.

The point of the narrative is a familiar one in Balzac's stories: talent or genius, expanding uncontrolled like a cancerous growth, transformed Frenhofer into a monomaniac. As his passion blinded him to facts, he entered a dream world, and the recognition of reality killed him as it had Stéphanie in *Adieu*. An obsession turned into the kind of consuming passion that destroyed Louis Lambert in *La Recherche de l'absolu*. The excessive use of a talent, as Balzac's own life proved, carried the seeds of its own death.

The *idée fixe,* however, also motivated the plot. Frenhofer was presented in a scene that established the master's skill, though Balzac withheld his identity for some time. In the first scene, at the painter's studio, a new mystery developed around the masterpieces his compulsion was driving him to create, but explanation of the mystery was reserved for a second act. Thus the plot falls into two sections: Frenhofer's dream, and its destruction, with a short transition on Gillette, the model, stitching them together.

As previously, Balzac needed most of his space to prepare the action. He had formed the habit of suggesting analogies between his descriptions and the works of painters, and now he welcomed the chance to air decided opinions on the world of art. He established Frenhofer's theories at the outset, "la mission de l'art n'est pas de copier la nature, mais de l'exprimer." The artist's capacity, theories, and ten years' search for perfect beauty, these were the conditions out of which the tale grew. The description, in effect, the local color so dear to the romantics, became a necessary justification of the plot. Balzac had simply to distribute the facts according to a pattern, then smash Frenhofer, like Stéphanie, with a return to sanity.

Again, so much care went into the arrangement of the story line that the characters suffered. Gillette scarcely appeared, although her name was given to half the story, functioning only to persuade Frenhofer to unveil his surrealist picture, while the other two artists, Poussin and Porbus, merely provided the means for shocking him back to reality. The emphasis fell on the monomania, on its symbol, the mysterious painting that provided the surprise ending.

So successfully did the recipe work that it became Balzac's principal and formalized manner of storytelling. It could also, he discovered, be explored more fully than previously. If the narrative were directed toward character delineation and stripped of romanesque details, if it were developed without reliance on so many contemporary tricks and mannerisms, the format could produce a bold and imaginative tale based on life-size portraiture.

Balzac tried just this when, on February 20 and 27, and

March 6 and 13, 1832, he published *La Transaction* in *L'Artiste*. Later entitled *Le Colonel Chabert,* it recounted the terrible misfortunes of an Imperial hero who suffered the fate of Enoch Arden. Colonel Chabert, the man who smashed the enemy charge and won victory at Eylau, had been left for dead on the field, stripped of his uniform, and tossed into a ditch. After he dug his way out of a mound of corpses, he found himself a vagabond without a provable identity. When he could substantiate his claims his wife, by then the Countess Ferrand, denied his existence, although she did persuade the colonel to sacrifice himself to her happiness. Six months later, Derville, Chabert's lawyer, saw his client, now an old tramp, being sentenced to perpetual detention.

Le Colonel Chabert contains a richness of topics unusual in Balzac's short fiction. Beginning with the theme of the returned husband or, as Balzac put it, "les morts ont donc bien tort de revenir," he made avarice and social climbing the motives for the countess' behavior, pairing off her moral depravity against Chabert's generosity. Her thirst for money and position provided movement as well as another set of contrasting themes: justice versus the law. Derville thought in terms of all justice within the law, but Chabert embodied the moral indignation of man. He rose from military hero to the greater stature of champion of decency in a world where the meek inherit the suffering and the moral find their reward in hell on earth; he was transformed into the personification of self-sacrifice. By balancing the themes against each other, intermingling forms of gratitude and ingratitude, Balzac gave the plot complexity, yet the obvious antitheses made it easy to follow.

This same principle was applied to the characters. Chabert has all the virtues his wife lacks. Among the minor personages, the countess's attorney, who uses the law to obstruct justice, presents a crooked caricature of honest Derville, the latter a more distinct personality than the others since he has already acted as Chabert's lawyer. His adversary, a shadowy figure at best, stands as the stereotype of the shyster in the service of his own purse. The portrait of the countess lacks clear definition since she constitutes merely a yardstick by which the colonel can be measured.

As in *Gobseck*, the main characters stand forth full-length. Since the story, like the history of the miser, was intended as a study of people under stress, events were arranged to force responses from Chabert that would outline his psychological profile. After a description of Derville's study, the colonel entered, cadaverous and tormented, permitting Balzac to ask the first motivating question: was the vagabond really the great hero? From this past he deduced the present character. Then Derville, patently the author's alter ego, discussed the moral problems basic to Chabert's case, and another question arose: what would the old man do? While the attorney prepared his case, he observed Chabert loyal to old companions and Chabert vengeful. A second flashback outlined the countess' position, while another visit to the law study, where the drama really unfolded, revealed a restored and optimistic colonel. But the conquering hero became putty in the hands of the wily wife when the sight of her children and her tears persuaded him to abandon his suit, for which he paid with his identity and his sanity.

The portrait of the old soldier stands out starkly despite the fact that Balzac again strayed into unnecessary detail. Chabert's skirmish with death is recorded in grisly terms as, tossed into a ditch with a tangle of naked bodies, he had to claw his way out of the gruesome pile. When his wife tricks him, the scene relies on sentimentality and the opposition of primitive virtue and sophisticated wile. The ironic incarceration of the hero provides a brutal ending to the plot in a savage comment on civilized behavior.

Since Balzac concentrated on portraiture, he fell back on the trusted flashback and the emphasis on dates to ease the static quality of the tale. Similarly, he indulged in humor, the teasing of the bewildered colonel by the clerks and the errand boy, the kind of heedless cruelty which symbolized society's attitude, because he could not permit the incidents to precipitate a sudden

climax. Twice Chabert visited Derville's study, once as sup-
plicant, then as potential victor, and his moral decision had to
be made in terms of the conditions set therein. As his plight
unfolded, consistent with the premises, his picture filled in
gradually through the slowly developed action.

This prescription for brief fiction produced perhaps its
greatest success in *Le Curé de Tours,* first published as *Les
Célibataires* in the second edition of the *Scènes de la vie privée*
(1832). Here, in a *drame bourgeois* that recalls the *romans de
moeurs* popular between 1825 and 1830, he created the pathetic
picture of a man "soumis aux effets de cette grande Justice
distributive . . . nommé par certains niais les *malheurs de la
vie.*" He united his power of observation and a strong imagination to produce a powerful account of ambition and hate in a
small town: the persecution of Abbé Birotteau, a gouty old
priest who aspired only to become canon of the metropolitan
chapter of Saint-Gatien in Tours and to inhabit a coveted
apartment in the home of Mlle Gamard.

The action, if such it can be called, rises from the conditions of provincial life as they operate on a weak personality.
The abbé Birotteau's character is not developed but stated at
great length, first with a physical portrait, followed by a minute
character analysis. The episodes serve to demonstrate the effect
of "distributive justice" on a guileless person, covetous of
creature comfort, with too much faith in the goodness of man.
His doom results from an incapacity to understand evil or to
cope with the harsher facts of life; his simple mind and tactless-
ness unwittingly generate the resentment that ruins his dream.
The saga has overtones of a morality play, as do so many of
Balzac's brief narratives, but with evil triumphant and the meek
gobbled up by the ruthless.

The themes of the story were arranged in a more complex
manner than usual, with the basic interest in ambition leading
to a consideration of petty provincial rivalries that broadened
into a concern for justice. Though Birotteau was abused by his
landlady, then bilked of an inheritance, his noble friends

abandoned him after they had advised a lawsuit. Thus, he became the agent of his own destruction, with many an assist from well-wishers, in whom Balzac pictured the degeneration of the aristocracy. The power of the Church, misused for personal reasons, brought his protectresses to heel through the machinations of that mysterious bogey of the nineteenth century, the *Congrégation*.

Through all this, Balzac wove another theme: the evils of celibacy. Mlle Gamard, unwed and hence embittered, physically and morally shriveled, was the classic *vieille fille* turned harpy who, like any other frustrated old maid, enjoyed hurting people. As the brief epilogue stated, "le célibat offre donc ce vice capital que, faisant converger les qualités de l'homme sur une seule passion, l'égoisme, il rend les célibataires ou nuisibles ou inutiles." Thus Birotteau, his rival, Troubert, and Mlle Gamard ran afoul of this "law." Since the first was an innocent, the other two pounced on him in accord with Balzac's theory of the social jungle. Egoism was for all three a dangerous monomania.

Balzac had put his favorite organization of brief fiction at the service of a major psychological portrait that illustrated his social theories and his concept of divine justice. The plot strayed little; Balzac, sure of his method, felt no need for coating a bitter didactic pill with the sugar of strange episodes. The story unrolled naturally, moved by personalities reacting to their separate ambitions, with the minor characters acting credibly as small-town busybodies. Only in the episode of Mme de Listomère's nephew, the officer whose promotion was threatened by the Congrégation, did Balzac's penchant for complications reappear. Otherwise, after a short parenthesis explaining the characters and their actions, he set up three sections: the beginning of the persecution, the expulsion of Birotteau, and the failure of a lawsuit that eventuated in the abbé's exile to a poor suburban parish. Since the process of describing the erosion of the priest's hopes would cover months, Balzac took pains to indicate time as a major ingredient of his action. The plot began with Birotteau's predecessor, with the sequence carefully

specified: the next morning, eight days later, after ten days . . .
it took almost twelve years of events to produce a full-length
Abbé Birotteau. He was contrasted physically, mentally, and
morally with Troubert, the successful competitor for the
canonry, a latter-day Hildebrand with no way of using his
talents for the social good. Although Troubert and Mlle
Gamard were contemporary stereotypes, Balzac made them as
individual as Birotteau. Only the minor characters remained
faceless, with one of them, a M. de Bourbonne, helping the
author explain exactly where the curate's simplicity would lead
him. Thus Balzac restrained his urge to intrude, though he could
not resist underscoring the moral of the tale as though he had
little faith in the intelligence of the reader to grasp the implications of a *drame bourgeois*.

By the time Balzac had completed *Le Colonel Chabert* and *Le
Curé de Tours*, his method had become almost settled as he
began to move from brief fiction into the novel. To be sure,
he would write this kind of story all his life, but not as a major
interest. Lack of time, the constant pressure of commitments,
rarely permitted him the leisure necessary to attain the maximum economy and effect. Moreover, the conception of the short
narrative at which he had arrived fitted his understanding of the
novel, and he used the same structure in both genres. Hence,
the more he worked with the longer form, the less interest
he had in experimenting with brief fiction. The kind of portrait
he achieved in *Le Colonel Chabert* and *Le Curé de Tours* was
precisely what he needed for the illustration of his social
theories in the *Comédie humaine*. Meanwhile, as more and more
he fell back on short fiction to raise money, he depended on
romanesque, tortuous plots like *La Marana,* and memories from
his pot-boiler days. Not all his productions were bad, but the
good ones came more rarely.

It was in portraits like *L'Illustre Gaudissart* (1833) that
Balzac showed how he could control his medium, given time
and a sympathetic subject. He had specialized in humorous and
satiric portraits during his stints on such journals as *La*

Silhouette and *La Caricature,* and this type of sketch matched
his talent and dream of immortalizing contemporary social
types. Gaudissart represented a figure new to the nineteenth
century, a gift of the expanding industrial economy: the
traveling salesman. When Paris companies discovered the
advantages to be gained from transforming the itinerant peddler
into the sales representative of non-competing firms, they flooded
the provinces with fast-talking men wise in the ways of country
folk. Inevitably Balzac added this striking figure to his gallery
of illustrious stereotypes.

L'Illustre Gaudissart is technically a full-length portrait, the
plot of which ironically describes the working habits of the
traveling salesman. Gaudissart, of course, has suggestions of
the Titanic, the biggest and the best, "le génie de la civilisation
et les inventions." Since Gaudissart could sell anything, he had
risen to become the Napoleon of his trade, wooed by manu-
facturers, insurance companies, and even newspapers. He left
for his adventure at Vouvray with superb confidence, but when
the arrogant huckster encountered the cunning Vernier, the
latter sent Gaudissart to sell insurance and newspaper subscriptions to a madman. To the delight of the population, the
lunatic palmed off barrels of bad wine on his caller while
Gaudissart sold Margaritis only a single subscription to the
Journal des enfants. The joke almost turned to tragedy when
the offended Parisian challenged Vernier to a duel, but the ad-
versaries prudently fired wide and fell into each other's arms.

In *Gaudissart,* Balzac indulged his sense of humor in a manner unusual for him. The subject invited it, and he happily
obliged. Gaudissart was a salesman to end all salesmen, the
epitome and nadir of the species, at once the perfect specimen
and his own caricature. Since he believed in his mission, he also
became a pathetic comment on the dubious benefits of the new
middle-class world. Using satire at no time delicate, Balzac
burlesqued the nobility of commerce: "Calembours, gros rire,
figure monacale, teint de cordelier, envelope rabelaisienne; vête-
ment, corps, esprit, figure s'accordaient pour mettre de la

gaudisserie, de la gaudriole en toute sa personne. Rond en
affaires, bon homme, rigoleur . . ." His consort was Jenny, a
fleuriste, the courtesan of the new age, at whose feet he laid his
conquests of subscriptions. He even talked like a feudal lord,
for he did not sell, but put products "sous ma protection." The
bravery of the old order had changed into the prudent canniness
of the new; a different conception of honor had been provided
for the bourgeoisie.

Using popular notions of provincial life, Balzac employed
the age-old theme of the trickster tricked. Only Gaudissart and
the madman remained unaware of the joke; the salesman plied
his trade as usual, but circumstances, as in a Maupassant tale,
provided the dramatic irony. The Napoleon of the hat trade
met his match in a simple-minded farmer in a combat whose
obvious humor lent force to Balzac's comment on society. The
argument leaned heavily on a familiar stock situation in which
stereotypes followed immediately recognizable patterns. A new
type entered an old plot, personifying urban arrogance about to
get its come-uppance, the city slicker undone by the wily hick
whose very provincialism endowed him with primitive virtue.

The portrait of Gaudissart unfolded as Balzac deduced him
from the general introduction, and the personality of the salesman unfolded from the premises of a previously stated character. The brash Gaudissart twice came a cropper, in the en-
counter with the lunatic and in the comic duel. Since Balzac
had become vaguely aware of the benefits derived from
changing point of view, he began by talking to the reader,
but then had Gaudissart explain his psychology to his mistress,
Jenny, in a revelatory scene; later, when Balzac fell back on
the epistolary device, the salesman entered the plot on his own.
The situation that resulted provided a sharply etched comic
sketch for the Human Comedy.

By 1834, Balzac was committing himself more and more to
the novel, partly from personal taste, partly because the first
quick vogue for the *conte* and the *nouvelle* was petering out. A
surfeit of writers eager for quick profits had cut down the sales

value of short fiction. Balzac's interest in the genre lagged, particularly since he felt he could put the lessons learned to better use in the longer form. This attitude became obvious in an anecdote like *Un Drame au bord de la mer* (1835), a first-person narrative concerning the spoiled, nasty son of a fisherman whose long-suffering father finally heaved him into the sea.

Balzac's interests, like those of his major characters, were assuming an almost compulsive force; he became fascinated with discovering the "natural laws" motivating the society that inhabited his vast imagination. His plots, therefore, tended to revolve around contemporary moral and religious problems, growing heavier with moral statement, as in *La Messe de l'athée.*

After 1835, Balzac's production of short narratives dropped considerably; by this time he had ceased experimenting. His plots tended to bog down in increasing complexity, although occasionally there were flashes of his great talent, as in *L'Interdiction* (1836). The tale recalls the treachery of Mme Chabert and the money-hungry Comtesse de Restaud. Once again Balzac relied on his trusted method to create honest Judge Popinot, but the economy of the story suffered from dependence on coincidence, misunderstanding, and a curious change in the sentimental and the melodramatic took over as lack of time encouraged haste, making the delineation of character almost accidental and incidental. *Facino Cane* (1836), for instance, combined the pathetic figure of a blind musician with a fantastic tale of adultery, a strangled husband, and escape from a dungeon into a cellar that contained the secret wealth of the Venetian government. Similarly, *Gambara* repeated the plight of a monomaniacal artist who played cacophonic music on a Panharmonium. The narrative bulged with complications surrounding the tragedy of an unrecognized genius as Balzac became involved in a long-winded attempt to blend fiction and a dissertation on music. The genius in a slum, the faithful wife who later deserted him, the handsome young man who purported to help the less fortunate, all these, with a large dash of sentimentality, were jumbled together in unhappy juxtaposition. Balzac relied too heavily on his stock arrangement to provide a neat solution for all his literary difficulties. As a result, the plot creaked along and the skeleton of his work never did fill out with any artistic flesh. Such was the case in *Massimilla Doni,* a complicated dissertation on ethereal and physical love, full of digressions, involving a host of characters in complicated and bizarre relationships. "Esprits purs qui peuvent se dépouiller ici-bas de leurs larves de chair . . ."

The old touch was disappearing as Balzac lashed himself on to meet his commitments. *Z. Marcas* (1840) unsuccessfully attempted a portrait as outstanding as that of Gobseck or Chabert. *Albert Savarus* (1842) described provincial life and the obsessively possessive love of Rosalie de Watteville, whose pursuit of Albert, worthlessly single-minded and brilliantly described, was buried in an uncontrolled mass of detail, along with essays on provincial political machinations.

But Balzac hit bottom in *La Dernière Incarnation de Vautrin* (1847), a rambling account of the master thief's conversion to virtue. The old method no longer served its purpose, although Balzac had the advantage of being able to use characters like Camusot, Popinot, Vautrin, and M. de Grandville, who by now had amassed extensive histories and full personalities. He established a story line so complicated that no character could escape its tangled web, indulged his interest in thieves' jargon, then expanded the narrative by explaining his theory of criminology. Balzac seemed to have lost his conception of brief prose, and he swamped the tale with moralizing. The genre functioned here only as a carrier for his theses, not as an autonomous art form. The more he worked with the novel, the more he tended to confuse the two media, to consider one a dehydrated version of the other. *Vautrin* seems an undeveloped novel, not conceived to benefit from the advantages of the short narrative nor adequately structured to provide the psychological motivation of the novel. In Balzac's mind, the longer form had won out after a minor debate.

Mérimeé

Caught in the tides of indecision, short fiction was suddenly rescued by Prosper Mérimée, perhaps the man least likely to be concerned with the development of a literary form. Mérimée's narratives come almost as a shock in the history of the brief narrative during the age of romanticism. He seems almost an anomaly alongside Nodier, Hugo, or Musset—for, unlike them, he never considered himself a professional writer. In an era when sentimentality marked most literature, his detached irony and acid wit set him apart from his colleagues. The symmetry, concision, and artistry of his work establish him as a talent among talents; the comprehension he showed of his medium, his deft and imaginative experimentation, make him the pioneer who deliberately forged the brief narrative into a mode of expression divorced from the various forms of didacticism so beloved by past writers.

How much acquaintance with an author helps explain what he wrote is a moot point, but there is no question about the effect of Mérimée's personality on his work. The tone is satiric and the humor bizarre—even savage—reflecting the paradoxical figure of the poised bureaucrat turned author.

Opinion on Mérimée's character is remarkably consistent. His mother, his close friends, and his enemies reacted similarly to the only son who had been spoiled in his upbringing. His father, a conscientious Republican, had made willing peace with the Empire, but his mother came from sterner stuff. An unreconstructed Voltairian, she was, as Stendhal put it, "capable d'attendrissement une fois par an." Perhaps it was she who saddled her son with the name he detested; at any rate, she saw her offspring with open eyes, "mauvais et gouailleur à taper . . . , maigre comme un garenne." When she painted his portrait, Mme Mérimée could not help putting the touch of malice in his glance which Stendhal recognized in his own description of Prosper as "laid avec son nez retroussé. Ce jeune homme avait quelque chose d'effronté et d'extrêmement déplaisant. Ses yeux petits et sans expression avaient un air toujours le même, et cet air était méchant." In 1830 Turgenev wrote his brother that he had met Mérimée, "le second Voltaire. . . . Dans la nature tout entière, il n'a rien trouvé à bénir." And George Sand, whose attempted liaison with him ended in disaster, summed up her opinion in one word, "ordurier."

Mérimée's public personality seemed to substantiate these remarks. Tall, slim, carefully shaven, grey eyes hidden under bushy eyebrows, he took pride in dressing and acting like an Englishman. He laughed little, presenting to the world the figure of an ice-cold man who rarely indulged in the luxury of permitting emotions even the slightest leeway. He seemed the perfect example of a nineteenth-century Frenchman's idea of the proper Briton.

However disturbing his restraint and ironical pose, Mérimée's conversation was carefully calculated to attain the maximum shock effect. The Count d'Haussonville noted that he skirted the limits of good taste in anecdotes which Pontmartin called gross obscenities. With an expressionless face he told outrageous stories, displaying that relish for the earthy that marks his letters to Stendhal. Musset called him common, a man with the mind of a peasant; certainly he enjoyed a type of humor not then socially acceptable. When he and his friends decided to play a joke on Duponcel, the director of the Opera, they scrawled "le feu Duponcel" an all available walls. Paris was mystified, and the grim joke was compounded when a man draped Duponcel's door in black and invitations were issued for the funeral. One day Mérimée allowed the adventurer, Doctor Koreff, to introduce him to a lady as Alfred de Musset, to Musset's marked displeasure. Even in his old age he continued his addiction to dubious practical jokes. As a grey-haired elder statesman at the court of Napoleon III, he enlivened Bismarck's formal visit to the palace by putting an effigy of the prime minister into the bed of a virginal lady-in-waiting.

Disreputable, many called him, and shook their heads over his choice of friends, the most intelligent and witty bad company in Paris. With Delacroix, with a Musset no longer the blond prodigy of early romanticism, he often dined at the Divan or the Café de Paris. There he might be joined by Sutton Sharpe, an English barrister who loved to sow wild oats in France, or Doctor Koreff, whispered to be involved in espionage and sorcery. Sometimes, after gargantuan repasts, as when Viel-Castel ate 500 francs worth of dinner, they wandered to the more fashionable brothels, where Mérimée shocked his companions with scabrous tales recounted in a quiet, even tone of voice.

Under the public personality, however, under the glacial exterior and the superficial cynicism, lurked another person, timid and unsure of himself. Sensitive observers like Turgenev noted the paradox with interest: "La sensibilité était le vrai fond de son caractère." The reserve protected a man intensely alive to moral suffering and who feared above all things any possibility of ridicule. At the age of ten he had sworn never to be anybody's dupe after he had caught his parents laughing over the effect of their pretended anger. He crawled into a shell, afraid to trust what seemed a hostile and cruel environment.

Life confirmed what his parents had taught him, and from this nightmare he forged his own protection. The world was a crawling ant heap, diverting to watch, frenzied in undirected activity, brutal for those unfortunate enough to be counted among the dispossessed or the weak. "Nous sommes dans ce monde pour nous battre envers et contre tous," he warned Jenny Dacquin. All the things other men believed in, he disdained as traps for the unwary.

He had never been baptized, and since he embraced the faith

of the Encyclopedists, religion remained all his life a hodge-podge of superstitions. When he watched the people sack the Archevêché, he found the spectacle amusing, especially the vandals who clothed themselves in chasubles and miters. An atheist, but never aggressively so, he enjoyed the reputation his lack of religion gave him in the salons; "nous autres païens," he chuckled. When, in 1850, a priest from the seminary at Carcassonne attempted to convert him, Mérimée politely acknowledged that faith was a gift he had never received and that, at his age, he had little of the enthusiasm needed for such exaltation. He held to the maxim of the seven Greek sages, that it was necessary to be a gentleman and to doubt. To Mme de Montijo he admitted that God seemed probable but immortality unlikely. Even after death he scandalized the devout by having stipulated that a Lutheran minister read a short service over his grave.

Mérimée had as little faith in this world as in the next. In an age noted for its sentimental approach to the little people, he stood as a staunch advocate of the rule of an elite. Democracy disgusted him and he regarded the electorate as one of life's grimmer jokes: "Je suis horriblement aristocrate quand je vois la démocratie et ses dégoûtantes manières." The handshaking, the double-dealing, the incompetence of 1848, all confirmed his belief that the common man could not control his own destiny.

The world he saw had little in its favor, particularly since a long career as Inspector General of Monuments had given him a jaundiced view of the provinces. Pleasure-loving and fond of witty company, he despised the lousy beds and the dull pleasures of soporific towns full of empty-headed citizens and fat, greasy women. "Je hais et méprise toute cette racaille autant qu'elle me hait elle-même," he confided to Stendhal. The petty meanness Mérimée found in government offices seemed to spread a grey pall over society. The salons teemed with the brilliant mediocrity of the *juste-milieu,* and his pessimism deepened as France succumbed to the "progress" brought by the Industrial Revolution. Railroads, machines, factories, all seemed the product of an evil genius. Often he fell victim to what he called the "blue devils," fits of melancholy; during one of these he threatened to join a monastery, provided he could find one where he need not pray. He sought refuge in dandyism, or turned to the dubious comfort of quick amours— never, however, permitting himself to become seriously involved.

Most of all, he stood aside as life passed, careful not to let it soil him. When his own vision of a better world increasingly diverged from reality, he protected himself with irony. He never mocked his country, his friends, or many other things dear to him, but trespassers on his inner self found themselves brushed away with a cruel joke, as happened to the lady who insisted that Mérimée, a grown man, submit to baptism. He agreed, providing she serve as his godmother and carry him to the font. No one was allowed to challenge the personal integrity he considered one of the few values society had not yet obliterated.

In view of this background, it is not surprising that Mérimée approached the art of storytelling with a keen sense of irony reinforced by a careful reading of Sterne. An acute perception of the ridiculous influenced his choice of subjects, his exploitation of character, and his comments on the meaning of the tales. All the usual types of satire can be found in his work, particularly romantic irony, the mocking of man's highest aspirations or noblest beliefs. This last constituted one of Mérimée's most common techniques, evident in his better narratives, *La Double Méprise* or *Le Vase étrusque*. Only his mind controlled events in his fictional world; the characters were suddenly confronted with dilemmas they never anticipated, at which point chance made a mockery of their intentions.

This is the substance of the *Mosaïque* he published in 1833.

Composed of six stories (*Fédérigo* would be dropped after the first edition), the book included all his work produced in 1829 and 1830, with the exception of *La Chronique du règne de Charles IX*. *Mosaïque* is just what the name implies, a collection of tales arranged in a pattern. Differing in subject matter and variety of narrative, the tales seem to have no discernible unity, although actually they do have a design. On the one hand they represent Mérimée's best efforts in the art of brief fiction; on the other, equally important to him, they sum up his comments on man in a violent world where coincidence and the irony of fate have a legitimate place. In a spare style, Mérimée offers his idea of the meaning of existence, a view uncomplimentary to his characters, their creator, and his readers. Despite this pessimism, Mérimée apparently enjoyed writing, but he never felt the need to jot down the principles of his art. Consequently, the only way to discover his esthetic is to inquire how he constructed his tales.

The locales of his stories cover the map of Europe. The themes reveal little considered extraordinary in his day: the fantastic in *La Vision de Charles XI;* religion in *Fédérigo;* slavery in *Tamango*: war in *L'Enlèvement de la redoute.* Such catholicity of taste discloses only a man close to romanticism and the popular subject matter of his time. His plots are peopled with ghosts, animated statues, slave kings, illicit lovers, gypsies, even a fallen girl who is the object of attempted regeneration.

The works themselves, however, reveal a far from ordinary talent. To be sure, *Mateo Falcone* (1829) came primarily from an article in the *Revue trimestrielle* of July, 1828, which contained the story of a Corsican shot by his relatives for betraying two deserters. Mérimée also turned to the abbé Gaudin for details on a land he had not yet visited, but to this basic material he brought the skill that would make him one of France's greatest storytellers.

Mateo Falcone is related like an anecdote, in a clean style, stripped to essentials, lacking even the colorful adjectives so dear to the romantics. The plot is handled with a sure sense of the dramatic, all elements united to produce a single effect. Mérimée thus produced a narrative that fits perfectly Poe's later definition of the formal short story.

Mérimée introduced the reader to the *maquis* with a fine sense of visual appeal, then fell back on the direct approach: "Si vous avez tué un homme . . ." To heighten the exoticism, he gave advice on how to prepare for a stay in these wilds. Then, abruptly, he presented Mateo as though he had known him personally: "Quand j'étais en Corse en 18 -- . . ." Mateo lived on the edge of the heath, a good friend and an implacable enemy, famed for his marksmanship. He had three daughters, which infuriated him, and a ten-year-old son, ironically named Fortunato, upon whom he doted.

Most of the story happened in Mateo's absence, although he dominates the action. One fall day he left with his wife to inspect the flocks, leaving Fortunato to mind the house. The subsequent plot is articulated almost like a four-act play. Act I introduces an escaping bandit, Gianetto Sanpiero, wounded and hotly pursued by gendarmes, who bought refuge in a haystack from Fortunato for five francs. Act II revolves around Fortunato's betrayal for a silver watch offered by Sergeant Tiodoro Gamba. In a scene forecast by Fortunato's bargaining with Gianetto, the sergeant tempts the child, thrice subjecting him to bribery before the boy turns Judas. Act III brings Mateo back, and when he appears the stage is set for an explosion. Characteristically, he thinks the soldiers have come for him, then finds himself in a dilemma when Gamba reveals Fortunato's treachery. Mateo faces his problem in Act IV. He smashes the watch the sergeant had given Fortunato and marches the child into the glen. Patiently he hears the boy recite his prayers, then shoots him. Without a glance at the corpse, Mateo orders his wife to send for a relative to replace his son.

Using the appeal of the exotic, Mérimée constructed the story around a point of honor, a subject dear to the romantics. For the sake of plausibility Mérimée interjected himself into the introduction, but once the story began he let the characters shape their own tragedy. Events slip by rapidly, their passing noted in phrases which indicate that Mérimée organized his material to keep psychological and reading time as close as possible to plot time. The action does not begin until Mateo has been absent a few hours, then Gianetto appears and is hidden in a matter of moments. "Quelques minutes après" the police appear, Fortunato succumbs in about the same time, and Mateo arrives as the bandit leaves on a stretcher. For ten minutes he ponders and, after about the same time, Fortunato dies.

The narrative ostensibly revolved around the Corsican code of honor. Fortunato occupied the stage most of the time but only to prepare the dilemma, as important to the plot as the wounded bandit. At this point Mérimée's ironical mind came into full play. Mateo was created according to the accepted recipe for the primitive but he failed to conform to the tradition of the "good" savage. Unlike the rational creature so dear to the eighteenth century, he never examined his own code. Family "honor" took precedence over all else and no transgression could be pardoned, even for a child. Mateo took all of ten minutes to decide on the murder of an only son who had informed on the killer of a policeman. Far from being a natural democrat, the good savage was an egotist who dared not challenge the local tabus.

This concern for the inexplicable violence man perpetrates on man led Mérimée to try his hand at narrating a famous episode of the Imperial wars in *L'Enlèvement de la redoute* (1824), the assault on the defenses at Schwardino that paved the way for the capture of Moscow. French military annals noted the battle as a major blood-letting in which some four to five thousand Frenchmen died, along with seven to eight thousand Russians.

Mérimée transformed the anecdote by adopting the hoary device of a story told by an old friend. He recounted the tale in the first person to give it a sense of immediacy. The point of view was placed within the narrative, a change from *Mateo Falcone,* where the action had historical perspective. Mérimée began the narrative with a brief introduction addressed to the reader, then let his hero recount his own baptism of fire. The soldier did not even understand what was happening, since he saw the battle as uncoordinated mass movement. Mérimée presented the struggle through the eyes of a participant inclined to view the hostilities in personal terms. As a result, the focus remains on the character and not on the events. The officers, particularly the pseudo-author, become the center of interest, with the attack a means of illuminating implicit comments on life.

No spectacular new techniques are used. Since the conclusion necessarily had to reflect the slaughter, considerable attention was given to foreshadowing. A young lieutenant, fresh from St. Cyr, came to a veteran infantry regiment as a replacement. He met his company commander, "ce capitaine, que je n'eus guère le temps de connaître," as substitute for an officer killed the day before. The tone is consistently tragic: an old veteran remarked that the moon shone red, a sure sign of bloodshed; the captain sensed danger when the lieutenant's hat was shot off, recalling that every time he was wounded the officer beside him died.

In a few pages of bare prose Mérimée described the baptism of fire. With the ink barely dry on his commission, the boy arrived on the eve of a major action. That night fear kept him awake; the bloody moon, loneliness, and thoughts of reputation shook him until fatigue dragged him down into sleep. The next day his great adventure began with the advance. Even when a shellburst knocked off his shako, he considered the danger of combat overrated until he faced the Russian artillery. He quailed at the captain's cynical "Bon soir," closed his eyes to the carnage, and fought mechanically. The colonel fell just before the Russians retreated, leaving the youngster as senior officer in charge.

The pattern of the narrative follows that of *Mateo Falcone,* although here Mérimée manipulates his material to achieve an almost perfect example of the sketch. He traces the effects of events on the mind of his protagonist, interested in reaction rather than action. No mention is made of time until the advance starts. A few lines allow the author to vouch for the facts, then the "friend" takes up the story. In a style bare of imagery, the lieutenant's thoughts are interspersed among descriptions of the military situation.

This organization allowed Mérimée to indulge his satiric bent. The hero, fresh from military school, ended up as commanding officer in his first action. Veterans might die, but not a lieutenant who, brave in new uniform and martial moustache, lacked the imagination to understand battle as more than a topic for salon conversation. After the engagement, the wounded colonel answered his solicitude with a rude remark: "Mon cher, mais la redoute est prise!" As the captain had warned earlier, the wrong man died; logic had no more place in the world of war than in Corsica, where accident ruled both mice and men as butts of a grim jest.

In *Mateo Falcone*, Mérimée took advantage of contemporary interest in the exotic and the primitive; in *L'Enlèvement*, he cast a shrewd eye on the growing Napoleonic legend and the pride of a peacefully bellicose middle class in the exploits of the Grand Army. It is not surprising, then, that in *Tamango* he dealt with slavery, a subject beginning to agitate the nation. Mérimée borrowed generously from many sources but mostly, and surprisingly, from Emerigon's *Traité des assurances* (1827). Once again the incident interested him because it emphasized the noble savage in action. Tamango, himself a slave dealer, was captured by Ledoux, captain of a vessel ironically named *La Bonne Espérance*. Arranged in five major scenes, the Bargain, the Capture, the Curse, the Revolt, and Justice, *Tamango* promised to be a sentimental thriller. But Mérimée had other ideas. Tamango was the betrayer betrayed, and his successful revolt aboard ship brought only slow, agonizing death to the slaves, of whom only Tamango was saved. To underline the thesis of man's inhumanity, Mérimée described life aboard the slaver, the whippings and deaths; to reinforce his idea of a world organized as a cosmic jest, Tamango was the one who survived, although he had created the entire predicament. But he lived to fall into the hands of a humanitarian-minded English governor who freed him to work for a pittance. Proud Tamango, once a chief, became a cymbal player in the regimental band and died of pneumonia and alcoholism.

Since Mérimée exploited the commonplaces of his age, it is not surprising to find that this unreconstructed rationalist wrote three short tales of the supernatural: *Fédérigo, La Vision de Charles XI,* and *La Vénus d'Ille.* Of the three, the first two had appeared in *Mosaïque; La Vénus,* not published until 1837, was considered by Mérimée as his best effort.

Fédérigo does not seem to fit into the pattern of *Mosaïque,* nor does it match the other early narratives. Supposedly from an old Neapolitan tale, it appealed to contemporary interest in legends. Fédérigo is a courteous scoundrel who dedicated himself to wine, women, and song, never went to church, yet won a place in paradise. The supernatural setting here is a popular one, in which heaven and hell function in human terms.

However, with *La Vision de Charles XI,* Mérimée drew on the supernatural for its frightening aspects as, once again, he found a ready-made subject. In 1742, when the Swedish royal family was struggling over dynastic succession, the backers of one of the pretenders circulated a prophetic "vision" of Charles XI. This document appeared in the *Vaterlandisches Museum* on June 16, 1819, and was forwarded to France by a diplomat. In all probability one of Mérimée's friends found it for him in the archives of the Ministry of Foreign Affairs, but he brought to the politically motivated anecdote an artistry that transformed it into a tale of mystery.

Mérimée deliberately introduced an alternate solution to confuse his readers. One autumn in 1676, Charles XI, sunk in a black mood, saw the great chamber come alight. He walked along a gallery draped in mourning, and in the hall witnessed a macabre judgment scene, in which a group of young men were beheaded; one of the heads rolled against Charles' slipper. When the king invoked the aid of God, a phantom prophesied that these events would later come to pass. The judges vanished, along with the executioners, the blood, and the funeral drapes. Back in his room, Charles thought he had been dreaming until he found a red splotch on his slipper. Thereupon he wrote an account of the event, its veracity vouched for by the royal honor.

In choosing a supernatural subject, Mérimée's problem was to present the seemingly impossible as historical fact, depending on a realistically handled background for verisimilitude. Tongue in cheek, he began with a quotation from *Hamlet*: "There are more things in Heav'n and earth, Horatio, Than are dreamt of in your philosophy." To beguile disbelief, he used historical personages and the testimony of four unimpeachable witnesses. At no point did he indicate the possibility of a political hoax as the basis of his tale.

Much later, in 1837, Mérimée turned again to the ghost story. Whereas in *Charles XI* he had kept to the "historical facts," in *La Vénus d'Ille* Mérimée gave freer rein to irony and offered the reader two solutions, both carefully substantiated, but neither sufficiently clear-cut to satisfy either the superstitious or the positivistic.

La Vénus d'Ille revolves around the Pygmalion theme, the statue come to life. The basic fable Mérimée claimed to have borrowed from a medieval legend reported by Fréher, but it may have come from Eckhardt's *Corpus historiarum*, which recounts the same anecdote. It also contains a great many reminiscences of Mérimée's travels in the provinces as Inspector General of Monuments. As such he puts himself in the tale, moving from the real and the probable to a suggestion of the supernatural.

The story concerns a bronze figure of Venus newly discovered in the Pyrénées-Orientales, a region Mérimée had visited in

November, 1834. He arrived in Roussillon just in time to see the malevolent-looking statue and attend the wedding of Alphonse, son of its discoverer. While the groom was beating a Spaniard at handball, he insulted him and was threatened with revenge. Coincidentally, Alphonse discovered that he could not remove the wedding ring he had slid onto the statue's finger. The morning after his wedding, Alphonse was found apparently squeezed to death. Logic indicated the Spaniard as the murderer, but the bride hysterically accused the Venus. When witnesses absolved the Spaniard, the police refused to accept the wife's fantastic explanation. The ironic Mérimée compounded the mystery by noting that when the goddess was cast into a church bell, the vineyards froze for two straight years.

The ambiguity of the ending permitted Mérimée to utilize the techniques of realism while building up the possibility of the Venus as the murderer. He had met people like M. de Peyrehorade, an amateur archeologist of the type that plagued the Inspector General with misinformation; his loutish son, Alphonse, who was marrying a girl for her dowry; and the practical mother. He had often seen rural weddings and munched many a heavy meal to the tune of insipid conversation. His discussion with the archeologist over the legend on the statue recalls a translation he once made, as far-fetched as that attributed to the father. The minor characters, the superstitions, the local patriotism, and the small town materialism he had encountered all too frequently. Curiously, the face of the Venus resembled the one he sketched over and over during boring moments at the Academy.

The cutting irony of the Parisian cynic appears everywhere. No one is spared, not even himself, whom he describes as a serious man with no time for women. He was certainly remembering his fiasco with George Sand when he cautioned the groom against drinking too much on his wedding night. The more esthetic of the peasants compared the beauty of the Venus to the town's plaster bust of Louis-Philippe, while M. de

Peyrehorade considered the marriage of his son a minor incon-
venience for his archeological studies. Mérimée summed up his
dislike of rural stupidity when he had the father melt down the
beautiful statue for a church bell.

The drama of the story increased with the gradual development of the goddess' personality. By liberal foreshadowing,
Mérimée turned the Venus from a topic of conversation to the
dominant figure of the narrative. She first appeared in a long
conversation between the author and his guide, a rare use of
dialogue for Mérimée. The guide stressed the evil in Venus,
who fell on a workman who struck her with a pick-axe, an
accident that led M. de Peyrehorade to note that the Latin
legend on her base began with *cave*. Mérimée watched a peasant
toss a stone at her, heard the man swear that she threw it back
at him. He was struck by the malice of her glance and translated the inscription as "Beware, if she loves you." Moreover,
the marriage took place on Friday, a day of ill omen.

Mérimée himself offered the logical explanation for Alphonse's death, but by then Venus dominated the imagination
of all. The ring lay beside the body, the bride swore that the
statue had killed him, and even M. de Peyrehorade began to
waver. Symbolically, the cock crowed just before the murder.
Just as in *Charles XI*, the mystery remained unsolved and the
reader was left with an uncomfortable feeling of the malevo-
lence of the inanimate.

Mérimée's penchant for twisting romantic themes reached a
peak in *La Partie de trictrac* (1830). Now his interest shifted
from plots cleverly constructed for a maximum of dramatic
effect to a fascination with emotional states. In this framework
story he exploited the theme of crime and punishment—punishment self-inflicted for transgression of the code of the gentleman.

Unlike many of Mérimée's narratives, the action of *La Partie
de trictrac* occurs over a period of weeks. The captain of a
vessel tells his passengers about Roger, a naval officer who fell
in love with Gabrielle, a capricious actress who refused his

flowers and gold. When colleagues from the army hissed her plays, Roger challenged all of them. Gabrielle capitulated and the couple led a happy existence until a Dutch frigate arrived. Roger gambled away all his money to a Dutch lieutenant, but with a last coin his luck turned and the bankrupted officer shot himself. Gabrielle tormented a penitent Roger who admitted he had cheated; then, in a feminine change of mind, she stole a watch to prove her love and even agreed to a double suicide. Before Roger could carry out this plan, his frigate was dispatched on patrol. He swore to let himself be killed and, when seriously wounded in an engagement, begged a friend to throw him overside. At this point in the captain's story, an ensign calls out that a whale has been sighted, and the captain rushes off, forgetting to finish the anecdote. "Je ne pus savoir comment mourut le pauvre Lieutenant Roger," Mérimée concluded.

The pace of the story differs from the previous tales. Once Roger fell in love, Mérimée focused attention on the young man's mental state; the lieutenant's defense of Gabrielle's dubious honor, his remorse for the chicanery, and his desire to kill himself when he understood why he had cheated. The drama turned inward as interest centered on when, not how, Roger would solve his problem. Only death could release him, and the reader was asked to guess whether in battle or by suicide.

The story is more loosely knit than *Mateo Falcone* because Mérimée understood that psychological inquiry required more leisurely analysis. He started slowly with a justification of the narrative, then prepared a second introduction containing detailed portraits of Roger and Gabrielle. Not until halfway through the story did Roger's confession establish a problem, and then its solution was constantly postponed.

Mérimée's cynicism threatened the unity of the narrative because, as usual, he had no affection for characters whom he considered fools. The quixotic Roger, gambler and rake, brooded overmuch about his honor; Gabrielle, "la plus capricieuse créature de son sexe," mistress of senators and generals, raged at Roger for cheating, then stole to prove her affection. Having sent the lover into battle, Mérimée chose to rescue a plot that had obviously lost momentum by suddenly breaking off the story. The satire here was directed at both the reader and the tale itself, verging on the cosmic irony so dear to the German romantics.

However, the lessons learned in *La Partie de trictrac* bore fruit in two of Mérimée's better works, *La Double Méprise* and *Le Vase étrusque*. The latter, a case study in jealousy, stemmed partly from a traumatic personal experience, probably his affair with Mme Lacoste. Auguste Saint-Clair had been planning to marry the widowed Mme de Coursy at the end of her mourning —until gossip tricked him into believing that Massigny, to him the dullest of men, had also enjoyed her favors. Furious, he jostled a friend on the way home and the subsequent hard words produced a challenge. That night Mme de Coursy explained away the presence of Massigny's Etruscan vase on her mantel, but Saint-Clair died the next morning in the duel his jealousy had provoked.

The tale revolves around the vase, which symbolized for Saint-Clair the rival he thought he had dispossessed. Because of it he believed the irresponsible chatter that inexorably led to his death. The urn functions to focus Saint-Clair's jealousy and, when Mme de Coursy smashes it, foreshadows his doom. This time Mérimée built a tight structure. Saint-Clair dominates the action as the author's alter ego, discusses himself wryly without any illusions about his personality or its effect on other people. He reveals himself as proud, ambitious, eager for the good opinion of others. Like the author, Saint-Clair had a protective wall of impassivity to shield a sensitive nature and consequently was not well liked. He seemed cold and distant, and never confided in anybody; he antagonized acquaintances by his self-sufficiency and calm disregard for public opinion. No one knew anything of his love life, but he was suspected of having an affair with Mme de Coursy on the curious grounds that he never mentioned her name.

The plot follows the standard pattern for stories about jealousy. Saint-Clair started out happy with his lot, but a casual conversation aroused doubts about how exclusive Mme de Coursy had been with her affections. He tortured himself as malicious rumor and coincidence seemed to confirm his suspicions. When the misunderstanding was cleared up, Mérimée could not leave his characters happy. A hostile Providence caused Saint-Clair's death at the hands of a friend, all because of a needless quarrel.

The gossip that upset Saint-Clair occurred at a bachelor dinner of the kind Mérimée enjoyed with Musset and Delacroix. Mérimée used it not only to motivate the plot but also to comment sarcastically on dandies, utilizing their fatuity almost in counterpoint to the tragic effects occasioned by their mindless babble. Furthermore, the portrait of the dandies provided Mérimée with a means of slowing the action, which otherwise would have sped to a conclusion that weakened his psychological analysis.

Mérimée's sense of humor fed on the ample material provided by the dinner scene. Adopting a confidential tone, he invited the reader to share his mockery by addressing him directly, even asking him to fill in some of the details. The conversation probably came from recollections of similar affairs: toasts to the modistes of Paris, to the tragedienne Judith Pasta, remarks on the theater, dramatic censorship, politics, English horses and, as Mérimée dryly commented, "par une liaison d'idées facile à saisir," the engrossing topic of women. Inevitably, they tried to reduce amorous success to a pattern, with a consequent debate on procedure, and Thémines was prompted to cite the case of Massigny, a dullard without manners or conversation, who proved an irresistible lover.

With the anecdote about Massigny, Saint-Clair suddenly

found reason to wonder about Mme de Coursy's generosity. The irresponsible Thémines flatly announced that Massigny had been her lover, a statement that recalled to Saint-Clair the Etruscan urn, a gift from Massigny which his mistress kept full of flowers. The vase obsessed him as a reminder of her easy virtue and his succession to the place of a boor. Jealousy led to a series of misinterpreted conversations, followed by the inevitable reconciliation. But Mérimée's view of life would not permit such an ending. He stressed the irony by noting that Thémines had not intended to kill Saint-Clair at all. As for the countess, she retreated from society and died of a popular romantic ailment, consumption.

To permit Saint-Clair ample time to grow jealous, Mérimée introduced Théodore Néville, a dandy just back from a quick trip to Egypt. In a digression badly integrated into the body of the narrative, Mérimée mocked local color and the contemporary rage for bric-a-brac. Théodore posed as an expert on Egyptian affairs, commented fatuously on Arabic literature, the Sultan, and even the Koran. Tourist fashion, he had seen all in six weeks.

Le Vase étrusque contains all the techniques normally found in Mérimée's work: the plot is stated, the action seen only from a distance through the author's eyes. Mérimée persistently interjected himself into the tale whenever it threatened to slow down or if events moved too quickly for his purpose. Once again he relied on the conventions of his time in a classic tale of misunderstanding. The story moves according to the emotional states of Saint-Clair, who is alternately happy or dejected as he fights waves of suspicion. The story is liberally sprinkled with trite remarks on human behavior, most of them on the plight of a man in love: "Un homme a l'air bien sot quand il reçoit froidement les cajoleries d'une jolie femme," or "un amant heureux est presque aussi ennuyeux qu'un amant malheureux."

The more he dipped into autobiographical material, the stronger grew Mérimée's protective irony. He invited the reader into a conspiracy against the characters, assuming a position of supposed objectivity, "mon devoir d'historien." So sensitive was he to potential criticism that he debated directly with the critics whether gossip could really create Saint-Clair's jealousy.

Along with the short tales, all but one of which form *Mosaïque*, Mérimée tried his hand at a few longer works. His first attempt, *La Chronique du règne de Charles IX* (1824), was an imitation of Scott that resulted in what he called a *genre bâtard*, wherein background and plot joined in an incompatible marriage.

The chronicle incorporated three different stories: the Saint Bartholomew's Day Massacre, Georges de Mergy's religious difficulties, and his brother Bernard's affair with Diane de Turgis. Bernard, arriving in Paris to live with Georges while serving as a Huguenot soldier, is saved from the massacre by Georges and escapes to join in the defense of La Rochelle. During a sortie, a detachment under his command mortally wounds Georges, an ostensible Catholic convert who dies refusing all religious comfort.

Mérimée proposed a history of the massacre, with a Protestant, a Catholic, and an atheist as eye-witnesses. Events are arranged in scenes calculated to reveal the mind-set of France in 1572, with the result that the religious tension always remains in the foreground. Riding into Paris to begin his career, Bernard sees the city with a tourist's eyes, but the point of view shifts and it is Georges who comments on the religious quarrel and describes the massacre. He had been converted formally to Catholicism, but he was an atheist, whose missal cover hid a copy of Rabelais. Like Mérimée he could say, "J'ai lu tous nos docteurs pour y chercher des consolations contre les doutes qui m'effrayaient, et je n'ai fait que les accroître. Bref, je n'ai pu et je ne puis croire. Croire est un don précieux qui m'a été refusé, mais pour rien au monde je ne chercherais à en priver les autres." While he lay dying in La Rochelle, priest and minister fought over his last moments, but he steadfastly refused their aid, his stoicism a counterpart to the behavior of the pseudo-atheist Béville, who confessed out of fear of the unknown.

The massacre provided not only a nucleus around which to build the narrative, but also an ending consistent with the savagery of the central event: fratricide over religious differences. However, the very grimness of the subject matter presented an insuperable obstacle: Mérimée's ironic view of human destiny prevented any understanding of the motives that prompted such uncivilized behavior; his sharp sense of the ridiculous hampered the creation of a unified work.

As a result, the characters were constantly pushed into awkward postures. Bernard de Mergy appears as a naïve bumpkin who instantly falls in love with the seductive Diane de Turgis. After Bernard encounters the marauding *reîtres*, he is robbed during the night and the next morning fights a comic opera duel with the inn potboys that smacks of *Don Quixote*. Even his affair with Diane has moments approaching burlesque, as when, on the eve of the massacre, Diane works mightily to convert Bernard in the soft comfort of her bed. The absurdity of the situation never occurred to this defender of the faith, who changed lovers as she did gloves, who practiced black magic and white, and who attended church twice daily only in order to be seen. Béville, the fop, belatedly denied his atheism from fear of hellfire. Only Georges received straightforward treatment; Georges held many of the author's opinions.

Occasionally, Mérimée indulged in romantic irony directed at his reader. While Bernard was discovering Paris, the contemporary literary recipe indicated the need for a series of historical portraits which Mérimée refused to provide. In a "Dialogue entre le lecteur et l'auteur," he argued against the practice of the "faiseur de romans," brusquely advising the inquisitive to go visit a museum to satisfy their curiosity. He fell back on the same technique at the end of the chronicle when he arrived at an illogical ending. Bernard had opened the tale, his love affair filled most of it, but Georges dominated the last and most important part. For those who wondered what would happen to Diane and Bernard, Mérimée offered only cold comfort: "Mergy se consola-t-il? Diane prit-elle un autre amant? Je le laisse à décider au lecteur qui, de la sorte, terminera toujours le roman à son gré."

The plot moved slowly, without the usual tension characteristic of the shorter tales. A failing he admits in the preface led him to introduce extraneous elements and sardonic digressions. A camp follower related the story of the Pied Piper; a burlesque battle in the inn was later matched by a scene in which Bernard and Captain Dietrich, disguised as monks, baptized two chickens *Carpam* and *Percham* at the insistence of country terrorists who craved meat on Friday. The action broke into a series of episodes on two topics, the love affair and the massacre, each manipulated according to Mérimée's whim. He enjoyed writing the story but could rightly dismiss the *Chronique* as a *genre bâtard*. Obviously, his imagination worked best at compressing his vision of the major moments of human life.

In 1833, Mérimée returned to a psychologically motivated plot with *La Double Méprise*, longer than *Le Vase étrusque*, but like it, an analysis of the effect of strong emotion, this time on a woman. "C'est un de mes péchés pour gagner de l'argent," he disclaimed his work protectively.

Almost clinically, Mérimée plumbed the mind of a Parisian lady whose marital unhappiness led her into adultery with an old friend. Julie de Chaverny, married for six years, finally realized that her husband was a complete clod. Chaverny lived in his own limited world of hunting parties and stag dinners, while Julie "était fière de se voir plaindre dans la société et citer comme un modèle de résignation. Après tout, elle se trouvait presque heureuse, car elle n'aimait personne." Mérimée moved slowly from this premise, establishing Chaverny's vulgarity and his consuming desire to become a *gentilhomme de la chambre*, which precipitated the affair. Chaverny committed the blunder of inviting the Duc de H . . . and his mistress to sit with Julie at the opera, then abandoned his wife after the performance. An embittered Julie met Darcy, an old friend just returned from Turkey, and hazy memories combined with the urbanity of the diplomat to transform Darcy into the man she should have married. A chance accident during a storm, and a ride home with Darcy, provided the occasion for Julie to succumb. Shame overcame her the next morning and she left Paris, but only to fall ill and die.

In his analysis of a classic case of incompatibility, Mérimée presented his story like a Racinian tragedy. The first page established the relationship between Julie and her husband, setting the scene for events that would rapidly culminate in an explosion of emotion. Not only the title but also a quotation from Calderón warns of impending tragedy. The characters are kept flat and single-minded, partly because Mérimée did not envision them as complete personalities, but mostly because he wanted attention focused on the interplay of emotions. Thus, Chaverny is "un assez bel homme, un peu trop gros pour son âge"; Julie is lovely, young, and flirtatious; Darcy is pale, deep-eyed, wrinkled, and beginning to lose his hair.

Since Mérimée wished to show how dislike for a husband could turn an honest woman to adultery, he carefully prepared Julie for meeting Darcy. Though the reader was immediately informed that Chaverny's wife "trouvait tout en lui repoussant," Mérimée set up a series of minor episodes to produce the first of the crises that propel the action: Chaverny, dining at his mother-in-law's home, was afraid of having to talk to his wife for twenty minutes on the way home. Vain, stupid, sure of Julie, he could not recognize her aversion to him. When commenting on his wife's dress, he inadvertently referred to his mistress, then clumsily tried to caress his wife simply because he was bored.

At a dinner party, Chaverny even had the bad taste to discuss Julie's legs as though he were describing a horse. Events came to a head when Chaverny compromised his unsuspecting wife. When she discovered what he had done, the stage was set for Darcy's appearance and by happy coincidence the newspapers announced his return from a diplomatic post in Constantinople.

Mérimée sent Julie into the country to a confidant using the time lag to have her recreate Darcy, the poor but handsome boy she might have married. Thus, when Julie arrived at Mme Lambert's, Mérimée had to slow his story, the momentum of which had rapidly accelerated, in order to give Mme de Chaverny time to react to Darcy's presence. Therefore, he introduced the salon gossip of Darcy's rescue of a Turkish woman whose angry husband was about to drown her. The anecdote was told twice, once by a woman who transformed the diplomat into the hero of Julie's dreams, then by Darcy himself, who stripped it of romantic trimmings. The digression thus served to corroborate Julie's illusions. To bring the two together, Mérimée used the coincidence of a carriage accident in a thunder storm. The use of such a device bothered him not at all. He well knew that a Providence in his own ironical image often forced human beings into ludicrous positions.

In the carriage, the plot reached the carefully prepared climax that permitted Mérimée to study a second emotional state: Julie's acceptance of seduction and her misconception of Darcy. When Darcy comforted her, Julie surrendered to an illusion after only perfunctory objection. During the rest of the ride, she began to see herself degraded to the level of her husband; in but nine hours she had maneuvered herself into an affair. Any hopes of escape from the predicament vanished when her lover calmly chatted of continuing their relationship in the traditional manner. He went home smugly satisfied with his luck, but she could not escape the consequences of an abrupt return to reality. Julie tried to escape the consequences of her adultery but died of chagrin and romantic illness.

Longer than the tales in *Mosaïque*, *La Double Méprise* suffered from Mérimée's need to move slowly for reasons of psychological credibility. Commandant Perrin and his friend Châteaufort furnished a mildly humorous episode based on the latter's misconception that Julie loved him, but neither added much to the narrative, though they usurped a good many pages and broke the unity of the plot. Similarly the twice-told tale of the *mama-mouchi* seems a needless extravagance. Because of these interpolations the action crawls along at first, then races at breakneck speed once Julie has committed adultery.

Like all of Mérimée's work, the tale was more than twice-told. As usual, the author adopted a position of omniscience, permitting himself the luxury of intruding, sometimes to discuss a situation, more often to criticize his characters. The portraits of Chaverny, Perrin, and Châteaufort bordered on caricature; only Julie received close attention. He delighted in pointing out that nobody understood the situation between Mme de Chaverny and her husband. "Comme ils s'aiment," her mother thought, a phrase Mérimée used in sarcastic contrast to the scene he was describing. His world was cruel, as Julie discovered, a universe in which only the author's mind operated rationally. The only kindness Mérimée could offer was to let her die quickly, albeit unmourned.

After a long silence, interrupted only by the appearance of the haphazard *Ames du purgatoire* (1834), Mérimée published in the *Revue des Deux Mondes* on July 1, 1840, what became one of his most popular works, *Colomba*. Generations of secondary school children have come to know Mérimée, however reluctantly, through the dramatic tale of a Corsican vendetta, complete with ambush, sudden death, and the dominant presence of a determined heroine. The structure of the story recalls *Mateo Falcone* in that once again Mérimée attempted to set a love story against an exotic background. This time, however, he avoided the difficulties of historical subjects by choosing for a background the then almost unknown island of Corsica. Moreover, he attached the love affair more firmly to the major plot by having Lydia Nevil not only fall in love with Orso della Rebbia but also act as the witness who cleared him of a murder charge.

Basically the tale is a simple one, though as violent as *Mateo Falcone*. Retired from the French army on half-pay, Orso returned to Corsica where his sister, Colomba, expected him to avenge his father's assassination by the Barricinis. Having lived most of his life on the continent, Orso thought the vendetta absurd. However, circumstances arranged by his aggressive sister provoked him to anger. He miraculously killed Orlanduccio and Vincentello Barricini with two shots when he was ambushed and thus unwittingly complied with the code. He escaped prison only because Lydia and her father testified that he had fired in self-defense.

Such a tale could have been treated in the manner of *Mateo Falcone*, but Mérimée preferred the more leisurely pace of the chronicle form to indulge his taste for anecdote and the description of the unusual. To that end, he added two characters, a retired British colonel and his tourist daughter. Sir Thomas was taking Lydia to Corsica because Italy bored her. They met Orso when he requested a ride on their boat, and the two young people inevitably fell in love.

But even the love story and the vendetta were insufficient to fatten the narrative to Mérimée's taste. To them he added a dissertation on the art of the *voceratrice*, a discussion of the *maquis* and of bandit habits in Corsica, and a history of the island. Contrary to his usual manner, he did not introduce his characters in a few deft sentences but sketched them leisurely. Colomba does not appear until the sixth chapter, up to which point Mérimée has been concerned with Sir Thomas, Lydia, Orso, and the extravagant local color of the island.

The author's irreverent smile appears everywhere. Although Taine claimed that in *Colomba* "l'auteur s'efface jusqu'à paraître absent," Mérimée's sense of the ridiculous sometimes threatened to turn the characters into caricatures. Sir Thomas, the retired officer, verges on the Colonel Blimp. He lives for hunting and catering to Lydia, a spoiled only child who visited Italy because it was the thing to do. Her efforts to collect conversation pieces unknown to her London friends had all misfired. She found Italian art mediocre, Vesuvius at its best an appalling disappointment. When she arrived in Segni only to discover that Lady Frances Fenwick had preceded her, Lydia pouted until a friend described Corsica, a place then unknown to Englishmen. She knew she had come upon something unusual when she learned why the young lieutenant was returning home. Orso, of course, was the reluctant hero, but events—and Colomba—conspired to force him into the role of avenging knight. Even the bandits have a touch of the comic, with their trained dog and plans for selecting a husband for their protégée, Chilina. Castriconi ran from the police, but he feared only the loss of his Latin and yearned for a copy of Horace. Colomba alone had Mérimée's respect, perhaps because she was the sole person who dared impose her will on events.

The love affair is a travesty of romantic conventions. The proper English girl imagined Orso as the Byronic hero hiding his deadly purpose under an air of insouciance. Colomba, who demonstrated the correct use of a stiletto, increased Lydia's interest in the della Rebbia family to the point where she gave Orso an Egyptian scarab bearing the ridiculous motto: "Life is a struggle." Orso, of course, was struck by the traditional *coup de foudre*, but it was a somewhat delayed bolt. While lying wounded in the *maquis*, he received a visit from Lydia, at which point his sister Colomba pushed her to Orso's side, placed her hand in his, and waited for nature to take its course. Lydia blushed; Orso declared himself unworthy of her; Lydia pressed his hand, and the two stared at each other until the police raided the camp. Even the secondary characters suffer from the author's sense of humor: the police always arrive too late; the prefect stalks pompously into a situation he cannot prevent; the Barricini boys pose like confirmed villains, scowling at an Orso who has no intention of fighting them. In fact, when Orso is finally provoked, he challenges them to a duel, something completely beyond their ken.

Mérimée took little seriously, even the tragedy he was about to unfold. The vendetta had begun over a relatively trivial dispute, then broadened into a disagreement that spawned forgery, perjury, and murder. Mérimée indulged his passion for violence and crime without compassion for the creatures he involved in the tangle of circumstances. Utilizing the techniques and conventions of romanticism, particularly the heavy use of local color, he irreverently poked fun at his own literary ancestry.

As in all the longer works, the plot was stretched to the breaking point. The narrative began *in medias res*, as Mérimée ironically explained, "to conform to Horace's precept," then in Chapter VI the author filled in the background, "now that everybody is sleeping." Colomba's case against the Barricinis was outlined in Chapter XV, but her suspicions remained unverified until the end, when the mayor, half mad, blurted out the truth.

The murder, however, forms only part of the background, as the reason for Colomba's manipulation of her brother. The drama of the tale springs from the question Mérimée kept unanswered almost until the end: would Orso comply with the rules of the vendetta; would heredity and environment overcome the training of civilization? Similarly, the love affair provided a target for cynical barbs and served to counterbalance Colomba's efforts. Orso sensed that his sister was directing him; his role ended happily in marriage but Mérimée could not stop there. His pessimism demanded a postscript, a comment on life's cruelty, and so Colomba, the winner of all the stakes, had to meet a broken old man mourning his sons and crucify him with a last remark before she rejoined the happy couple.

With the publication of *Carmen* in the *Revue des Deux Mondes* on October 1, 1845, Mérimée reached the end of his major production in the short prose narrative. Perhaps his best known work, the story shows clearly how secondary the creation of fiction had now become for him. Subsequent tales, *L'Abbé Aubain*, *Lokis*, would be dashed off to amuse and shock a feminine audience. Mérimée had begun to lose interest in a writing career and whatever concern he had for his art slowly dissipated as other matters intruded.

In *Carmen*, Mérimée fell back on a story told him by the Comtesse de Montijo. It was, he wrote her, a *conte* framed in scholarly considerations. The exact source is not known, but the finished product reveals how much he depended on the pastiche, and to what extent he drew his material from bookish sources. *Carmen* is a simple tale: the love of a Basque soldier for a fickle gypsy girl that led him to desert, turn bandit, stab a rival, and finally, after killing Carmen, to seek death by surrendering to the police.

Mérimée chose a framework structure into which he interjected himself far more than customarily. First he told of encountering José while he was traveling on the Cachena plain. Later, in Córdoba, Mérimée met Carmen, who promptly stole his watch. Thus the author could vouch for the reality of both his characters, and two months later he discovered José in jail and heard from him the details of the tragedy.

As Sainte-Beuve noted, *Carmen* has more than a casual similarity to *Manon Lescaut*. In both the sorrowing lover blurts out his tale of woe to an observer. Manon and Carmen are interpreted only as they affect the hero; they are subjective creations of minds under great emotional stress. Both women have strong personalities that let them dominate plots which concern the degradation of two essentially decent men destined for the priesthood. José and Des Grieux have their dilemmas solved by death, and bury their mistresses in lonely graves dug with their swords. The girls are fickle, a quality that lends movement and drama to the plots, but for the men love comes at first sight and life pushes them to become what they least wish. They are led helplessly by emotions that reason cannot control, and seem weak and vacillating.

The comparison, however, cannot be pushed very far, for

Carmen warned José of his probable fate at the very outset. Though Mérimée generously compared the hero to Milton's Satan, José seems banal and conventional, introduced as the mysterious stranger in the tradition of Hernani, a "symbole de l'amour viril soumis à la femme et humilié, déshonoré." Like Orso, José was manipulated by a woman despite the protests of his queasy conscience. Even when facing death he could only say, "Pauvre enfant! Ce sont les Calès qui sont coupables pour l'avoir élevée ainsi."

Carmen, on the other hand, resembles Colomba more than Manon. Both the Corsican girl and the gypsy display the primitive nature and feline qualities which Mérimée admired in cats. Carmen cheats and Carmen lies; Carmen steals and Carmen begs; but nonetheless Carmen stays true to her code, unlike José. Mérimée made her a good savage in reverse, inevitably bound to clash with her lover because of their differing cultures. Sketched in light, successive touches, even as seen through her lover's dazzled eyes, she dominates the action, amoral, whimsical, powerfully feminine, yet ready to accept death as part of her existence.

Stripped of excess baggage, *Carmen* proceeds from one emotional crisis to another, as Bizet noted. But the published narrative contains a long semi-humorous introduction about a search for the true site of Munda. The asides and personal comments indicate a tale written for a special audience privy to the author's life and mind-set. "J'étais alors un tel mécréant, il y a de cela quinze ans, que je ne reculai pas d'horreur en me voyant à côté d'une sorcière." Mérimée poked fun at the Spanish army, delicately referred the reader to Brantôme for a Spaniard's idea of beauty, discoursed on bedbugs in country inns, and described women bathing in the river. He expected to enjoy his own story, even at the expense of the reader. Since he had been studying gypsies, he appended a short essay on the life and customs of the Bohemians which almost ruined the illusion as the reader passed from the world of Carmen to that of the archeologist. Mérimée's whims might well destroy the balance of his narrative, but at this point he did not care. The amusement of a salon full of friends, a sardonic smile at human folly, an interesting anecdote, meant more than reputation as a conscious artist.

In the history of short prose in the first half of the nineteenth century, Mérimée stands out as a man to heed well. He theorized little, since he never felt compelled to establish an esthetic for either self-explanation or self-defense, yet he understood the limitations and advantages of his medium as well as any contemporary writer. To be sure, most of the techniques he favored were common currency: plots shaped in sequential narration, articulated by causality, told by a pseudo-author who persistently intrudes with caustic observations. The tales are often presented as stories within a story, well seasoned with foreshadowing. Mérimée dipped deep into the pool of romantic conventions for such clichés as the exoticism of the faraway, primitivism, dreams, visions, folklore, and the catchy excitement of blood-and-thunder situations. Each story contains a calculated dose of local color which particularizes such stereotypes as the Noble Savage, the Good Priest, the Luckless Lover, the Regenerated Whore, or the Jeune-France.

Yet Mérimée offers more than a catalogue of commonplaces. He unblushingly used the themes in vogue but, having learned his trade from Diderot and Sterne, he arranged them slightly out of focus. Unlike the major romantics, his writing lacked the grand images and symbols so appealing to a Hugo. He followed the oral tradition, as Diderot recommended; many of his tales were written to be read aloud—particularly to young ladies. Some contain asides for the critics the thin-skinned Mérimée feared, and in the *Chronique* he stopped the plot to debate heatedly the question of local color. From this sense of irony came not only the broad mockery of *La Chambre bleue* and the rapier thrusts of *La Double Méprise,* but also the open ending of the *Chronique.*

The stock plots were given strange twists. Mérimée delighted in ambiguous endings that left the reader on a split stick, wondering whether the statue of Venus really crushed the bridegroom, or whether Charles XI actually had a vision. Certainly the pure in heart will never understand *Lokis.* The Abbé Aubain resembles a clever and scheming Jocelyn. Tamango by office and culture is a noble savage, but a stupid one who lands in the kind of slavery only an abolitionist British government could imagine. Arsène Guillot, courtesan, gets religion on her deathbed, to earn a place in heaven and a romantically inscribed headstone, while her reform-minded benefactress and erstwhile lover live to enjoy a more earthy reward. And how Mérimée must have chuckled over the plight of Orso, the accidental hero, or the memory of Diane de Turgis as she tried to convert Bernard de Mergy in the warmth of her sheets.

This kind of orientation makes his work interesting, although Mérimée deserves high praise for bold experimentation and major contributions to the art of short fiction. For all his mockery, for all his seeming indifference to literary reputation, this confirmed ironist took his work seriously. A close scrutiny of his stories reveals a variety of modes of expression that could not fail to enrich the genre. At long last, a writer had appeared who refused to load his tales with the heavy burden of commonly accepted morality. He accepted the short narrative as an autonomous art form fully capable of rich expression, provided the author understood its limitations as well as its possibilities. Intrude he did, but without any claim to omniscience. Unhampered by tradition or the urge to write novels, he became the first French writer to treat brief fiction as more than a dehydrated novel or a miniature long romance.

He chose the short narrative deliberately as a fitting expression of the way in which his imagination grasped subjects that attracted him. Mérimée was not primarily interested in the development of incidents multiplied around a boy-girl entanglement, which would have led him to the romance, nor did he wish to create rounded characters by the slow erosion of cause-effect on a personality, which would have brought him to the novel. Both these forms required settings spatially and temporally elongated. He preferred to draw on the dramatic possibilities of life's ironies at selected moments, to exploit the tension which compression made possible. The choice limited him to the brief narrative: the handling of a selected number of incidents focused to produce rapidly a maximum of effect, or the development of character in one major mood or situation. Both of these would be restricted by considerations of time and space, the psychological time of the reader as well as the chronological time of the characters, the space of the fable as well as the geography of the plot. With full appreciation of these limitations, Mérimée worked at solving the problem of manipulating characters in short spans of time and space within the bounds of his medium. As a result, he produced some nineteen stories, no two alike, and used a multiplicity of techniques for such varied works as *Mateo Falcone, La Double Méprise, Colomba,* and *L'Enlèvement de la redoute.*

Within the very brief narrative, his concern for psychological time caused Mérimée to experiment in treating incident variously, depending on his conception of the event. Thus, *L'Enlèvement* occurs over perhaps an hour, during which period Mérimée caught people at a highly interesting moment. On the other hand, in *Mateo Falcone* and *La Vénus d'Ille* everything is directed to the creation of a single effect, concentrated and stripped to essentials. All action is exteriorized and passes in rapid tempo through a single crisis to explode in the climax, then decline in a brief dénouement.

The longer forms, too, include the same range of technical capacity. The *Chronique* closely imitates Scott with its historical background, and weaves through this extended setting a much shorter story than the romance structure demanded. He repeated this "bastard genre" in *Les Ames du purgatoire,* when he tried to use a box-car series of episodes to describe an epic of sin and redemption. As in *Colomba,* this kind of story necessitated giving the reader a sense of elapsed time, since the subject would normally take longer to mature. Because overcompression would destroy the desired effects, as in *La Double Méprise,* Mérimée had to learn how to slow his tale. He was not now concerned with exposition but with the psychological delineation of a personality.

Mérimée's productions were interesting, historically meaningful, and artistically distinguished, but the world in which he set them was mean and small. A master *pasticheur,* he placed his characters in a hostile world, although they seem unaware of the situation. They appear as pawns in an enormous practical joke on mankind played by an ironical Providence; however rationally they try to act, they ultimately fall victim to irrational impulses, or are driven into behavior rejected by their logical minds. Under such circumstances, heroism becomes impossible, and moral values are constantly subject to attack because the human ant heap offers no security and, at best, a precarious happiness. The repetition of this view makes his stories monotonous and the constant irony upsets readers, most of whom view the world more optimistically. This, perhaps, is why Mérimée never attained the stature of the major romantics. However clever his plots, however amusing his jibes, the universe he portrayed contradicted the one which the nineteenth century hoped to forge: optimistic, ultimately benevolent, and based on a progress guaranteed by a number of philosophies of history.

And, yet, despite the reservations with which his age received him, Mérimée's work indicated unmistakably how rapidly short fiction had matured. He had scrubbed it clean of its popular origins, demonstrated how much more it offered than mere anecdotal possibilities, and tested its capacity for intellectual content without challenging its artistic integrity. The infant genre was growing into a lusty and attractive child.

✤ ✤ ✤ ✤ ✤ *V* ✤ ✤ ✤ ✤ ✤

The Major Romantics

THE CAUSE of short fiction so capably furthered by Mérimée received little aid and comfort from the great generation of French romantics. Lamartine, Hugo, Vigny, Musset, poets all, had fought the good fight for their artistic principles, finally winning over the laggard traditionalists of neoclassicism—but their esthetics held no room for so plebeian a form as the short narrative. The kind of imagination they possessed, their epic feeling for a world a-borning, their concern with the great problem of the age, all these combined to keep them from becoming enthusiastic over a medium too limited for imaginations tinged with Titanism. For Lamartine, Hugo, Vigny, and Musset, verse seemed a more natural way to express their vision of the world. When they did turn to the *conte* or the *nouvelle,* they did so as great poetic revolutionaries. For them prose had the taint of the second best; the brief tale seemed restrictive and suitable only for anecdotes. They thought of narration in terms of length, not understanding the literary rewards they might reap from concentration. Conservatives in this sense, they perpetuated a form conceived as separate from content which had been evolved over centuries, with the incidents related chronologically to support the heavy burden of a moral or political thesis.

Lamartine

Lamartine, the senior member of the romantics, reveals clearly their uneasiness in coping with the short narrative. The illumination he experienced near Naples on January 10, 1821, which outlined the grand plan of the universe, occurred to a mind not interested in the microcosm. His talent led to the panoramic, to the story done in full strokes; his ego, as large as any of that time, brought him to the organic theory of genius and, with it, the Messianic mission of the artist. Understandably, then, he favored a confessional type of literature, highly personal, entitled *Les Confidences* and *Nouvelles Confidences*.

He came late to prose, after a long, successful career as poet and statesman. But the great years had passed, and during them he had depreciated his talent for political gain. For a while Lamartine seemed to have chosen wisely; he rose to head the provisional government in 1848. Then he tumbled suddenly into political oblivion and financial disaster. His only asset now lay in his pen, but he had come to realize, like others, that the money he needed could come only from prose. In the years since 1830 the novelist and the short-story writer had usurped from the poet the tangible rewards of success.

This Lamartine knew, but he misinterpreted other signs of social change. Brought up in the country, as he loved to boast, he had become a landed aristocrat of considerable holdings. The seats he held in the Chamber were for agricultural regions; he understood rural problems because he knew these conditions of life at first hand. But the nineteenth century had spawned a new class, the urban workers, who behaved in disconcerting ways. As a politician Lamartine had come to dislike the proletariat, given to violence, inhabiting squalid slums, uneducated, and with no sense of tradition or respect for position. He blamed his humiliating fall from power on what he considered the ingratitude and inconstancy of the worker.

In dislike, then, and in the last surge of his Messianic compulsion, he constructed a world more acceptable to his ego than that of the bickering, socialistically-minded plebs. Lamartine fell victim to the myth of the good peasant and proposed for France a morality based on the example of kindly folk who trusted in God and never complained about their lot. *Geneviève* and

Le Tailleur de pierres de Saint-Point were exempla which Lamartine hoped to spread over rural France to combat the materialistic attitude of the industrial cities.

Geneviève, histoire d'une servante first appeared in 1850, appropriately enough in *Le Conseiller du peuple,* a newspaper Lamartine dedicated to the moral rearmament of the nation. Everything happened to poor Geneviève: her mother died, her brother was drafted, her father took to drink. When sister Josette died bearing a soldier's child, Geneviève took the blame for the abandoned baby. She lost her good name and became a drudge, finally dedicating herself to Jocelyn, a mountain priest. In a final scene of incredible complication, Geneviève met a boy who turned out to be Josette's son and went off with him to enjoy a legacy given by the soldier's aunt, who unexpectedly proved his legitimacy. "C'est ainsi que fait le bon Dieu," Geneviève summarized the plot.

Le Tailleur de pierres repeated a like tale of woe. Claude des Huttes left home and his cousin Denise so she might marry his blind brother, Gratien. Claude wandered for years before returning to find the family impoverished and Gratien dead of heartbreak because of his brother's sacrifice. The premature explosion of a heap of powder Claude was using to celebrate his marriage killed Denise and her two children. Claude's mother perished from shock, and the mason atoned for his error by practicing Christian humility and charity.

Both *Le Tailleur* and *Geneviève* are leisurely *récits villageois* for simple folk. Lamartine propounded a pastoral primitivism based on the myth of the honest, deeply religious peasant with few wants. The tales are structured like poems, broken into *chants*, and bump from one emotional crisis to the next. Consequently, the narratives burst with pathos and are punctuated with floods of tears. Each has a framework: Lamartine recalled his own life, then introduced the major characters, who recounted their frightful experiences. He was present at the ending of both as the sympathetic squire interested in the affairs of his people, who could not resist interrupting the action with lyrical outbursts on nature, the love of animals, or resignation to the will of God.

Since Lamartine also hoped to present a public personality to his readers, he used *Graziella* and *Raphaël* to add dimensions to his self-portrait, with thinly veiled but censored episodes from his youth. *Graziella*, in fact, had formed books VII through X of a volume enticingly called *Les Confidences*. Here the squire was replaced by the young Lamartine, poet aspirant just beginning to make his way into emotional maturity.

Graziella was purportedly an episode from his Italian trip, recalled almost totally. In his first love, Lamartine became involved with a fisherman's daughter who rejected her cousin for him and, when the poet returned to France, died of a broken heart. The story is awash with the characters' tears; often the plot is disregarded to permit comments on love, liberty, and God's will. The tale contains all the paraphernalia of romanticism: storms; a visit to Vesuvius, on the summit of which a poet can solve his problems; a pilgrimage to Graziella's hut; and the plaintive cry, "J'ai aimé, j'ai été aimé." The primitive level on which the Italian family lived enchanted Lamartine but, though he approved of it for the "classes inférieures," Graziella's simple background made marriage impossible. With this slender thread he wove the tenuous plot.

Raphaël, the story of Lamartine's great passion for Julie Charles, supposedly came from the diary of a consumptive friend. Raphaël-Lamartine, reversing the *Graziella* theme, fell in love with an older woman. Using a deceptively autobiographical manner, Lamartine penned a classic of romantic love. Raphaël, an unpublished poet, was suffering from an aggravated case of the *mal du siècle* when he met Julie at Aix and the strength of their Platonic love brought them to the brink of suicide. When she returned to Paris, he borrowed from his mother's savings, even pawned her rings for funds to live in the capital. Raphaël planned to meet Julie again at Aix, but he arrived there only to learn that she had died.

All four stories demonstrate why Lamartine never succeeded

in short fiction. He tried to spin out slender narratives to volume length with only the technique of effectism, which permitted no shades of meaning and little subtlety in characterization. Events were strung together without any attempt to establish causal relationships. Inevitably, because Lamartine insisted on playing a role in them, the focus became double, sometimes on the hero or heroine, sometimes on the author, producing long-winded lectures smug in purpose and narrow in their view of the world.

Hugo

Curiously, the versatile Victor Hugo did not take brief fiction seriously either. Poetry was his first love, and when he did dabble in prose, only the ample dimensions of the historical romance could hold his gigantic imagination. The two short narratives he wrote were titled *La Légende du beau Pécopin* and *Claude Gueux*. The latter is a social tract aimed at the abolition of the death penalty. On July 6, 1834, Hugo published in the *Revue de Paris* the facts concerning the execution of Claude which he had gleaned from the *Gazette des tribunaux* of March 19, 1832. Claude, an illiterate worker who lived with his mistress and child, was jailed for stealing to feed his family. In prison he was terrorized by a sadistic director until Claude killed him in a rage. He was executed, but not before he put the moral of the tale by asking the jury, "Pourquoi ai-je volé? pourquoi ai-je tué?"

Claude's story furnished the text for Hugo's sermon as the condemned man acted out a thesis that would later figure in *Les Misérables*. An expert propagandist, Hugo used the story in standard fashion to build a series of emotional crises that culminated when the handsome Claude, the good criminal of romantic mythology, found himself immolated to society. He suffered one ignominy after another until, once he was convicted, the law demanded punishment instead of the regeneration of a man who could distribute his last possessions to the poor before mounting the scaffold.

When Hugo did try to create a fictional world, with its own unity and existence, it was to write *La Légende du beau Pécopin* in approved pseudomedieval style. Published as letter XI of *Le Rhin, La Légende* told how Pécopin was about to marry the lovely Baldour when he went hunting. Pécopin wandered for years, protected from aging by a talisman until, in a dark forest, the devil in the shape of a wild horse carried him dizzily over the earth to a palace where Nimrod was entertaining the world's greatest hunters. At dawn he found himself home with a Baldour who had grown old during the century of his absence. Pécopin tore his clothes in grief, the talisman fell, and he, too, aged as the devil laughed and the birds called out that it would have been better had he stayed with Baldour.

Hugo enjoyed a story that put his verbal virtuosity at the service of a lively imagination. He lovingly described exotic countrysides and ancient customs, even unexpectedly indulged in broad humor at crucial moments of a tale supposedly for children. When Pécopin discovered that the devil had kidnapped him, he shouted that he was going to purge the hall, the walls of which were covered with mottoes, the largest being: "Adam a inventé le repas, Eve a inventé le dessert!" With admirable poise, the devil handed him a recipe for his own favorite purge. *Pécopin* bears a slight superficial resemblance to the *Saint-Julien* Flaubert would write in 1875-76, particularly in the hunting and wandering episodes, but comparison only shows how carelessly Hugo organized his narrative. The scale of conception is large, with the elements of the plot loosely held together, bearing only the wispiest ideological burden. Unlike Flaubert, he did not shift back and forth from the real to the surreal but began and continued in make-believe. The legend form followed the classic structure of the fairy tale. Hugo strung out fantastic episodes as long as he could, multiplied incredible adventures, then staged an eerie night hunt. With only a minor statement to make, one that could have been given at any stage of the tale, he played with words, punned, and generally amused himself. Obviously he had no intention of taking the short narrative seriously.

Vigny

Although Alfred de Vigny cherished his reputation as a poet as much as Lamartine or Hugo, he paid closer attention to the short prose forms. He had tried his hand at the historical novel in *Cinq-Mars,* but its lack of success induced him to try more fertile fields. Despite the fact that his stories run a good hundred pages each, the plots are simple, the number of incidents restricted, and the cast of characters limited. And whereas history had entangled him in *Cinq-Mars,* now he created a completely fictional world. The brief narratives still betrayed a passion for philosophical theses but the ideas gained force, not through the ponderous majesty of the historical romance, but by repetition in thrice-told tales.

The trilogy of *Les Consultations du Docteur Noir* stemmed from an idea that obsessed Vigny. In *Cinq-Mars* he had dreamed of the poet as ruler in a coming age of intelligence, but this expectation died of blight during the July Revolution. From high optimism Vigny swung to dejected pessimism. Using the case histories of Gilbert, a contemporary of Louis XV, Chatterton, an English poet of the late eighteenth century, and André Chénier, he portrayed three victims of social injustice to underscore the thesis that poetry stood to lose under any form of government.

L'Histoire d'une puce enragée was published on October 15, 1831, in the *Revue des Deux Mondes,* and the legend of Chatterton, long known in France, on December 1, 1831. These two, with a third added, appeared in book form in 1832, set in conversations between Stello, a poet, and Doctor Noir, a mysterious physician with the ageless experience of the Wandering Jew. Both characters symbolize aspects of Vigny at war with each other in a dialogue over the author's problems. Stello represents the heart, the "divine" side; Doctor Noir stands for "life," the rational approach. The latter's reasoning always reduces Stello to silence; he is sad and cynical about human behavior, the antithesis of the sulking poet. Vigny polarized the pair to reveal the ambivalence of his own attitudes and to describe the rise and fall of a romantic dream.

The entire work concerns a call the doctor made to cure Stello of the "blue devils," the treatment for which consisted of anecdotes as "excellents remèdes contre la tentation bizarre qui vous vient de dévouer vos écrits aux fantaisies d'un parti." Surprisingly, since the subject indicated serious treatment, Vigny adopted a light touch. The poet and his mentor showed a whimsical illogicality, emphasizing the unsuspected importance to human events of the infinitely small.

Vigny, in effect, tried to marry the traditional French manner of storytelling to Sterne's techniques. The three tales were told in a straightforward fashion, with interjections by Stello, followed by the doctor's explanations. In contrast to his manner in *Cinq-Mars,* Vigny adopted a bantering tone when introducing the major characters. Stello was sketched vaguely as a child favored by destiny, happy and lucky, whose spells of dejection were cured by Doctor Noir, Vigny's version of a psychiatrist. The grave and cold physician, whom Vigny never delineated, guaranteed to cure Stello's migraines by making him understand his mental condition.

The first consultation concerned the poet Gilbert and a fat Louis XV. Mlle de Coulanges, the royal mistress, was awakened from her boredom when a flea sent her into chattering terror. When the anxious king summoned the doctor, the physician came to treat Mlle de Coulanges and at the same time begged royal aid for the ailing Gilbert. But Louis XV wanted no truck with poets, who too often bit the hand that fed them. On his return to Gilbert, the doctor found him dying in his garret, yet still able to write his own epitaph: "Au banquet de la vie infortuné convive . . ."

Since Vigny was working with a simple anecdote, the interjections served to make the tale seem longer and to permit the presentation of ideas on another level:

"Je crois en moi, parce que je sens au fond de mon coeur une puissance secrète, invisible et indéfinissable, toute pareille à un pressentiment de l'avenir et à une révélation des causes mystérieuses du temps présent. Je crois en moi, parce qu'il n'est dans la nature aucune beauté, aucune grandeur, aucune harmonie qui ne me cause un frisson prophétique. . . . Je crois fermement en une vocation ineffable qui m'est donnée, et j'y crois à cause de la pitié sans bornes que m'inspirent les hommes mes compagnons en misère, et aussi à cause du désir que je me sens de leur tendre la main et de les élever sans cesse par des paroles de commisération et d'amour."

This boundless pity Vigny expressed dramatically in a story that falls into scenes, flashing back and forth from the Trianon to Paris, and from Stello to the doctor. The interruptions were sandwiched between episodes treated in imitation of Shakespeare's comic relief. By contrasting the attitudes of Louis XV and Gilbert, Vigny relied on antithesis to emphasize the injustice of society. He kept his hero nameless until the last possible moment, when a bit of verse revealed his identity.

The second example hammered home the same point, but this time in a constitutional monarchy. In *L'Histoire de Kitty Bell* the ubiquitous Doctor Noir gave an eyewitness account of how Chatterton, a young poet who had successfully forged the work of "Monk Rowley," ironically discovered he could not market his own verse. When Mr. Beckford, the Lord Mayor, and a red-faced, red-nosed caricature of John Bull, refused his protection with a discourse on the good, the useful, and the businessman's outlook, the poet melodramatically cast his poems into the fire and raced up to his garret to swallow opium. Kitty Bell, the beautiful Quaker landlady, had been the only one to understand him.

In this story, Vigny dropped his light touch, treating essentially the same plot in a heavy manner. Even more than its predecessor, the narrative was conceived in dramatic scenes, but monotonously, without relief. The Lord Mayor is a caricature, Chatterton the most adolescent of poets. Once again Vigny began the action almost at its climax by using an epistolary device to reveal the hero's mindset, and confronted two allegorically conceived characters to make his point. The comments of Stello and the doctor took on a sharper edge as patient and psychiatrist exchanged views on the unfairness of life. They grew pedantic over oratory and wit in Paris and compounded digressions in a tale arranged to demonstrate a thesis with great pathos.

Episode three took place during the Terror, at Saint-Lazare, where Doctor Noir was visiting André Chénier. He described the imprisoned aristocrats sentimentally as, ladies and gentlemen to the end, they remained brave and gay. Chénier displayed more fortitude than Gilbert and Chatterton; he waited for execution by discussing with the physician the theory of the poet as seer. He and his fellow prisoners were contrasted sharply with Saint-Juste and Robespierre. Portrayed as an irresponsible madman, the latter toyed with his caller, then signed Chénier's death warrant after a lecture on the poet as counterrevolutionary.

The background of this story intrigued Vigny more than Chatterton's London. He peopled the plot with a host of minor characters, painting miniatures more striking than the larger portraits of the principal figures. The bad revolutionaries range from an objectionable little street urchin who summoned the doctor for Robespierre, to the loutish officers who called out the condemned. Saint-Juste appeared as a maniacal mystic who had concocted a new social structure for France based on a mixture of communalism and vegetarianism. So much did Vigny hate the Revolution that he associated all its aspects with dirt, vulgarity, drunkenness, and brutality. But the royalist sympathizers received kinder treatment. Rose, the jailer's daughter who tried to save Chénier, was clean, smelled of herbs, and radiated kindness, while Blaireau, the doctor's servant, carried on his body a succession of tattoos that listed the political passions of his adult life. A cannoneer temporarily in the doctor's service, he represented the people; but, for Vigny, since his biggest tattoo was a fleur-de-lys, he symbolized the enlightened segment of the masses. He and Rose hornswoggled the first official who came for Chénier; later the gunner and his mates refused to obey the drunken General Henriot, thus causing Robespierre's downfall. He was the grain of sand that turned destiny to a new direction.

The frame of the story was not only the doctor's consultation but also the fact of revolutionary terrorism. Curiously, it was the supposedly practical physician who lapsed into a sentimental defense of the landed aristocracy. As spokesman for Vigny, he even interrupted a dramatic scene in Robespierre's home to refute Joseph de Maistre's theory of the Revolution as a national expiation. He railed at terrorists drunk with the continued emotion of assassination who lived off the death of their betters; they were creatures who dirtied the name of republican.

In the epilogue, Doctor Noir lectured on the social uselessness of the arts, listing the unappreciated great writers of the past. The general and the many became the enemies of the personal and the particular. Vigny resented the encompassing pressure of the mass toward conformism, objected to the religion of material success that had replaced the worship of beauty. He contended that the doctrine of the divine right of the poet led to beauty, hence to truth, an unpopular stand, for the man of power and the man of art were destined enemies. Thus, his "blue devils" dissipated by righteous anger, Stello could take consolation in the dubious notion that God must love poets since he had made so few of them. When Doctor Noir prescribed flight to an ivory tower, Vigny ended in a manner reminiscent of Mérimée: "Stello suivra-t-il l'ordonnance? Je ne le sais guère. Quel est ce Stello? Quel est ce Docteur Noir? Je ne le sais guère."

Vigny's other short narratives, incorporated in *Servitude et Grandeur militaire*, closely resemble Doctor Noir's first consultation. Three tales concern another set of social outcasts, this time the military. Remembering the dreary futility of his own service, Vigny prefaced the trilogy with a disquisition on the fate of the modern soldier, lionized in war, a pariah in peace. A military life had been his birthright but the sudden end of the Imperial epic had cheated him; like many of his contemporaries, he felt he had been born too late for glory. Writing from the bitterness of personal tragedy, he broadened his own experience into that of everyman by seeking the general in the particular.

Once again he attacked the false gods of contemporary society, although, in direct contrast to Lamartine and Hugo, he ridiculed the practice of creating a public personality. No such "singerie littéraire" could make him hide his essential beliefs, so he proposed to defend his position by exposing the ingratitude of a whole nation. Bitterly resentful of Joseph de Maistre's concept of the military as the instrument of a vengeful Providence, Vigny repeated his assertion that the modern bourgeois state had perverted the values of a happier age.

By the time Vigny came to write *Laurette, ou le Cachet rouge, La Veillée de Vincennes,* and *La Canne de jonc* (1835), his conception of short fiction had stabilized. The tales move chronologically as in *Stello*, but this time they concern the period from the Directory to the second emigration. Doctor Noir and Stello were gone, replaced by the omniscient *I* in three illustrations of military abnegation, the theme of the struggle between blind obedience and personal conscience. A hoary device stating Vigny's position framed the collection but, since two of the stories had already appeared in the *Revue des Deux Mondes,* he added introductions and conclusions for each part.

The first tale, *Laurette,* smacks of the melodramatic. During the Bourbon retreat to Belgium, Vigny met an old soldier who provided the required anecdote. The officer had been a merchant captain who one day received a young couple as passengers, along with sealed instructions ordering him to have the young man shot. This he did, arranging for the wife to go out in a boat during the execution but, at the moment the rifles fired, the girl went mad. The captain resigned his post, joined the army, and took the young girl with him everywhere, caring for her even during the retreat from Moscow. When he died at Waterloo, the girl survived only three days.

The drama of the tale sprang from a letter endowed with sinister appearance. It dominated the background, its three red seals glowering down from a clock to symbolize blood and approaching death. The anecdote moved along so quickly that Vigny slowed it down with interpolated remarks, occasionally even portraying the officer's grief. The young man's crime, that of exercising free speech, was revealed at the last possible moment, and Laurette's fate withheld until the very end.

Vigny found himself in the position of having to manipulate the plot to his ends and for the enlightenment of a mass audience. Hence the characters are patently allegorical, with a touch of strangeness. The captain represents human decency; though not sufficiently inquisitive to inquire the names of his passengers, nonetheless he could offer to abandon his ship to live with them in Cayenne. This strange officer forgot important sealed orders, and had to consult a map to discover his position relative to the equator. The young lovers were just that—and no more. The boy died bravely, as befitted a victim of tyranny, and the girl lost her mind at the instant of his execution, clasping her head as if she, too, had been shot. The incredible captain immediately accepted her as a moral charge with which he would be burdened forever.

The second story, *La Veillée de Vincennes*, turned to the theme of military responsibility. In 1819, Vigny and a friend, Timoléon d'Arc, met Mathurin, an old adjutant who lived in constant fear of a reprimand that would spot his record. One night he told them how Marie Antoinette had helped his childhood sweetheart train her voice; Sedaine wrote a play for her; and the young folks married on the proceeds of the only performance Pierrette ever gave. Vigny and Timoléon returned to quarters to be awakened shortly after by an explosion.

Mathurin, anxious to prepare for an inspection, had accidentally set the magazine afire.

Vigny used a structure based on Doctor Noir's first consultation: an introduction in which two men discussed the main point of the tale and related it to the general argument, an anecdote interspersed with reminders of the main theme, and an epilogue that stressed the principal points. The technique had worked well in *Stello,* but here Vigny seemed only to be following a pattern. He and Timoléon might well argue for the rights of the military, but the old soldier seems unbelievable. He had fought for the Revolution, then for Napoleon, yet his loyalty had presumably always remained with the Bourbons. For all his years of service, he broke regulations by carelessly entering a powder magazine with a lighted lantern, killing himself and jeopardizing the fort.

The old recipe failed because the plot had little connection with the principal thesis. Neither Mathurin's love story nor his neglect can be associated with responsibility or love of danger. Moreover, Vigny and Timoléon substituted poorly for Stello and his strange doctor. Timoléon, about to leave the service to please his fiancée, contributed only his presence, his dilemma remaining extraneous to the argument. Instead of considering the difficulties of the professional soldier, Vigny approached the sentimentality of a Lamartine. The family scene stressed togetherness, and Mathurin's love story contained such familiar ingredients as a curé who instructed poor children, a gracious queen who miraculously solved the lovers' problems, and a respectful peasantry that knew its place. Stuffed with emotional recollections of the author's military career, the tale has little unity; even the interruptions meander. Timoléon interrupted the adjutant's anecdote to poke fun at comtemporary literary fads, unaware of the unconscious irony of his remarks. Vigny attempted to pull the plot together by using a symbol, a hen and her chicks living under a cannon, but even the picture of a belligerent chicken that disliked the pacifist bourgeois could not rescue a badly planned narrative.

In the third episode, *La Vie et la Mort du Capitaine Renaud ou la Canne de jonc,* Vigny abandoned the device of the two friends to repeat "word for word" a story told him by its hero. One night in July, 1830, he happened upon an old friend who explained how he had earned the nickname "Malacca cane." The first of the three episodes revolved around Renaud's meeting with Napoleon at Malta, where he had gone with his father, a general officer. The dazzled youngster was under the spell of the magnetic Bonaparte until he witnessed a royal tantrum during which the Emperor admitted his religion of success. After a spell as the prisoner of Admiral Collingwood, Renaud earned his nickname in a tragic night skirmish near Reims, where he killed a Russian child-officer armed only with a malacca stick. Conscience-stricken, he carried the cane everywhere until in 1830 he was shot by a child while retreating with the Guard to Saint Cloud.

The real hero of the narrative is Napoleon, even though legitimist Vigny tried to depict the imperial epic as the work of a power-mad general. The key scene occurred when Napoleon browbeat the Pope, performing like a spoiled adolescent. Collingwood was used antithetically as a modern Bayard while Renaud moved from blind adoration of ruthlessness incarnate to comprehension of devoted service to country and, finally, to the paradoxical position of soldier-pacifist. In the end, the legendary Napoleon won over both the captain and Vigny. Renaud shook the Emperor's hand in forgiveness after the action at Reims, and Vigny could not help admiring the tragic figure of 1814. He was, after all, a Frenchman.

In his effort to communicate to even the dullest, Vigny created a black and white story in which the major characters assumed allegorical proportions at the cost of verisimilitude. Napoleon was a petty, egotistical tyrant, Collingwood a maritime Washington. While establishing this antithesis, Vigny so overlooked the problem of historical accuracy that his Moslems drank wine at Ali-Bonaparte's banquet. Renaud's father was 78 at the time he wrote from prison, 60 at the captain's birth, which would have made him one of Napoleon's oldest generals, though obviously a lusty one. Collingwood had been to sea variously for 33, 40, or 49 years, depending on how much Vigny nodded. Since the outbreak of hostilities, the Admiral had spent only ten days in port, had not seen his family for years. A most peculiar navigator, he calculated his position seated on a gun, and conned his own vessel. Landlubber Vigny even reported that in his zealous patrol of the French coast, Collingwood had worn out seven ships in five years.

Because Vigny understood the brief narrative as an instrument for philosophizing, his thesis often dictated the arrangement of the fictional elements. He tended to overload simple anecdotes, and his constant interruptions and persistent didacticism almost destroyed his fictional world. In the *Canne de jonc* the villain overshadowed characters who supposedly portrayed the correct attitudes. Renaud became only an observer who, after the skirmish, faced the dilemma of the soldier who refuses to kill. The major symbol referred not to his struggle to attain Collingwood's concept of honor, but to the irrationality of war. The good people emerged only as pale shadows in a world dominated by the gigantic man of action. Since Vigny sought in brief fiction only a vehicle for ideas, his work suffered from a kind of bifocalism of thesis and narrative, to the detriment of the latter. He left the possibility of subtleties in prose fiction, the use of implication rather than exposition, unrecognized. In effect, he preferred the more congenial medium of poetry.

George Sand

The tradition of the feminine author had been temporarily suspended by Napoleon, who disapproved of women outside the home, but after his fall Mme de Charrière, Mme de Souza, Mme Cottin, Mme de Krüdner, and the Duchesse de Duras busily fill in the gap. George Sand differed from other lady writers by virtue of a greater measure of talent, but contrary to what might have been hoped, her early handling of brief

fiction showed no more understanding of it than her sister
writers had displayed. True to the cause of feminism, the
advocate of the equality of the sexes concerned herself with
the more vivid aspects of love.

George Sand had her usual difficulty restraining a penchant
to verbosity when she recounted in *Métella* (1833) the sad fate
of a rich Genevan, Olivier, and his elderly mistress, Métella
Mowbray. She spent half the story relating the meanderings
of Olivier's affair and the jealousy of his predecessor, Count
de Buondelmonte, with the result that after the Count left the
plot, Métella's niece, Sarah, had to keep events moving by
making the aunt jealous. The two sections resemble each other:
in the first, the Count resented a young rival; in the second, it
was the aging Métella's turn. Mme Sand intervened to discuss
the incidents or to make such sententious remarks as: "La vie
ressemble plus souvent à un roman qu'un roman ne ressemble à
la vie." She agonized over the problem of a fading beauty who
felt herself cast aside, even managed a story within a story when
the count, picked up by Olivier after an accident, heard from the
young man the story of his own affair. Métella, jealous of her
niece, ironically lost Olivier at the moment she decided to
relinquish him. But George Sand's study of a woman's dilemma
never jelled because her interest in the problem overrode any
concern for organization. She attempted to reach a conclusion
through increasing emotional effects but could not make the
story believable.

In *Mattea,* she dealt with the escapades of silk merchant
Jacomo Spada's daughter, a rebellious girl who was desperately
trying to escape a domineering mother. After pursuing a Turk,
she ran off with a young Greek, and three years later returned
with her husband to take over the family business. Although she
was dealing with young love, a subject sacred to her, George
Sand unexpectedly showed a sense of humor. Jacomo was a well-
henpecked husband and his patroness, the Princess Veneranda,
was a thin, elderly attraction for confidence men. Mattea single-
mindedly pursued Abul, a Moslem merchant, to avoid being

forced to marry a dull cousin, but when she fled to his home, there ensued a scene of burlesque comedy. Since neither spoke the other's language, Abul interpreted her presence as an invitation to seduction; only the appearance of Timothée, the Greek interpreter, saved her honor. Timothée, a caricature of the sharp merchant, manipulated all the other characters to his advantage, like the shrewd valet of French comedy. As for Mattea, she assumed some of the author's traits: she had fashioned her own religion as part of her revolt against her parents, "personnelle, pure, instinctive." She lived like an orphan, trapped between a weak father and a violent mother. All the characters were exaggerated, and the plot stumbled along in accord with the unplanned reactions of conventional figures. The effect approaches satire, with George Sand displaying a playfulness unusual in a full-fledged romantic.

Love, however, was too solemn a subject for her to keep joking about. In *Melchior,* she returned to a serious discussion of the plight of a young Breton sailor, whose wealthy uncle and cousin decided to return home from India aboard the boy's ship. During the long trip, Melchior fell in love with his cousin, Jenny, but they could not marry because Melchior had once been trapped into wedding a mercenary Sicilian. One night the unhappy Melchior leaped into the sea, dragging Jenny along; he was saved, but she perished. He went mad when, on landing, he learned that his wife too had died.

George Sand's principal difficulty was that she wrote before she thought. *Melchior* needed considerable help from the author to reach a conclusion. A long introduction discussed an intricate family setup, Uncle Henri's affairs in India, and the tragedies that overcame Melchior's thirteen brothers and sisters. A complicated web of circumstances kept the youngsters from falling in love immediately, then a half-forgotten marriage intervened to separate them at the moment they realized their love.

She stuffed the tale with romantic clichés. The Lockrists came of a poor, honest family fallen upon hard times. When Uncle Henri made a fortune, he lived in Oriental splendor, even dispatching an elephant to fetch his nephew. Fate pushed the lovers together in romantic inevitability when Melchior sheltered Jenny in his room during a storm. With the ship almost foundering, they became married in the eyes of God as Melchior cried, "Tu ne peux me refuser." But their happiness had to be doomed. Unable to solve their problem, the boy attempted suicide and a murder which led to the ironical ending, leaving him with no choice but to go mad. This strange collection of unarticulated episodes originated in George Sand's urge to wring as much pathos as possible from the situation. As a result, she compounded structural clumsiness with logorrhea. Obviously, short fiction so restricted her crusading spirit that she produced only précis of longer works. Brevity was not her virtue.

Dumas, *père*

Perhaps the least conscious artist among the major romantics, yet certainly one of the best natural storytellers of the nineteenth century, was Alexandre Dumas, *père*. Brash, exuberant, and a perpetual adolescent, he possessed beyond most of his contemporaries the gift of spinning a fascinating yarn. Never interested in theorizing, he fabricated stories from memories, stole plots, or simply rewrote old tales, alway infusing them with his own high sense of excitement. He built episodes of derring-do that have kept his works alive while those of more polished contemporaries have sunk into literary history.

In his early years, when romanticism stirred his blood, he discussed his share of unfortunate lovers predestined to tragedy. But as he grew surer of his talent, he tended to emphasize a restricted number of themes: loyalty to an ideal, to a monarch, to friends, the sanctity of the gentleman's code. His fictional universe, never overly complicated, was primarily that of a young man, in which his characters translated his beliefs into violent action as they upheld the virtues a simple man admired. He liked the excitement and strangeness of the past, and liberally seasoned his tales with colorful crowd scenes, medieval ritual, or carefully explained historical background. Life seemed simpler then, more direct and honest. He never discussed ordinary folk, only those with some quality, good or evil, in large amount, monolithic, hence easier to handle. But Dumas did not consider brief fiction as other than elastic anecdote. Never one for theory or the subtle, he used the form time had proved most successful: a simple tale told in a straight-forward manner.

Like most of the major romantics, Dumas preferred the longer prose forms to spin such popular favorites as *Les Trois Mousquetaires, Le Comte de Monte-Cristo,* and *Vingt ans après* in volume after volume. The historical romance partic-ularly suited his temperament, and he drove his heroes from one thrilling adventure to another, cleverly exploiting a pre-scription that mixed action with sex. Yet, as a practical man well aware of all aspects of his profession, he was among the first to understand the business side of the short narrative when he wrote the *Nouvelles contemporaines* in 1826. Unhappily only four copies were sold; the vogue for brief fiction and the work of Dumas had not yet begun.

One of these tales, *Blanche de Beaulieu,* Dumas later (1831) published in the *Revue des Deux Mondes.* The narrative con-stitutes an act of filial piety, concerned as it is with an episode supposedly from the career of the author's father. In December, 1793, when Generals Marceau and Dumas were pacifying the Vendée, Marceau rescued Blanche de Beaulieu, daughter of the rebel general. He was arranging to hide her in Nantes when Delmar, Robespierre's representative, arrived to have the prisoners shot. Blanche and Marceau fell in love, but Delmar had the general transferred and the girl arrested. Marceau married Blanche in the prison, gave her a red rose, and then rode off to Paris to arrange a pardon. He returned in time to see the executioner hold up a blond head with a rose in its teeth.

The story reveals how shaky Dumas' hand was when he first began to write. His characters came straight from a fledgling romantic's baggage: General Marceau, for example, had the fatal sadness of those destined to die young. Overconscious of the readers, Dumas kept reminding him of events, digressed on the horrors of night fighting, the thoughts of a young man in love, revolutions and violence, Robespierre, and the events of '94. General Dumas' presence merely gave his son the opportunity to brag about his father.

But the ingredients of a typical Dumas story stand out despite the novice's ineptness. General Dumas trapped a spy with primitive detective work. The two forces fought a night engagement around an altar before which women and children prayed. With a keen sense of public taste, Dumas introduced Delmar, an agent of evil. A tender love story was overcast with gloom, and the hero galloped from Paris on an errand of mercy. Dumas drained every drop of excitement the story contained, even ending with the gruesome, if improbable, picture of a head with a rose in its teeth.

In 1835, after the phenomenal success of his play *Antony*, Dumas capitalized on his popularity with the *Souvenirs d'Antony*, a continuation of the *Crimes célèbres*. He had discovered the kind of articulation that provided the skeleton of most of his stories: He would ask a simple question and use well-tested ingredients in response. In this case, he wondered why priests were handsome and vigorous, answering that "pour que le prêtre soit à la hauteur de sa mission, il doit jouir de toute la plénitude de ses facultés physiques et intellectuelles." The case of the abbé Chambard proved his point in reverse. A timid man, the abbé became involved in the affairs of the Siadoux family when a butcher named Cant asked to marry the widowed sister of Saturnin, head of the household. Saturnin was killed when he went to investigate a rumor that Cant already had a wife. His sons threatened the priest unless he revealed a secret heard in the confessional. On his frightened admission that Cant had committed the murder, the boys dragged the butcher to the police. Cant went to the wheel; the abbé was burned alive.

Dumas claimed that the story had been sent to him, as he did in *Un Bal masqué*. At an artist's ball, Antony met a young woman who was frantically seeking her husband. When they discovered the man with his mistress, the angry wife gave herself to Antony, then disappeared, to be seen again only in Antony's fevered dreams. He searched in vain until a letter advised him to visit Père-Lachaise, where he found her grave.

Antony had been urged by fate, as he told Dumas, to an adventure which he might have dreamt. But there were no dreams in *Cherubino et Celestini,* two young Calabrians turned bandit. As children they had killed a famous robber and sold his head to the French, then turned bandit in their turn. Years later, as Jacomo and Hieronomo, they were trapped in the mountains by French soldiers. Jacomo led the band to safety but unfortunately had to kill his own baby to keep it from alerting the troops, for which his mistress, Maria, shot him. She cut off his head and sold it to the French.

Both stories had plots well-worn even when Dumas used them. The masked woman in search of an errant husband, Antony's instant passion for an unknown, her swift surrender and subsequent guilty love, all sprang from a belief in the spring tides of romantic emotion. A great love had to be tragic, its emotional impact strong. The bandit tale incorporated the evil genius, in this case the traitor, plus the excitement of a pursuit and incredible escape. Maria killed her lover in ironical revenge, which she expiated fully in a convent. For the Frenchman of 1830, the tale had the added glamor of being laid in the land of the Mafia during the French occupation.

Most of Dumas' stories contained even more action. In 1838 he wrote a fictional account of Murat's death, though he claimed he was merely reproducing a manuscript given him by an Italian general. History furnished him with a bottomless plunder chest into which he constantly dipped, rearranging fact to make the exciting more so. Thus, in 1841, he published *Dom Martins de Freytas, Praxède,* and *Pierre le Cruel. Dom Martins* concerned one of Dumas' major themes, loyalty to a monarch, an idea which perhaps recalled his father and Napoleon. Dom Martins, who had sworn eternal loyalty to the boy king of Portugal, remained faithful even when Don Sanche was deposed. He surrendered only when assured that his liege was dead. *Pierre le Cruel* repeated the same theme, though here the loyalty went to an ideal of justice. Appointed *primer assistente* of Seville by a monarch who recognized his complete honesty, Juan Pasquale cleaned up the city, and even had the king judged guilty for the murder of a policeman who interrupted his amorous dalliance. The royal person was inviolate, but the police chief extricated himself from an impossible situation by having the head lopped off a statue of the monarch. In *Praxède,* Dumas again stood for justice as young Count Raymond Bérenger defended the honor of the Empress Praxède of Germany, falsely charged with adultery. The Emporer, Henri IV, had kept her imprisoned for 364 days and, without a champion, she would die on the morrow. Raymond arrived in time to kill one of the accusers in a joust; the other turned coward.

Even when Dumas told a ghost story, he focused on the subject of loyalty. In *Les Deux Etudiants* (1849), Beppo dreamed that his friend, Gaetano, had been killed by bandits while he was returning to visit his sick father. Gaetano's ghost guided him to the spot where the murder had been committed, and Beppo isolated the bandits by destroying a bridge; a year later, he married Gaetano's sister, thus fulfilling his friend's dearest wish.

With an uncanny sense of good story, Dumas continued to satisfy the public's appetite for adventure. Ghost stories, tales of adventure snatched from history, sea stories, translations, even, in *Les Fous du docteur Miraglia,* a discussion of the use of the theater in the psychotherapy of the criminally insane. He exploited practically all the basic romantic themes though, by perference, he turned to the long ago and the far away for historical exoticism. But always he trusted in time-honored techniques. What he had to say fitted snugly into old formulae which he had no desire to change.

Musset

For his part, Alfred de Musset came late and reluctantly to the short narrative, not because the bad boy of romanticism had misread the signs of his age, but because he struggled harder than the others to maintain his poetic virginity. Prose meant the common and the ordinary, the practical and the plebs, one of the few beliefs he shared with Boileau. He held out as long as he could, until the need for money drove him to the hated genre. As he wrote in the *Poète déchu,* "Il est juste que je me serve d'un langage que je méprise, d'un grossier instrument sans cordes dont abuse le premier venu." The remuneration might help to satisfy his large tastes, but the confirmed poet despised even the novels of Balzac and George Sand. "Que les Dieux immortels vous assistent et vous préservent des romans nouveaux," began the first *Lettre de Dupuis et Cotonet;* as Musset more succinctly put it "J'aimerais autant être marchand de chandelles." Consequently, he scribbled *finis prosae* with great pleasure on the manuscript of *Croisilles* (1839), although he later had to retract the statement.

Musset accepted a contract for short narratives from the *Revue des Deux Mondes* on March 15, 1833, but four years passed before he honored it, and then he approached the task cavalierly. His career as a writer of tales ran from 1837 to 1853, with half his work produced between 1837 and 1839, most of the rest from 1842 to 1846. So little concerned was Musset with the genre that he named *contes* the stories published before 1839, the later ones *nouvelles,* merely to differentiate the two time periods.

It was his audience that determined, in part, Musset's subjects and mode of composition; his readers dwelt within the narrow confines of the aristocratic Faubourg Saint-Germain or the Chaussée d'Antin. His characters sprang straight from salon conversations, as did the predicaments in which they managed to involve themselves. Brittle conversation fill the tales, and easy maxims, and often a bit of préciosité. Never are the plots permitted to grow dull or lag, even at the cost of poor composition. The incidents revolve around subjective judgments and are grasped statically; most concern purportedly contemporary characters and deal with the emotional involvements of a few people. Addressed to a feminine audience, they are chatty, nearly free-association lectures on love that incorporate a limited conception of the world. Musset never took a moral stance, since he assumed that the mere fact of being in love legitimized an affair. His concern lay only with human quirks, or the sentimental education of a young boy or girl. As an expert on the behavior of teenagers, he explained the psychology of flat characters to readers uninterested in technique or causality. Freed of the discipline of poetry, he permitted his stories to lose concision and proportion, too often indulging in trivia, badinage, or unnecessary explanations. But Musset's visual imagination succeeded in producing a series of sharp, clear portraits of adolescents wrestling with the perplexing vagaries of the affections.

His was a closed universe, unrelated to most experience, the values of which stemmed from love as the supreme good. Normal mentality had no place here, for the concerns of ordinary people lay beyond his ken. He lived in a private world, involved only with his own ego and memories. Musset therefore preferred the old oral tradition, which permitted close relationship with the reader, and avoided the necessity of organizing a fictional world with its own integrity. Usually his tales came in related pairs: the emotional education of a young boy, or a young girl; girl, then boy, hoping to marry out of her, or his, class. Because he was a portraitist (as he admitted in the subtitle of *Mimi Pinson*), he intended to sketch only a single person, with plot and minor characters restricted to the necessary backing for his youngsters. He manipulated events and people carelessly, used coincidence often because, after all, why should he waste time on detestable prose?

From the first, his tales delighted subscribers to the *Revue des Deux Mondes. Emmeline* (1837) set a pattern that Musset generally followed: a short introduction addressed to *Madame* that set the problem, then the characterization of the boy and girl, their brief adventure, and an ending variously happy or unhappy. In this tale, Musset proposed to explain the marriage of wealthy Mlle Duval to a penniless older nobleman, M. de Marsan. Mademoiselle refused all suitors until she met M. de Marsan at a hunt and a year later married him. In 1829, after her husband had left on a trip, Emmeline grew bored, ripe for an affair, and temptation arrived in the person of Gilbert, the experienced romantic hero, pale, with long, dark hair. Emmeline finally surrendered but her happiness lasted only until M. de Marsan discovered the truth two weeks later. Emmeline tried suicide, after which an understanding husband walked with her along the *Allée des soupirs* as she repented.

Musset wrote chattily: "Ce n'est pas un roman que je fais, madame, et vous vous en apercevez bien." When he introduced Gilbert, he intimated that he was presenting one of *Madame's* friends. The plot moved only in terms of the single emotion depicted, its progress made jerky by intrusions and digressions on man in love. The world he encompassed excluded all but this one fact. The characters were stereotypes, never intended as real, with personalities meaningful only to salon society.

Emmeline has a didactic side, to explain the emotional education of a poor rich girl in love with two men, a plot which Musset reversed in *Les Deux Maîtresses* (1837). When Valentin could not choose between a coquettish marquise and a quiet widow, he declared himself to both unsuccessfully. In desperation, he wrote passionately to Mme Delauney—and mailed the letter to the marquise. His luck changed immediately. That night he kissed a cooperative widow, and the next day emerged from hiding in the marquise's pavilion to become her lover. For six weeks he tried to choose between these demanding mistresses until reflection brought wisdom: "L'une est la folie et le plaisir, l'autre est l'amour." Valentin escaped the dilemma by returning to his mother.

The plot rambled even more than that of *Emmeline*. Interested only in the special logic of young passion, Musset was bothered by neither coincidence nor improbability. "Vous trouverez peut-être, madame, que je vous fais un conte invraisemblable. Je connais des gens d'esprit, dans ce siècle de prose, qui soutiendraient très gravement que de pareilles choses ne sont pas possibles, et que, depuis la Révolution, on ne se cache plus dans un pavillon. Il n'y a qu'une réponse à faire a ces incrédules: c'est qu'ils ont sans doute oublié le temps où ils étaient amoureux." Since Musset had discovered with *Emmeline* the appeal of a gossipy style, *Madame* again became his confidante in *Les Deux Maîtresses*. For her he outlined another case study of the emotions that fascinated the salons, swearing that he had heard the anecdote from a Valentin who kissed and told. Musset cared little that such incredible events occurred in so short a time. He was interested in the reactions of "notre étourdi," about whom *Madame* and he held the same opinion. "Le devoir d'un historien est de raconter et de laisser penser ceux qui s'en amusent." Musset liked the type of narrative in which he could act simultaneously as mentor, critic, and master psychologist.

Inevitably he came to the case of the *grisette* in *Frédéric et Bernerette* (1838), where he outlined the classic tale of the provincial student in love with a young hat-maker. Bernerette was a veteran of many affairs yet, for her, Frédéric refused his family's choice. When he finally broke off, she tried suicide, and Frédéric stayed with her in the face of parental pressure until she found another lover. He finally married, but Bernerette killed herself and he tried to end his own life.

In *Frédéric*, Musset was working with the hoary tradition of the *mésalliance* and the true love of a girl no better than she ought to be. Frédéric was a country boy who learned about life in the big city the hard way; he grew up at great cost to himself and to the mistress who sacrificed her own happiness for him. The situation permitted Musset to squeeze a tear from *Madame* over the plight of a nineteenth-century Des Grieux.

Not until he wrote *Le Fils du Titien* did Musset abandon

the structure used for the first three tales. Since this one originated from his own love for Aimée d'Alton, he prudently set
the action back to 1580. To be sure, all the *contes* contained
autobiographical information: Emmeline was Mme Jaubert,
Gilbert was Musset himself, but *Le Fils du Titien* thinly veiled
his gratitude to the woman who tried to save him from himself.
Like the author, Tizianello was wasting talent and fortune until
an unknown sent him a purse and a note on thrift. When he
sought its donor, he found Béatrice Loredano, of a great Venetian family, who was planning to force him to paint as well as
his father. To this end she became his mistress and nagged
him into doing her portrait. He created a masterpiece but never
worked again despite her insistence. The two long lived "comme
deux époux," and after their deaths her more moral family
destroyed the portrait.

With its thin overlay of local color, *Le Fils du Titien* also
concerned a *mésalliance* produced by love and talent. Musset
teased about woman's irresistible urge to remake man according to preconceived notions. Tizianello, however, succeeded in
having Béatrice and his own kind of life by disregarding the
carping, thus achieving a happy ending. Yet the stuff with
which Musset wove was no stronger that the gossamer of the
previous stories, nor had he abandoned the tradition of the
anecdote. By now these had become the only tools he knew
how to use, and he had no intention of trying to control a larger
fictional world.

For *Margot*, Musset again drew on memories of his own
youth when he lightly sketched a peasant girl's unrequited love
for her employer's son. Margot went to Paris at fifteen, as companion to Mme Doradour, and fell in love with Gaston, a
hussar who never recognized her existence. When he married,
Margot tried to drown herself but was rescued by Pierrot. Ten
years later, Gaston, an officer in the defeated Imperial army,
saw Margot and Pierrot happily surrounded by five children.
This was Musset at his best, understanding a teenager in love
with a man unaware of her presence. As usual, the plot was

hopelessly trite and the characters were names acting out conventional circumstances. But he focused attention on a child's discovery that first love and hero worship can burn worse than fire, and he made the point that love does not conquer all, particularly not a major discrepancy in social rank. The emphasis raised the tale from a trite observation to a subtle study in adolescent psychology.

Croisilles (1839) cannot be included among Musset's best. The plot is cruder than usual, the contrived ending preposterous. Because love had to conquer with the aid of a clever young lady, Croisilles blundered into a good marriage. This was the manuscript on which Musset scribbled *finis prosae*. Perhaps he was running out of ideas; certainly this story must have discouraged the artist in him.

However, financial considerations drove Musset back to brief fiction in April, 1844, at which time he resuscitated a plot Nodier had already exploited: the love of two deaf mutes, Camille and the young Marquis de Maubray. Musset came close to melodrama in *Pierre et Camille,* when he stooped to basing the plot on pure pathos: Pierre Maubray is an orphan, Camille a rejected child. The two unfortunates achieve happiness through coincidence, love at first sight, and the mythology of a hard-hearted grandfather who melts at first sight of a grandson.

He did improve, however, in *Le Secret de Javotte* (1844), which recalls Mérimée's *Vase étrusque.* The hero, appropriately named Tristan de Berville, had been wooing Mme de Vernage in competition with M. de la Bretonnière. When Madame intimated that he had acted cowardly in an affair of honor, Tristan challenged La Bretonnière and was killed in a duel.

Le Secret de Javotte was as complicated as Musset ever made his short narratives. Love, jealousy, the irresponsible and unaccountable ways of women still concerned him, but he added the theme of a gentleman's honor, one of the few matters he considered more important than love. Mme de Vernage enjoyed the attentions of two men in her role as an unprincipled coquette, while Tristan was a gentleman who took his code seriously. Armand, his brother, functioned as common sense, with M. de la Bretonnière as the older, less quixotic man who got what he wanted by gamesmanship. Tristan went to his death because he conformed to his value system after fate had made it impossible for him to disprove the thoughtless jibes of a flirt. Love can kill, Musset noted, but a man's honor transcends all other considerations.

In December, 1845, Musset attained perhaps his greatest success with a second portrait of the *grisette* in one of his better-known tales, *Mimi Pinson*. The carefree and good-natured whore had such contemporary interest that the romantics made a fortune with it. Mimi was a perfect example of the species—witty, hardworking, fickle, charitable, and silly. She could pawn her dress to help a friend, and she never thought of the morrow. She was the joy of student supper parties, sang and danced well —and stole cake for the less fortunate. At any moment Mimi could turn from one gentleman friend to another. "Triste joie," Musset summed up what even he recognized as a "profile," the most successful in his gallery of sketches.

Plot had now been reduced to a minimum, the characters to pure stereotypes drawn from contemporary mythology. Musset defended his *grisette* and her sorority for their kindness in a long comparison to good King Robert, digressed on ladies' hats and student mores, and even composed a poem to Mimi. The surprise ending, where the two students were caught sympathizing with young women who could take care of themselves, fitted the half-teasing little story: "Qui dit ce qu'il sait, qui donne ce qu'il a, qui fait ce qu'il peut, n'est pas obligé à davantage."

Reading one of Musset's stories can be amusing, but reading more than two is to court boredom. The subject matter appeals primarily to the very young, to those close to similar problems.

Musset had the talent to analyze interestingly the process whereby his puppets fell in love, suffered frustration, and broke their fragile hearts. Boy met girl or girl met boy in frothy tales of a special never-never land. Nonetheless, thin as his narratives may be, Musset helped Mérimée strip off the overlay of moralizing that was shackling the development of the short narrative. He cared little for the genre, yet by avoiding too much explicit didacticism and relying on his plots to make implicit commentary on life, he indicated the direction the modern form would take. Ever the gentleman, he granted brief fiction the right to speak for itself.

VI

The Second Generation

THE *petits romantiques*, the second generation of romantics, boasted fewer distinguished names than the original group, but they made up for this lack in devotion to a cause. Their faith in their destiny flamed even higher than that of the founders of the movement; they developed an overpowering sense of the sanctity of their mission. Tragically, most of them possessed a modicum of talent but no genius, with the result that their work scarcely outlived them. Most were devout poets who, like their predecessors, turned reluctantly to the brief narrative as it became an accepted mode of literary expression. Yet some of them, Gautier, for instance, would help raise short fiction to a level where it could stand unashamed alongside any of the other genres.

Gautier

Like Mérimée, Théophile Gautier brought a sense of art to the short narrative; like him, he stood out from his contemporaries in his sure knowledge of the possibilities of brief fiction. Whenever the crushing necessity to earn a living permitted, he could produce works with perspective, balanced in emphasis, and cleverly constructed. Though inclined to verbosity and easily enticed into long descriptions from the intoxication of reading his own words, he had a sense of form known to few of his fellow romantics.

Life, however, generally refused him the leisure to polish his narratives. Like Balzac, he struggled incessantly to satisfy a horde of nagging creditors. For a good thirty years, while others were building major reputations, Gautier worked like a hack to liquidate his debts. He debased his large talent by grinding out *feuilletons* because of the legal paper that regularly snowed down on him. Thus, one of his special crosses was a constant need to sacrifice a strong sense of integrity for monetary gain. For example, from April to December, 1848, he produced at least ninety *feuilletons* for *L'Evènement, Le Journal,* and the *Revue des Deux Mondes,* approximately four volumes in eight months.

Under the pressure of time and need, Gautier made everything grist for his mill, but mostly he drew on himself and his friends. His heroes are generally Gautier in disguise, characters drawn from the environment he knew well, or contemporary stereotypes. His protagonists recall the companions of the *Jeune-France* group, slightly eccentric and passionately dedicated to the pursuit of love and beauty. The autobiographical content runs high in many of his stories, which also contain his dreams and hopes. Harried as he was, he still managed to cling to the belief in the dignity of artistic creation he so eloquently defended in the preface to *Mlle de Maupin.*

In his first story, *La Cafetière,* published in *Le Cabinet de lecture* on May 4, 1831, Gautier showed a sense of public taste when he took advantage of current interest in phantoms and the possibility of return from death. As with many of his tales, the story was told in the first person. After a trip to Normandy the sleepless hero was terrified when, as the clock struck eleven, a Falstaffian man stepped from a tapestry and released the other figures. The narrator leaped from bed to waltz with a beautiful girl who called him by name. He lost track of time until his partner fell to the floor at dawn and he, too, fainted. His friends found him dressed in the garments of his host's grandfather and clutching some broken porcelain. Later he moodily began to sketch a coffee pot that stood in the room, producing instead a portrait of his host's sister, Angela, who had died two years before. "Je venais de comprendre qu'il n'y avait plus pour moi de bonheur sur terre!"

In *La Cafetière*, Gautier had written in the temper of his age. Like Nodier and many subsequent imitators, he passed from the real to the hallucinatory to stress the actuality of the dream substance. He arranged his story to provide a logical explanation, a tired man having a nightmare in a strange chateau. Gautier firmly believed in spiritism and the occult. A tapestry come alive, a coffee pot turned beautiful girl, were only devices to introduce the land of the ever present dead. Angela remained faceless because Gautier wished to deal only with the love of a man for a phantom. Consequently, instead of explaining the vision rationally, he introduced the ancient clothing and the portrait of the host's sister. The romantic theme of love forever lost and never enjoyed ended the story.

La Cafetière represents an important point both in Gautier's career and in the history of short prose fiction, despite its trite and conventional nature. He joined Mérimée in moving toward a conception of brief fiction that recalls Poe's definition of the formal short story. The plot was organized toward a single effect, the sudden, sorrowful comprehension of the lover's plight. The dream itself constituted the major portion of the fantasy, economically structured although slightly commonplace. More important, however, he had turned his back on the contemporary habit of padding a story with moralizing digressions.

For more that a year Gautier neglected brief fiction; then, in August, 1832, he published in *La France littéraire* a take-off on Hoffmann, *Onuphrius ou les Vexations fantastiques d'un admirateur d'Hoffmann*. However joking the title, Gautier had the serious intention of reproducing the attitudes of a man verging on schizophrenia. As Balzac normally did, he began *in medias res*: Onuphrius, a full-fledged member of the lunatic fringe of romanticism, arrived late at a rendezvous with the excuse that all the clocks said he was early. When he took

Jacintha to his studio to finish a portrait, he found his painting decorated with a pair of moustaches; as he tried to finish the work, a blow jiggled his elbow, though nobody was present. The next day, four toughs dressed as harlequins threw an unidentified white object under his horse. Onuphrius went to bed, to slip into a nightmare in which he was nailed into a coffin and buried. In the grave, he composed poetry about "la vie dans la mort." Thenceforth Onuphrius lived with his hallucinations. When asked to recite some verse at a salon, he found an ironical young man catching the lines and swallowing them before they could be heard. As his mind slipped, Jacintha cared for him, but Onuphrius persisted in thinking that the devil had made off with his body. He wandered into the world of fantasy and never returned.

While he was writing *Onuphrius*, Gautier's own memory was working well. The plot smacks of *Le Mort ressuscité*, published in the *Mercure de France du XIXe siècle* in 1829; Gérard de Nerval had used the idea of the revived corpse in *La Métempsychose* in 1830. Hugo, Chamiso, Gavarni, Daumier, all provided material; Hoffmann furnished the scene in which Onuphrius recited his poetry; and Gautier even borrowed from his own *Albertus*.

Within a structure similar to that of *La Cafetière*, Gautier stitched these bits and pieces into a coherent whole. As he told Mélanie Waldor on July 26, 1832, "Il y a une idée philosophique dessous." Gautier wanted to describe a man so concerned with watching himself live that his imagination pulled him away from reality. "A force d'être spectateur de son existence, Onuphrius avait oublié celle des autres, et depuis bien longtemps il ne vivait plus qu'au milieu de fantômes. . . . Il aurait pu être le plus grand des poètes, il ne fut que le plus extraordinaire des fous."

Gautier introduced this *romantique forcené* lost in mystical poetry and the study of sorcery at the moment Onuphrius' mind first began to totter. Somewhat of a misanthrope, he fled into the past, into the mystic, the marvelous and the occult, which led him to attribute life's small annoyances to hostile supernatural forces. Gautier intervened to vouch for the nightmare, slipping from the facts to the hallucinations that his friend had described to him. He repeated an idea used in *La Cafetière* when Onuphrius imagined his own funeral, symbolically the death of his mind, to celebrate which he composed *La Vie dans la mort*. The last scene portrayed his divorce from reality, and his insanity took the form of satanic persecution involving the loss of his body. And young Gautier could not refrain from pointing out cynically that Jacintha a year later could not recall his name.

Onuphrius led Gautier into the sketch of a young man who took a ridiculously exaggerated romanticism so seriously that he made it a way of life. He continued working in this vein by creating the portrait of *Elias Wildmanstadius ou l'Homme moyenâge*, prepared as a text for an English engraving of Saint Sebald Square in Nuremberg (1832). The portrait, patterned on Célestin Nanteuil, a friend from the time of the *petit cénacle,* drew on memories of the carefree days of the rue d'Enfer and *Le Camp des Tartares*. For the benefit of "friend reader," Gautier drew up a list of the varieties of *Jeune-France*: *artiste, viveur,* Byronian, with or without beards. Of them all, the type *moyenâge* was most numerous, as, for example, his friend, Elias, presently deceased. Elias had been born too late (an unfortunate historical accident). He lived apart from his fellow man in medieval style, surrounded by medieval furniture, dressed in medieval clothes, sometimes even clanked around the house in armor. He enjoyed a lonely splendor, in which he could sculpt or make miniatures, leaving home only to visit the cathedral. He died two years before Gautier wrote the story, at the same hour lightning struck the church.

Elias Wildmanstadius, like Onuphrius, had lost contact with the world, but he took evasive flight into the supposed simplicity of the past. He had judged his society and, much like Gautier himself, found it repulsive. He was as "dépaysé qu'un sauvage des bords de l'Orénoque dans un cercle de fashionables parisiens." His plight was sketched in a manner reminiscent of Balzac, describing his habits, his home, and the attitudes of a man trying to turn back the clock.

In August of the following year, 1833, Gautier continued exploiting the promising vein of his recent past by publishing the *Jeunes-France, romans goguenards,* composed of six stories and preface. Of these, *Onuphrius* and *Elias Wildmanstadius* had already appeared and were now retouched for the present publication. To them he added *Celle-ci et Celle-là, Sous la table, Le Bol de punch,* and *Daniel Jovard.*

The deliberate satirization of his recent companions seems surprising at first glance. However, two of the stories in this *décameron fashionable* had been intended for the *Contes du bousingo,* a collective enterprise the *petit cénacle* never completed. *Onuphrius Wphly, Elias Wildmanstadius,* Gérard de Nerval's *Main de gloire,* and probably some of Pétrus Borel's *Champavert* had also been intended for the abortive joint effort. Now Gautier's two entries were revised for the *Jeunes-France* in a manner that gave the collection a sharp satiric edge. Superficially, they are humorous tales about the posture of extreme romanticism that mirror the attitude of contemporary literary rebels toward virtue, the social conventions, and bourgeois snobbery. However, Gautier had outgrown his carefree rebellion by 1833. The decline of romanticism into a fad seized on by a lunatic fringe had frightened the bourgeoisie to the point where the conservative *Figaro* launched an attack on what it considered the socially delinquent. Then the great promise of the *petit cénacle* turned into a snare and a delusion as most of its members faded into oblivion, frustrated, never fulfilling their first bold promise. The leader, Pétrus Borel, wildest of them all, would even abandon lycanthropy for a career in the civil service. Others, faddists and extroverts without the seriousness of purpose that distinguished this first Bohemia, were discrediting the romantic movement with their extravagance. Hence, to protect his friends, his memories, and the dignity of his artistic principles, Gautier tinged the sketches with overtones of satire.

He was decidedly not joining the bourgeoisie, but he could not stomach the antics of the eccentrics he listed in *Elias Wildmanstadius*.

Gautier used a sense of humor rare among the romantics in the fashion he had learned from Sterne. He claimed to have written the book because "il est indécent aujourd'hui de ne pas avoir fait un livre, un livre de contes tout au moins." Like Daniel Jovard, he had been converted to the doctrine of the *Jeunes-France*. "Je parle art pendant beaucoup de temps sans ravaler ma salive, et j'appelle bourgeois tous ceux qui ont un col de chemise." The sneer broadened. He hoped to make a mattress of his mistress's hair: "Il ne me manque vraiment que d'être bâtard pour que je sois parfait." Mocking the latest literary trends, he swore that his book contained neither myth nor allegory; in fact, it contained no ideas.

Each of the four added tales dealt with some aspect of life among the imitators of the *bousingos*. Their morality, for example, provided the material for *Sous la table, dialogue bachique sur plusieurs questions de haute morale,* in which Gautier captured a moment in the night life of Roderick and Théodore: At 2 A.M. both lay drunk under a table, where they solemnly discussed virtue, of which they disapproved. Roderick complained of the purity and coldness of his mistress, Théodore criticized the insatiable fire of his own. Before they fell asleep, they agreed to exchange mistresses, but one month later, under the same table, they chorused "Au diable les femmes!"

To the picture of the *Jeunes-France* who escaped into superstition and madness, and of those who fled into the past, Gautier added comments on their easy cynicism, tomcat morality, and evasion through alcohol. The result remains a sketch, despite the story-within-a-story of Roderick's adventure with a poor working girl, satiric in intent, interesting as a glimpse at the antics of the gilded youth of the age. The narrative was drawn out, a fact apparent even to the author: "Les détails sont tout, sans les détails, il n'y a pas d'histoire. D'ailleurs c'est de la couleur locale." The concision, the organization of the first

stories, had been sacrificed because Gautier was writing the kind
of portrait Balzac favored in satiric vindication of his friends.

Le Bol de punch, another sketch of the lunatic fringe, recalled the famous "orgies" of *Le Camp des Tartares* which had
frightened conservative neighbors and contributed to the legend
of the *bousingos*. Gautier described the tale as a "conte panthé-
istique et palingénésique," a jibe at poor Ballanche, his own
particular bête noire. "Notre ami Philadelphe" lived amidst
bric-a-brac, broken furniture, a stuffed peacock, a yatagan, and
a missal. His friends sported beards ranging from the carefully
tended to the deliberately wild. When the *Jeunes-France* decided
to honor Théodore's house with a party, the costumed young
men loudly disagreed on proper procedure. The over-happy
guests noisily indulged in horseplay by throwing a girl out
the window, and the next morning the police led them away to
preserve the peace and security of a middle-class world.

The sketch was intended to interest the morbidly curious in
the mythical high life of the *avant-garde*. The irony deepened
to include the reader in "ce conte véridique." Recalling Paul de
Musset's *Table de nuit*, Gautier discussed with the reader such
points of craftsmanship as the correct use of dialogue and local
color. He punctured the legend of Bohemian life by revealing
the weakness of his own stomach in a tale more loosely woven
than his earlier works; his purpose had shifted from gentle
humor to an attack on the genre itself. While the characters
were exposed as shoddy imitators of hard-working artists, the
author busily pulled the leg of the bourgeois reader by debating
with Albert and Théodore over how to conduct an orgy. In
this tale the digressions stood forth as more important than
the plot itself.

In *Celle-ci et Celle-là ou la Jeune-France passionnée*, Gautier
deflated another misconception of the proper romantic with the
tale of a young man who decided to celebrate his majority by
having "une passion . . . volcanique." Full of wine and high
purpose, Rodolphe decided to seek an affair with a lady he saw
at the Tuileries. Alone with Madame one morning, Rodolphe

moved quickly. Closing the door to avoid a draft, he began kissing her passionately, putting his hand on her breast; Madame succumbed as Rodolphe quoted wildly from *Antony* and *Hernani*. Gautier interrupted here with an irrelevant offer of an engraving of Rodolphe's hand to purchasers of the 19th edition. He claimed that the chastity of the French language prevented his describing the seduction in detail but promised to append the omitted scenes to the next printing so that his lady readers could more easily find them. Rodolphe played out his part by trying to make the lady's bald husband jealous; he even proposed that his friend Albert court Madame so that he might discover the treachery and stab them both. When Rodolphe returned home to find Mariette, his maid, packing to leave, he suddenly discovered his ideal, and Albert entered to explain the moral of the tale: "Il faut être bien fou pour sortir de chez soi dans l'espoir de rencontrer la poésie. La poésie . . . est en nous." Rodolphe apparently heeded his advice, for "Mariette, le lendemain, n'eut qu'un lit à faire."

Gautier called his tale an "histoire libertine, écrite pour l'édification des petites filles." To mock a contemporary critical fad, he solemnly added an explanation of his "myth" for the benefit of a reader whom he called "garde national." Rodolphe represented the human soul in its youth; Madame was classical poetry, brilliant and false; Monsieur stood for coarse common sense, "la prose bête"; Mariette symbolized true poetry, and Albert reason, "la prose fine et délicate."

Celle-ci et Celle-là contains a great many literary reminiscences: Mérimée's *Double Méprise*, Paul de Musset, Walter Scott, and Hugo are well represented, though Gautier showed a fine sense of organization in reshaping these disparate elements. The story follows a common pattern: search for an ideal, deception, and the discovery of the true ideal. Similarly, the plot was structured around old themes: the quest, the pursuit of happiness, the great passion, the eternal triangle, and home is where the heart is.

But Gautier set these out of focus with an irony that threatened the form he practiced. He had almost as little love for prose as Musset, and the current vogue for short fiction annoyed the poet who understood how seriously the popularity of prose was affecting the reception of poetry. Moreover, he was continuing his exposure of the adolescent and untalented imitators of his hard-working friends in a satire as acid as that of the preface of *Mlle de Maupin*. This intent led Gautier to end each scene in ridicule. Thus, Rodolphe the romantic met his ideal wearing a bourgeois night cap. In great shame he leaped off the Pont Royal. As he flew toward the water, he gloated that his death would push the sales of his poems to twelve, but when he rose to the surface he swam to the bank, hat and all. The seduction ended peacefully in a discussion of Racine; and even when he tried to betray himself, the husband laughed and beat him at cards. Rodolphe was a sorry imitation of Don Juan who lived in a dream world fashioned from the untrustworthy matter of books.

The interruptions Gautier set at the end of each scene demonstrate how lightly he took the narrative. He discussed Rodolphe's morals with the lady reader, commented on Mariette, no better than she ought to be, and reviewed the love habits of the French. As an unreconstructed advocate of male supremacy, he proposed an Oriental role for women, "à la maison et au lit." Gautier had as little fondness for his characters as for his plot. Rodolphe constantly smashed his nose against reality: Madame refused to behave in the volcanic manner he expected; Albert would not agree to woo Madame so that he might be stabbed. Rodolphe could not even commit suicide with dignity; he was a perfect example of futility.

Yet the portrait of the inept hero revealed as much of Gautier as of Rodolphe. He was striking at sham, at shoddy recipe literature. Albert spoke for the author when he said, "La poésie . . . est en nous." For him the honest and faithful Mariette *did* represent true poetry. The edge to his complaint came from the deeply wounded feelings of the most vocal representative of art for art's sake, the defender of young poets who resented the fact that a middle-class society was erecting a system of values that excluded them.

This mood carried over into *Daniel Jovard ou la Conversion d'un classique,* the last portrait in his gallery. Daniel, a conservative young Voltairian and an excellent lotto player, went one evening to the Comédie Francaise to perfect his diction. From a *merveilleux,* he learned a new art which so enflamed him that Daniel burned his classics, threw away his conservative clothes, and called his father "garde national." Daniel began to write for the little magazines and drew attention to himself with violent clothes and a wild beard. Since he had a novel and a long poem in preparation, his literary name appeared in catalogues: M . . . us KWpl. . . . He was, as Gautier pointed out, on his way to becoming a publicly recognized talent.

This last story pointed up the reason for Gautier's bitterness. The *petit cénacle* had been hard-working, serious, and committed to artistic integrity, but now he saw Johnnies-come-lately, self-appointed geniuses, reducing others' theories to clichés. Daniel Jovard (the name is a pun on *jobard,* a sucker), metamorphosed from an ordinary citizen into a shaggy literary radical, an obscenity in the eyes of an honest writer. Matters had come to a sorry pass when a beard and an unpronounceable name substituted for real ability.

After the *Jeunes-France,* Gautier turned perforce to other subjects. Satire might satisfy his soul, but he had a precarious living to make. How much the pressures of haste and need would affect his work was revealed in 1833 when he published *Laquelle des deux? Histoire perplexe,* the story of a man unable to decide which of two sisters he loved. The tale lacks the concision of his satirical portraits; inconsequential in plot, it depends primarily on a strange dilemma for interest. The interruptions to chat with the reader, to defend the peculiar story, and to offer asides to *Madame* indicate that, like Balzac, Gautier was falling victim to a salable formula.

Soon, however, his growing interest in the unusual and his

professional's sense of appeal led him to an ancient and honorable theme, the work of art come alive. *Omphale ou la Tapisserie amoureuse, histoire rococo* took him into the world of fantasy he had entered in *La Cafetière*. Told as autobiography, the story concerned the adventures of a boy fresh from a *collège* who came to live in his uncle's pavilion while he learned the trade of *conteur fantastique*. On his wall hung a tapestry representing Hercules at the feet of Omphale. That night the lady left the tapestry to seduce the lad; she returned every evening thereafter until the boy's listlessness moved the uncle to pack away the tapestry and order the youngster home. Years later, the author found the tapestry in an antique shop, and when it was bought by an Englishman, he bowed his head in a moment of silent pity for the unsuspecting purchaser.

In *Omphale*, Gautier used the technique of the dream, common currency at the time, to describe a boy's education. The anecdote revealed characteristics that would become hallmarks of his brief narratives. The irony is still there, but gentler: the uncle's taste in literature was limited to *L'Epître à Zétulbé*, while the boy aspired to become a hack writer. Omphale herself preceded a long line of worldly women whom Gautier delighted in portraying in their boudoirs, dressing, undressing, or bathing. His penchant for long descriptions was now becoming more evident. The uncle's house, the pavilion, the tapestry, and the insatiable lady lent themselves to an attempt to create word pictures that could match paintings, a transformation of one medium into another.

This marriage of the bizarre and the occult with plastic prose reappeared in his next tale, *La Morte amoureuse* (1836). For three years a country priest named Romuald had lived a dual life, by day a conscientious curate, by night a worldly rake— even though he never left the presbytery. Romuald led a separate existence with the beautiful vampire, Clarimonde, whom he had raised from the dead with a kiss. The country pastor struggled unsuccessfully to escape Clarimonde until the abbé

Sérapion disinterred her body. When holy water finally turned her corpse to dust, "une grande ruine venait de se faire au-dedans de moi."

La Morte amoureuse came close to what Poe would define as a short story, with all details arranged to produce "a single narrative effect with the greatest economy of means that is consistent with the utmost emphasis." Baudelaire, who counted this tale among Gautier's masterpieces, noted "le vertige et l'horreur du néant," an end toward which the themes converged. To this purpose the familiar figure of the country priest was transformed into the *Doppelgänger* and Romuald committed sacrilege by succumbing to the traditional *coup de foudre* at the moment of ordination. The abbé Sérapion, acting as Romuald's conscience, furnished the standard against which the priest was measured, a latter-day Tiberge, the voice of doom and the constant friend. The inevitable dream assumed the texture of a nightmare when a mysterious negro servant summoned Romuald and they flew over a desolate plain to his downfall. The themes of the schizoid personality recurred as the hero fell into the uncertainty of not knowing whether he was priest or hellion. Even the solution maintained the tone of horror as, at the witching hour, the two priests dug up the corpse and destroyed it with ritual incantation. And, true to form, Clarimonde's ghost returned to bid Romuald a sorrowful adieu.

Gautier's conception of the story as a letter from a priest to his brother involved him in the problem of handling space and time on different planes. Romuald never left the church, yet traveled over large expanses of the earth; not only a split personality, he led two lives, the drama of which took place in his mind. Hence he faced the necessity of deciding what was dream and what reality. Since Gautier believed they touched, he had to surmount the same artistic difficulties Flaubert would later handle so well in the legend of Saint Julien. But Gautier never satisfactorily solved the problem of how to express simultaneity of action or to show motion over timeless space; he had at his command only the techniques elaborated over the past, none of them suitable. Both Balzac's solution of the flashback and the romantic devices used in nightmare and horror literature proved inadequate for creating the illusions involved in shifts from the clear outlines of time to the vague, distorted shape of fluid dreams. He narrated chronologically in blocks: the *coup de foudre,* the first meeting, the fall, and the rescue, separating the sections as stages of the action. The dream quality he indicated by reiterated explanatory statements and strange events. It would be too much to expect him to solve these problems without the benefit of prior experimentation.

His drift toward exotic subjects led him to publish *Fortunio* in 1837. Musidora, a blond courtesan of great reputation, fell in love with the mysterious Fortunio, spent an idyllic day with him at his country estate, then was jilted for Soudja-Sari, a slave girl bought for three oxen.

Gautier might write to earn a living, but he did not have to like "romans à grandes prétentions," or his own brief narratives, for that matter. In a facetious preface he declared that *"Fortunio* ne prouve rien. . . . *Fortunio* est un hymne à la beauté." Gautier obviously meant to enjoy the story as he deliberately slowed the action by inserting an irrelevant section on Musidora's cat and by arguing constantly with the reader. When the courtesan capitulated almost instantaneously to the hero's well-described charms, Gautier felt it necessary to explain away any objections. Yet he complained of the long, peripatetic novels, with their great platonic passions, duels, and abductions. With his lady reader in mind, he discoursed on clothing, furniture, feminine emotions, even corsets, adding teasing comments on feminine virtue. To her he offered all the popular irrelevancies he thought she would like, even at Fortunio's expense: "Nul héros n'est plus incommode."

Actually, *Fortunio* represented an attempt by Gautier to escape from a world hostile to his conception of poetry and to the manner in which he projected his mind into the fictional world of his daydreams. The belligerent preface of *Mlle de*

Maupin had not long been off the presses with its fierce con-
demnation of modern society. Fortunio lived the life of which
Gautier approved. He had been raised in India so permissively
that at fifteen he had a harem of 500 slaves. His home near
Paris was luxury itself, boasting a private lake on which he
and Musidora floated in amorous dalliance. Fortunio lived as
his weird humor dictated, even whimsically setting Musidora's
house afire and killing her servant; he was subject to no law
but the exclusive ownership of what he wanted. When he finally
decided to blow up his palace and return to India, he casti-
gated France as poor, Paris as dirty. Bourgeois dress, bourgeois
music, newspapers, and railroads he loathed as fit only for the
undiscriminating. Gautier even included a satire on the learned
savants of the Institut. When Musidora found Fortunio's papers
written in a strange language, she consulted a bemused professor who thought the visiting courtesan was a duchess enamored
of him after reading his treatise on Manchu punctuation.

With mockery the overriding consideration, the construction
of the story suffered from a plot that consisted of a string of
unrelated episodes interspersed with sarcastic irrelevancies.
Moreover, Gautier indulged a taste for long plastic descriptions.
The courtesans were described like Titians, the negro servant
like a Veronese. Not too long out of classes under the painter
Rioult, he enjoyed noting color and line, literally painting his
characters with the meticulous art of his beloved Flemish artists.
He lingered over Musidora rising and Musidora bathing. Fortunio's estate, Eldorado, fascinated him, though when he came
to the love scene, he used one of his old tricks: "Il ne nous est
plus permis de rester dans le petit salon."

His days as an angry young man were obviously fast fading.
Not that he approved of the world, but life no longer permitted
him the privilege of complaints. He had to write fast and often
to relieve the pressure of stifling debts, but he could at least
fulfill some of his wishes in stories like *Une Nuit de Cléopâtre*,
in which a queen bored by royal loneliness was pursued by the

love-struck Méïamoun. "Assurément je vais t'aimer," she greeted him. "Je te ferai tuer demain; ta vie pour une nuit."

Une Nuit de Cléopâtre illustrates the kind of structure Gautier came to favor: two or more almost independent scenes, each with possibilities for plastic portrayal. In his successful works he achieved a unity of effect, but the needy Gautier also made the disastrous discovery that he could attain a narrative of the desired length by stringing together a series of such segments. Thus in *Cléopâtre* he portrayed the queen on the Nile, in her bath, and at Méïamoun's last banquet. These pictures formed the key points of the story and permitted full descriptions of the river, the royal barge, Méïamoun, Cleopatra naked, and an Oriental feast. He gave himself full license to describe settings, customs, and clothes, particularly the last. "Nos lectrices seront peut-être curieuses. . . ."

The plot offered Gautier as much of an escape from reality as he had planned for his readers. Like Stendhal, he held in high esteem the powerful of the past who lived life fully, even violently. An arrogant elite untroubled by the petty annoyances that beset the nineteenth century, they seized great pleasures avidly. As he wrote wistfully on the grandeur of life in the ancient East, he contrasted the poverty of constitutional monarchs and the "néant de l'uniformité" to the "existences énormes" of the Pharaohs. The giants had disappeared in France, where it had become impossible even to imagine an orgy. The narrative constituted for him a kind of primitivism, a vision of happy people in happier times who could bargain for perfect happiness, even for a night, though it cost them their lives. Méïamoun shot into the queen's chamber an arrow that carried a declaration of love, then swam the Nile to escape the guards; Méïamoun prowled the grounds until he found an entrance to the palace through a water conduit that led to Cleopatra's bath. In a way, Gautier was also advising the ladies of the nineteenth century on how to act.

His desire to transpose into prose the techniques of the

painter and his yearning for a great, if fictional, love led him to publish *La Toison d'or* (1839) : Tiburce, an artist, journeyed to Antwerp where he was thunderstruck by Rubens' "Descent from the Cross," particularly the portrait of Mary Magdalene. When sixteen-year-old Gretchen fell in love with him, her heart was broken when she heard him talk to Rubens' picture. Tiburce continued to dream of Magdalene until, one day, dressing Gretchen in sixteenth-century costume, he saw a *tableau vivant*. Tiburce promptly forgot Mary Magdalene and married the young girl.

The *Toison d'or* was a variation of an oft-used Gautier plot. The tale rested on the quest theme, with the moral that of *Celle-ci et Celle-là*: the treasure sought afar may be right at home. The narrative consisted of a discussion of Belgian art and architecture unhappily wedded to a love story. Tiburce, an original if lazy artist, did not find nature "true," and began a search for blond beauty which permitted Gautier to present a kind of guidebook. The love story, appended to justify the art criticism, contained all Gautier's usual mannerisms. He challenged his own choice of Gretchen. "Est-ce bien l'héroine qui convient à notre héros?" Unlike the heroines of most contemporary novels, she could not play the piano; she was not thirty years old, nor a princess. Tiburce conformed to the romantic pattern when he followed Gretchen to her door, dropped a note, and sent flowers. Gautier lectured his hero, as he had Rodolphe, on paying attention to the beauty at hand; he solved the inevitable misunderstanding with a stroke of his pen.

By 1839 Gautier had apparently given up any idea of treating short fiction respectfully. It could not measure up to the magic of poetry and it gave him only the solace of withdrawal from an angry world, a means of expressing complaints or seeking wish-fulfillment. *L'Ame de la maison ou la Vie et la Mort d'un grillon* (1839) reveals how badly Gautier felt life was treating him. Not only had he lost his original purity, but his illusions had vanished as practical men tramped over his soul. He retreated into daydreams of better days, to the kitchen of his uncle, a canon with whom he had lived. In this story, on winter nights he and little Maria sat by the fire listening to a cricket that conversed with them. Unfortunately, one day Jacobus Pragmater, the schoolmaster, pulled a leg off the cricket. After the canon left on a trip, no one heard of him for months until, one night, Jacobus watched the priest slide down a moonbeam into the library. The boy learned afterwards that his uncle had been killed in a fall; Maria died soon, then the cricket and Pragmater. Years later, the lad felt that he, too, had become a wounded cricket as he wrote verse and thought of Maria and what might have been.

In this short sketch, the theme of retrospective love was transformed into a kind of fairy tale. In the world of the youngsters, the cricket symbolized the soul of the house, stolen by Jacobus Pragmater. Gautier, who believed in the spirit world, introduced the uncle's ghost not only to maintain the illusion of the fairy tale but because he considered its appearance possible. Skepticism and adult cruelty, intruding on the innocence of a child's dreams, brought disaster to an entire household by destroying a happiness founded on simple belief.

The fable, however, has another meaning when read as a witness of Gautier's bitterness toward life. Gautier blamed the middle class for his having missed the glory acquired by Hugo and other members of the *cénacle*. Jacobus Pragmater, cast in the role of fatality for the fairy tale, was, as his name indicates, the materialistic bourgeois, the exponent of Voltairian doctrines who set contemporary values. A schoolmaster, Pragmater had the matter-of-fact attitude toward the magic of poetry which had brought disaster to Gautier and his friends. It was the coincidence of these two stories that gave the narrative a consistent tone, a mood of sadness that carried overtones of the frustration and disappointment that had been Gautier's lot. Like little Maria, he had lost a dream, that of leading a great poetic movement. Told in a straightforward manner, the melancholy reminiscence indicated what Gautier might have done if he had consistently taken his work seriously.

A growing compulsion to escape, a preoccupation with the occult and the mysterious, led to *Le Chevalier double* (1840), the story of a young knight with a split personality who finally conquered the incubus that dwelt within him. That same year, he published a *conte étranger*, titled *Le Pied de momie*, a first-person narration of a young man's love for the daughter of the Pharaoh Xixouthros, dead thirty centuries. Two years later, with unconscious irony, the great enemy of the middle class published *La Mille et deuxième nuit* in the *Musée des familles*, a mass-medium family magazine. "Once upon a time" young Mahmoud-Ben-Ahmed, a lazy poet, became the lover of the beautiful *péri* Ayesha, who promised to protect him from all harm. In all three tales he could turn his back on the industrial present, fly to medieval France or the East, court a Pharaoh's daughter, or be protected by a lovely fairy. In any case, the hero lived happily ever after.

He used his great skill at evoking the past when, in 1844, he returned to the serious exploitation of antiquity in *Le Roi Candaule*. Five years after the Trojan War, King Candaule married Nyssia, daughter of the satrap Mégabaze. Candaule became so fascinated by his wife's charms that he embarrassed Gygès, captain of his guards, by discussing conjugal delights, and even ordered him to peep through the keyhole as Nyssia undressed. Unfortunately, the horrified queen saw his eyes shine and resolved to wreak vengeance for the ocular adultery. Nyssia drugged Candaule and the captain stabbed him; later, after the Delphic oracle conveniently picked him for the new ruler, Gygès married Nyssia, but nobody ever saw his wife's face.

As on other occasions, Gautier had borrowed the main lines of his narrative. Berthoud's *L'Ami de mon oncle Bertrand* had used the Candaule legend; Boissard had exhibited a *Roi Candaule* in the Venetian style in the salon of 1841. The combination of pictorial and written sources admirably suited Gautier's aim to transpose one art form into another. Just as the beauty of Ctésias had been a major factor in determining the direction of the plot of *La Chaîne d'or*, just as the hero's love for painted beauty formed the basis of *La Toison d'or*, now the intrigue of *Le Roi Candaule* pivoted on the loveliness of a queen. The regression into the distant past gave his imagination great latitude for the major scenes: the marriage, Nyssia's beauty, the betrayal, the queen's anger, her bargain with Gygès, and the murder. Of these, all but the fourth were constructed to let Gautier exercise his considerable descriptive talents. The background, the people in the streets, the wedding procession, the statuary, the palace, all received full treatment. Nyssia fascinated Gautier as much as she did Candaule. He described her preparations for bed with such obvious relish that the well-exposed Nyssia commented ironically that Gygès would soon tire of seeing her disrobe.

The plot received far less attention than the descriptions, with the characters, except for Nyssia, subordinated to the author's passion for creating effects normally produced by the visual arts. Thus, the story was fitted between a series of major descriptions, some of them expanded far beyond proportions useful to the plot. Crowd scenes, regal splendor, strange rituals, Nyssia's strip-tease, all enticed Gautier away from his purpose though they did contribute to reviving the ancient grandeur and exotic aura of the legend. Actually, the facts of the story needed this kind of prop since they consisted of such worn devices as love at first sight, a palace plot based on ambition and jealousy, and a woman's revenge.

Gautier wrought so well that the tale held together despite his readiness to play with words or indulge in irrelevant humor. He remarked on modern tragedy when Candaule decided to seek a confidant, discussed women's feet as Gygès stared goggle-eyed at the naked Nyssia. Furthermore, unlike the normal romantic hero, the captain rushed off to take a cold tub after peeping at the queen. But Gygès fell victim to events he could not control when the king forced him into the ridiculous posture of voyeur. In this world of barbaric violence, two views of life, that of the cultured and sophisticated Candaule and that of the cloistered but savage Nyssia, created tragedy because neither

could adapt to the other. Spartan aggression destroyed culture
when pride in the possession of artistic perfection led Candaule
to commit unpardonable blunders.

When Gautier reluctantly returned to his own times, it was
only to publish *Le Club des Hachichins* (1846), a reminiscence
of the romantics' experiments with drugs. The dream sequence
not only appealed to contemporary interest in mental states,
but also exploited bourgeois convictions on the conduct of
artists. The participants were conveniently described as bearded
men of strange behavior who arrived on the Ile Saint-Louis one
foggy night to pursue their search for an artificial paradise. The
initial descriptions set the atmosphere for the subsequent hallucinations and irrational states so dear to the romantics. Gautier
wrote of a world without logic, beyond thought, where color
and sound merged, where forms shifted fluidly in a universe
without temporal or spatial references. In fact, the visions persisted until a monster released the clock hands he had im-
mobilized.

After the *Hachichins*, Gautier forsook the inspiration of
personal experience and hid in the long ago, the far away, or the
occult. In September, 1846, he published *Le Pavillon sur l'eau*,
a tale of the love of a Chinese boy and girl, "a quelle époque,
c'est ce qu'il importe peu de savoir, les contes n'ont pas besoin
d'une chronologie bien précise." Three years later, in 1849, he
followed this with a children's story, *L'Enfant aux souliers
de pain*. "Ecoutez cette histoire que les grand'mères d'Allemagne
content à leurs petits enfants."

The old touch was missing from these tales, obviously pot-
boilers, but it reappeared in *Arria Marcella, souvenir de Pompeï*
(1852), a curious story involving the same kind of retrospective
love he portrayed in *La Cafetière* and *Omphale*: Young Octavien had gone to Pompeii in search of a dream. As he wandered
in the moonlight, a delighted Octavien slipped back through
time to 79 A.D. to find a beautiful girl whose voluptuous bosom
convinced him she was the woman he sought. Invited to Arria
Marcella's home, he made passionate love until the girl's father,

bearing a cross, made her vanish as the Angelus rang out. Octavien later returned to Pompeii, but never found Arria again.

Gautier cleverly adapted the device of the story within a story to present a young tourist at Pompeii where, as Octavien explained, the truly passionate could make the dead relive outside of time and space. "Dans ce monde où je flotte invisible. . . . En effet, rien ne meurt, tout existe toujours." The world about him was filled with phantoms: "La figuration matérielle ne disparaît que pour les regards vulgaires, et les spectres qui s'en détachent peuplent l'infini." A belief in spirits and the ultimate conquest of time bound the inner story to the outer.

The last days of Pompeii, during the reign of Titus, seemed happy ones to Gautier: *Hic habitat felicitas*. The colorist in him took over in the three sections that constitute the inner story: Pompeii alive, Arria at the play, Arria on her couch. Inspired by the picture of the city which Guérin had exhibited in the Salon of 1841, Gautier painted in prose; incidents were pushed aside in favor of descriptions, and the plot moved along hastily once the picture possibilities had been exhausted. The world into which Octavien passed grew out of Gautier's emotional primitivism. Long ago and far away people lived grandly, loved passionately, and respected the arts. The moral of his fable pointed out that Christianity had ruined a perfection the modern age could not even imagine. The theme of the fated love, the quick invitation more quickly accepted, the instant seduction, the conventional old man with his more conventional curse, all these clichés mattered little to Gautier; he wanted only to establish the dimensions of an era into which he could have fitted. The plot served only to provide space for his mural, while the characters remained faceless stereotypes.

As his debts piled up, Gautier forced an overworked pen to write *Avatar* and *Jettatura* (1856), his last two tales, which he expanded into *feuilletons* by complicating the plot. He abandoned any thought of form for a narrative adjusted to the space requirements of a newspaper. Full of *feuilletoniste* tricks, dreams, superstitions, and improbable events, these tales became a succession of "chapters" arranged like the traditional "cliff-hanger." It was a sad close to a career in short fiction that had once seemed so promising.

Gautier's success in brief fiction came despite his religion of verse and, paradoxically, because of it. The poet in him could not have cared less for plots or character delineation. His heroes resemble Gautier or his friends, projections that provided ready-made personalities. Generally speaking, they represented his own sentiments, were satisfied with a restricted life, and dreamt of a great love. The stories coalesced around the descriptions, and his plots became a succession of loosely connected scenes, each of which provided plastic possibilities. The major portion of his work, then, depended on color, not controlled form; he worked with silhouettes rather than in clearly defined relief, translating the visual into the written. As a result, most of his narratives lack proportion and concision. Technical distinctions seemed to mean little to him, since *Avatar* and *Jettatura* were first labeled *contes*, later *romans*. Despite this, Gautier stands forth as one of the earliest to construct a formal short story. In the *Nuit de Cléopâtre*, *La Cafetière*, and *Le Roi Candaule*, he arranged episode with a sense of perspective and carefully regulated tone and emphasis; in *Arria Marcella* he came to an understanding of the potentialities and limitations of short fiction. Along with Mérimée and, to some extent, Musset, Gautier helped short fiction shed its burden of moralizing. The implicit took over from the explicit and the genre was permitted to speak for itself. Content helped shape form, with the result that, once again, after Mérimée, he pointed out that the brief narrative might function as more than a frame for an anecdote. It could, his work indicated, serve to create the sketch, the portrait, and, most important of all, the formal short story.

Pétrus Borel

As an acknowledged leader of the young men who formed the second generation of romanticism, Gautier summed up the attitudes of the *petit cénacle* toward life and literature. This group had furnished the combatants who filled the balconies at the battle of *Hernani;* it was they who had recognized the implications of the romantic revolution in poetry and eagerly seized on the principle of a poet's poetry. They dreamed of becoming the apostles of a new gospel. "Quel que soit le tumulte de la place publique, que l'art persiste, que l'art s'enquête, que l'art reste fidèle a lui-même, *tenax propositi.*" The cult to which they adhered required the rejection of the utilitarian, prose, and a grubby industrial civilization. Only the pure in heart could be admitted into its arcana after long initiation. As Gautier had proclaimed, "il faut laisser le prose aux boutiques du boulevard." In the preface of *Mlle de Maupin,* he advised the suppression of newspapers, attacked modern economics, and ridiculed nineteenth-century morality. But the youngsters ran into one hard fact: except for the work of giants like Hugo, poetry no longer sold. They persisted in ignoring this fact, and, at one time, as Philothée O'Neddy pointed out in an unpublished fragment, *Une Fièvre de l'époque,* some six thousand neophytes burned to serve the new cause.

But the climate of opinion between 1830 and 1848 remained cold to such exuberance, since the middle class preferred material benefits to the intricacies of experimental verse. Businessmen sought in literature the defense and illustration of the penny saved and the bird in hand, while writers like Pétrus Borel, Alphonse Rabbe, O'Neddy, Lassailly, Esquiros, Jules Lefèvre-Deumier, and Jean Polonius resented the dampening effect of double-entry bookkeeping on their genius. Their deep sense of frustration produced a series of attitudes calculated to extract revenge for their repudiation, and the newspapers retaliated with open hostility toward men it considered antisocial. When the *bousingos* found that the current conception of culture did not include them, the *poète maudit,* a version of the Byronian hero, came into existence, the isolated man hounded by ruthless fate, distinguished from his fellow man by a *feeling* of difference. He and his kind huddled together in a Bohemia which moved to the political left in its disdain for the reign of Louis-Philippe but, paradoxically, also scorned the common man, "ce peuple imbécile." In their revolt, the *petits romantiques* came to picture themselves in the image of Satan, the greatest rebel of them all.

Though poetry may have been the nourishment of their souls, it put little fat on their bodies. They had, it seems, the misfortune of being born with a little talent but no real genius, though this they would discover too late. And their antagonism toward society infuriated the critics, the papers, and even their readers. With no market for their verse, they turned to short prose for an uneasy living, a few even trying their hand at novels like *Trialph* or the *Martyrs d'Arezzo.* But, as they moved to brief fiction, most of them overlooked the lessons taught by Mérimée and Gautier. With little interest in the short form, they fell back on easily salable anecdotes which, in turn, they charged with their own prejudices and their peculiar brand of humor.

Pétrus Borel, with Gautier a leader of the *petits romantiques,* furnished an outstanding example of the second generation romantics. Supposedly endowed with artistic principles of impeccable purity, he nonetheless found it expedient to stretch them when necessity demanded. At first he had had his fiery say when he introduced in the preface of *Champavert* a short essay on "Marchand et voleur est synonyme":

> C'est un oiseau le barde, il doit vieillir austère,
> Sobre, pauvre, ignoré, farouche, soucieux,
> Ne chanter pour aucun et n'avoir rien sur la terre
> Qu'une cape trouée, un poignard et les cieux!

Yet, when he came to write *Madame Putiphar,* the prologue conveyed much of the sadness that pervaded the young romantics as they finally came to suspect the illusory quality of their dreams. They would storm no castles, create no revolutions, leave no flaming monuments to their genius.

> Une douleur renaît pour une évanouie:
> Quand un chagrin s'éteint c'est qu'un autre est éclos;
> La vie est une ronce aux pleurs épanouie.

Early in his literary career, this former architect had become an editor. In 1832 he founded *La Liberté, journal des arts,* a weekly dedicated to expounding principles that would set straight both the Institut and the academic critics. During the few months of the periodical's existence, he worked for "des hommes dévoués . . . à la gêne sous un régime bâtard"; he issued a constant stream of pugnacious articles and manifestoes, then was astonished when the general public failed to support him.

Encroaching economic malnutrition drove this *ci-devant* literary radical to take advantage of the fad for short narratives with *Champavert.* The subtitle, *contes immoraux,* set the tone of a preface in the tradition of *Mlle de Maupin*: "Pétrus Borel s'est tué ce printemps: prions Dieu pour lui, afin que son âme, à laquelle il ne croyait plus, trouve merci devant Dieu qu'il niait, afin que Dieu ne frappe pas l'erreur du même bras que le crime." Like any good romantic, "il portait en lui une tristesse, un chagrin indéfini, vague et profond, la mélancolie était déjà son idiosyncracie."

The *nouvelles,* as he called them, were built around the *bousingos'* favorite themes. In *Monsieur de l'Argentière, l'accusateur,* Apolline, engaged to the prefect who had raised her, was raped in the dark by her fiancé's friend, the public prosecutor. Cast out by the prefect, she abandoned her baby in a sewer and was condemned to die on the scaffold by her attacker. "Il n'osait lui parler de son Dieu juste et bon; sa providence était trop compromise par cette vie fatale."

Borel's short narrative revealed a high-handed but unoriginal manner. The tale began with a long architect's description of a dining room in Louis XV style, actually irrelevant to the plot. Borel's theme came straight out of the mythology of his group: the wicked rich, the poor orphan, unjust justice, the futility of organized religion, and simple virtue conquered by sophisticated evil. All these were arranged in scenes, and each, in contemporary fashion, bore a title: *Was-ist-das?; Mater dolorosa; Moïse sauvé par des eaux;* and *Very wel.* Apolline was a naïve soul who fixed her own doom by asking the prefect to visit her mysteriously at night. This amazing girl received a man in the dark, was loved by him, and only too late realized he wore a beard, hence could not be her fiancé. Pétrus described her torments with meticulous care, his sarcasm steadily growing heavier; the prosecutor mocked Apolline's story and demanded the death penalty; no one could recognize obvious truth. Borel shifted from satire to horror, to pathos, to irony, his incidents regulated to show government officials in the worst possible light. For this reason, the prefect and the prosecutor received harsh treatment, the former given the supreme insult, "plus qu'un porc, c'était un préfet."

Two of the narratives, *Jaquez Barraou le charpentier* and *Three Fingered Jack l'Obi*, took place in exotic parts of the world. Jaquez, a negro husband jealous over his best friend's suspected attentions to his wife, was led by a misunderstanding to battle Juan savagely to the death. *Three Fingered Jack* concerned an outlawed obeah man who rescued Abigail from her picaroon abductors. When her suitor, Quasher, planned to capture Jack and use the reward to buy freedom for himself and Abigail, she tried to warn Jack. Quasher killed him, but wasted the money on women, for which Abigail stabbed him and escaped into the mountains.

Pétrus was merely reworking old tales in his own *bousingo* manner. *Jaquez Barraou* might have been an ordinary story of misunderstanding and the defense of marital honor, but Borel made the jealousy monumental. Much of the narrative was told in dialogue, a technique unusual for a romantic, with local color spread on lavishly. Inevitably he worked in the black humor so characteristic of his group. When Juan shot Jaquez, and the latter insisted on pursuing him, Amada could only exclaim "Jaquez, au moins changez cette chemise; vous exhalez le sang!" In the midst of the murderous fight, while the convent bell tolled, the combatants interrupted their struggle to kneel for prayers. *Three Fingered Jack,* written with *Hernani* in mind, was a tale told by a grandfather about a slave girl with the energy of a Renaissance heroine whose rescue from the white slavers was accomplished by no less than an obeah man. Her lover, Quasher, dreamed of great deeds: "dans mes veines ruissèle un sang qui me ravale . . . ," but was stabbed for infidelity. Pétrus vouched for the authenticity of the tale but retracted with a characteristic sneer: "Ce n'est pas vrai, j'en ai menti par ma gorge. . . . C'est de l'histoire." Because his tale ran short, Borel introduced a "Tiresome Chapter" to discuss his borrowings from Dr. Mosely and the etymology of *obi*, then concluded with a violent attack on slavery.

To these exotic bits, Pétrus added two on medieval subjects, *Don Andréa Vésalius l'anatomiste* and *Dina, la belle Juive*. Vésalius was a figure Borel could shape to his weird tastes. The great scientist, now old, married a young girl who soon proved faithless. Four years later, feeling herself dying, she tried to humiliate her husband by flaunting her adulteries, but he led her to his laboratory where he displayed the skeletons of her three lovers. That night Vésalius added a fourth skeleton to his collection.

Andréa Vésalius was a humorous tale from the point of view of the *petit cénacle*. Pétrus had offered it to Pichot of the *Revue de Paris* as the translation of a Danish story by Isaïe Wagner. Pichot knew better than to offer such strong meat to his readers, though he thoughtfully borrowed the manuscript to write his own *conte anatomique*. The *nouvelle* opened with a riot; the people stormed Vésalius's house, incited by a boy in a brown cape just as the wedding was taking place. Inside, the bride flirted openly with another young man. When the wedding feast ended, Pétrus could not resist the traditional humorous remarks on a May-December marriage. Because the impotent husband could only offer to read to his wife about love, Borel moralized: "Pubères et nubiles, voici l'enseignement que vous pouvez trouver en ceci: C'est qu'il ne faut pas, autant que faire se peut, si vous avez les passions ardentes, épouser un docteur des facultés." Later Amelia thought she had exacted vengeance from the old man, but Pétrus preferred male justice. With

gruesome joy, the author paraded the reader through the dissecting room, with its ornaments of arms and legs. However, in
the interest of fairness, he reported how the anatomist was
exiled at the demand of the superstitious and died of starvation
after a shipwreck.

This taste for the macabre carried over into *Dina,* a tale of
the love of Aymar de la Rochegude for Dina, a Jewess from
Lyon. When Aymar defied his father over marriage with her,
the old man drove him out with a curse. Meanwhile, the unfortunate Dina was raped by a boatman and heaved into the
river. Aymar, who arrived just as she was being buried, asked
the diggers to enlarge the grave, despatched his cloak to his
father, then killed himself.

Pétrus reveled in romantic commonplaces dealing with the
sense of evil and justice. Young love was frustrated by anti-
semitism, because of which a Christian father wounded his son
with an arquebus. A loving child defied his bigoted parent; a
beautiful girl was assaulted and killed by a scoundrel who then
dared demand a fee for rescuing her body. Pétrus jibed at
middle-class values by making the "good" Christians suffer
from comparison with the "lowly" Jews. He could not resist
attacking marriage as a social ill: "Celui qui a inventé le noeud
du mariage a trouvé un bel et spécieux expédient, pour se
venger des humains." His taste for the horrible seemed insatiable; he described Dina's death as minutely as he had the
dissecting room. Like *Andréa Vésalius,* the story proceeded
according to the formula for effectism, but, in this case, moved
from presentiment to increasing horror, then to the double
burial.

Passereau l'écolier combined horror with the triangle theme,
no innovation except that Pétrus passed far beyond the usual
volupté décente to an overt consideration of sex and the *crime
passionnel* in deliberate violation of all contemporary tabus.
Passereau, a student, discovered Philogène, his mistress, to be an
avid reader of Aretino and too close a friend of Colonel
Vogtland. The next day Passereau took Philogène for a walk

through a dark lane and, when she stumbled into an open well, dropped rocks on her head. Passereau then provoked a strange duel with the colonel, the winner of a game of dominoes to kill the loser; Passereau lost but, before the colonel fired, he directed him to the well.

The tale was the usual hodge-podge arranged to permit acid comment and romantic black humor. Passereau could almost fit into Gautier's *Jeunes-France* except that the characterization lacked Théo's gentleness. The story opened with an interpolated anecdote told by one of Passereau's friends. Albert, a self-proclaimed expert on women, was received warmly by his mistress, Estelle, early one morning, only to find in her apartment a cigar, a cane, and a strange pair of shoes. When a man sneezed in the closet, the suave Albert protested: "Mais ce cher collaborateur doit avoir froid, c'est impoli, laissez-moi lui ouvrir!" He politely requested the naked man to join them and, when the latter expostulated at the intrusion, remarked acidly, "Monsieur fait de la poésie un peu classique, dommage." The stranger apologized that he had met the lady only the day before. "Je ne l'aurais pas fait, vieux comme je suis, si mon docteur Lisfranc ne m'avait spécialement ordonné l'accointance pour dissiper une oppression et des congestions sanguines." With great savoir-faire, he invited the student to breakfast with him; and when Estelle asked Albert to return, he coldly demanded her price.

Borel's peculiar sense of humor inevitably interfered with his plot. Passereau dropped in on *his* mistress, to be met with ambiguous statements. When the maid entered the boudoir, Passereau tried to kiss her breasts, "vrai Parnasse à double cime," but the experienced servant cooled him with a quotation from Boileau. The disillusioned lover did not know whether to kill himself or get drunk, and was so confused that the next day he put on his pants backwards, "c'est une distraction royale et Mérovingienne." Though it was raining, he refused to carry an umbrella, "quintessence et symbole de notre époque," and plodded through the puddles declaiming from

Hernani. He sought out Señor Verdugo, M. Sanson, and begged to be guillotined in a corner of the garden. When the executioner regretted, Passereau wrote the Chamber of Deputies proposing that suicides could fill the national treasury by paying a fee for the use of a factory for pleasant self-extermination. And after Philogène fell in the well, her lover called down that he would ask the colonel to fetch along a copy of Aretino. Even as his hero faced death, Borel did not alter his banter. The student insisted on dining with his enemy Dutch treat and quarreled over the merits of Casimir Delavigne.

The last item in the collection was Champavert's testament. This romantic purist believed in the primitive life, but circumstances had robbed him of happiness, "car mon amour est fatal, car je suis funeste comme un gibet." Since he had promised his mistress that she could die with him when he could no longer stagnate in the "étang croupi de la société," he went to Montmartre to inform Flavia of his decision. He spat at heaven, "monde atroce, il faut donc qu'une fille tue son fils, sinon elle perd son honneur." Against the usual background of thunder and lightning, Champavert dug up his child with a dagger while Flavia wept. He soothed his mistress in a manner calculated to horrify the Philistines: "Ne pleure pas, Flavia, qu'est-ce donc? rien: un enfanticide . . . Loi barbare." He tossed the body into the road, stabbed Flavia, then went to Montmartre to commit suicide.

Champavert forms a companion volume to the *Jeunes-France,* with many of the same themes, but, whereas Gautier was mocking the lunatic fringe, Pétrus was reproducing the hurt reactions of the *petit cénacle,* and without Gautier's sense of form. Life overflowed with agony; love, generally for a mistress, met the frustrating disapproval of a stodgy society. Since Borel understood the brief narrative only in terms of length, he simply beaded episodes together to express the *petit romantique*'s sick humor, his young sense of lusty love, and his desire to ruffle the middle class. He brought little to the genre beyond the bizarre incidents of his now faded stories.

In this he represents the reactions of youngsters who despised prose because they considered themselves poets' poets. Borel was the original angry young man in an age that punished its angry young men by placing them in literary Coventry.

Pétrus rapidly discovered this fact of nineteenth-century literary rebellion, as *Jérôme Chasseboeuf* proved. Published in two issues of *L'Artiste* in 1834, it was a syrupy Horatio Alger story about Jérôme, the musically brilliant son of poor parents who left for Russia, where he hoped his music would sell. Jérôme married a baroness by posing as a French noble, then became a famous composer under a pseudonym and faithfully sent his parents an allowance. Poor Pétrus had lost most of his fire; the only remnant of his rebellion showed in his description of Jérôme as an apostle of the new music who, like Berlioz, had gone abroad for recognition. Otherwise the hero exhibited all the standard virtues: he loved his parents, was honest, patriotic, hardworking, and fearless—an obvious candidate for the Chamber.

The last shred of his diminishing talent went into *Le Trésor de la caverne d'Arcueil,* published in April, 1843. An ancient buried treasure, a beautiful sorceress, and a magic show provided the interest. The tale supposedly came from a mysterious prisoner's account of how a rich miser and his nephew had been trapped in an underground vault and died amidst their treasure. Pétrus liberally sprinkled oaths throughout the tale, but nothing could help. He had come to the end of the line and would suffer the cruelest blow a former *bousingo* could receive: poverty drove him to accept a post in Algeria as a government employee.

Xavier Forneret

Only dire circumstances could drive a proper *Jeune-France* to prose, as Borel's case demonstrated, yet one of their coreligionists, though not actually a member of the group, produced startlingly interesting experiments in short fiction. During this seed time of the short narrative not many of the younger romantics had seen the possibilities of a form which, *a priori,* they considered vulgar. Curiously, however, a latter-day purist showed that the ban placed on brief fiction by the unreconstructed poets of romanticism was ready to be lifted.

Xavier Forneret had come to Paris too late for the hectic days of the battle of romanticism, after a discouraging start in his home city of Dijon. When the capital proved no kinder to his talent, he returned home, where he already enjoyed a reputation as an eccentric young man. His play, *L'Homme noir,* put on at his own expense, had been announced in the city streets by halberdiers and heralds in medieval costume. The play failed, an event Forneret mourned by having it printed in white on black. None of his subsequent publications ever received general circulation either, possibly because of the way he advertised them: "Le nouvel ouvrage de M. Xavier Forneret n'est livré qu'aux personnes qui envoient leur nom et leur adresse à l'imprimeur et après examen de leur demande par l'auteur." His major works were typographical curiosities, some printed on the recto, some with only one line per page, all in large letters. Their very titles were disconcerting: *Vapeurs ni prose ni vers, Encore un an de sans titre,* or *Rien . . . Quelque Chose.* Sometimes the author wrote *fin* in the middle of the page, then continued his tale, a manifestation of the kind of black humor that distinguished Pétrus Borel and the *petit cénacle.* Folks in Dijon looked at him askance, since he always wore black and silver and slept in a coffin.

Not all of Xavier's stories rose above the dismal average of the age. *Alabrune ou un Pauvre du soir* repeated the Rastignac theme, more tragically but less competently. Alabrune, a poet, left Lombardy to mend his family's fortunes, leaving behind an aging father, an ailing mother and sister. In a big city, Signora Pudora received him warmly, and agreed to put on his play, sending him home at daybreak to the tolling of the church bells. Warned of the signora's appetite for young men, Alabrune fled to France to escape the woman scorned. On the night a note informed him that his play was to be read, his father arrived to report the death of his mother and sister. Alabrune expired of hunger and fatigue, whereupon his father leaped out the window.

A poor tale, it showed its threadbare quality, as did *Un Crétin et sa harpe,* the pathetic story of a beggar who watched a *grand salon* and died in the cold listening to the music of a glorious soprano. Or *Un Oeil entre deux yeux,* the love of a one-eyed Spanish beauty, Blondina, for the handsome Muguetto, the usual touchy and jealous Spaniard. Blondina was a wealthy, mysterious orphan who had been abandoned as a baby by monks. In love with Muguetto, she was coveted by Sangouligo, who raped her after an epic struggle, then cut off her hair. Muguetto refused to believe her story, whereupon she died, and the bereaved lover committed suicide by grinding up her glass eye and swallowing it.

The tale of hot Spanish passion thus ended in the twist of a romantic convention. Forneret began the tale properly as Muguetto and Blondina discussed the problem of exacting vengeance for infidelity, setting the tone of the narrative and foreshadowing the ending. Blondina, of course, had been foredoomed when the two monks dropped her baby basket. Muguetto had a vision of her death; an old friar told of seeing a spider run over the church's relic. Xavier followed the formula with excruciating accuracy. An orphan of unknown birth, a wild love affair, secretive monks, a vengeful suitor, and rapine—strong stuff, but the literary fare young romantics of Borel's persuasion liked to dish up. Death, of course, followed a misunderstanding.

On occasion, however, Xavier turned his taste for the lugubrious into tales that would arouse the enthusiasm of André Breton and the surrealists. *A neuf heures à Paris* introduced a few fresh ideas into an otherwise commonplace narrative: Fabius, a young Italian, met Anna, a Spaniard, in a brothel, each of them suffering from thwarted love. Anna had been adored by two men, one of whom came to hate her. One night, awaking to find her lover's severed head on her bosom, she slipped into madness. Fabius' father was a political prisoner who had agreed to permit experiment-minded doctors to drain the blood from his body to escape the disgrace of public hanging. Stumbling from the cell, Fabius was kicked in the head by the executioner's horse and carried to a neighboring house where Catherine, a young widow, cared for him. When he discovered that she was dying of consumption, Fabius clumsily tried to kill himself but only succeeded in stabbing her; she died in the sick bed he had just left. Overcome by their grief, Fabius and Anna prayed together, then he killed her and committed suicide.

Superficially this is only a gory catalogue of the varieties of romantic death. In the tradition of *Champavert,* Forneret piled horror upon horror without relief, and these of a kind calculated to remove all concern for verisimilitude. To top it off, Xavier set the scene in a house of ill fame. The tone is consistently grey, since Forneret did not indulge in asides, a unity he reinforced by adopting a first-person point of view for both boy and girl. His story thus became two complementary narratives, with that of Fabius occupying the major portion. Events happened *to* the characters, as in the majority of romantic works, because Forneret envisioned them as puppets upon whom fate acted, always to their sorrow. Happiness was impossible in a mediocre world hostile to all but the conformists. The exceptional were defined in terms of emotional, not intellectual, capacity.

Yet Forneret added something his confrères had overlooked. Unlike his predecessors, who were keenly aware of historical process and the specific, Forneret moved from Fabius and Anna to *the* Italian and *the* Spaniard. Using the technique of the fairy tale, he removed his plot from time, even space, and shifted to a generalized narrative. Most important of all, he successfully introduced poetic devices into brief fiction. His fellow revolutionists did not grant prose much of a measure of respectability but Xavier, by inheritance relieved of the necessity of catering to contemporary taste, chose to try to wed prose to his sense of poetry. He called the tale a "caprice," its themes set around a concern for evil. When Anna spoke, she lapsed into poetic prose of the variety used by Guérin:

> Il y avait bien loin devant le monde qui marche, tout près du soleil, des découpures faites comme par des anges;
> Il y avait des nuages violets qui formaient comme des croisées du Ciel, ouvertes sur la Terre;
> Il y avait des rubans de velours rosé, des pierreries de toute espèce, des soies de toute couleur. . . .

Forneret shifted time planes, and then introduced the concept of silence as an integral part of the narrative. Anna and Fabius executed a series of chants and responses, building a tragic tone incrementally, then Forneret inserted a blank space to heighten the effect. When Fabius addressed his "Anna *de Tous,*" he broke the continuity for dramatic purposes with an indicated silence, as he did when "l'Italien et l'Espagnol se rapprochèrent et se turent; ils priaient." Or, at the climax of the tale

> Ces dernières paroles expirèrent dans un râlement affreux.
> A ce moment, tout, excepté la vie de Fabius et d'Anna, tout d'eux—disparut; ce qui fit un silence.

> .   .   .   .   .

To be sure, the theory of dramatic silence was an old one, formulated by the Greeks and known in medieval times. More recently, Papa Haydn had toyed with it, to be followed more impressively by Beethoven, but Forneret seems the first to have used it as a modern literary artist in his experimentation with brief fiction.

As Xavier continued to write, he moved into dream literature in *Un Rêve c'est,* into the exploitation of the unconscious. "Un rêve. Ne m'interrogez pas; je vous le montre comme je l'ai eu; regardez-le.—Il m'a semblé que c'était ce soir." Forneret lived the inexplicable and unrelated convolutions of a nightmare, during which, like a man writhing in migraine, he saw that "le soleil se promenait sur un carré long de bois, sur lequel il y avait un drap jauni par le temps, sali par les hommes. C'était aussi l'or sur le cuivre." He broke down this image to produce six candles, the coffin of a young girl, holy water on the floor, dried flowers, and an old woman praying by the bier. "Je vis de la mort humaine. Dieu doit me prendre en pitié, mais je crois bien qu'il ne m'exauce pas." Then Xavier began his chant: "Et je vois . . ." Blinking lights, verdigris in the bottom of a vase, a row of headless bodies "qui pourtant ont l'air de tirer une langue dans une bouche sans dents." A woman danced, pursued by a weeping girl, then disappeared under the mantles of four men. "Je l'abandonne.' Xavier woke to see 'une longue ombre sans cheveux, à visage violet, avec des yeux blancs qui s'allongent." He fell out of bed, to hear an owl cry, see a feather fall, "cette plume à l'odeur qui m'étouffait dans mon rêve."

The dream sequence followed the romantic pattern. *Un Rêve c'est* revolves around the picture of a dead girl attended by her mother, and progresses from the major image to the exploitation of its components. Then Xavier shifted to cadenced prose as he had done in *A neuf heures à Paris*. When he finally awoke, Forneret taunted his readers: "Si cela signifiait bien quelque chose, ce ne serait point un rêve." The fantasy, unlike an actual dream, did not wander, but was carefully structured. Colors, black, red, yellow and green, reinforced the eerie gloom of twilight mood. Short, compact, and cadenced, *Un Rêve c'est* is as good as the best of Nodier.

Forneret's masterpiece, perhaps, is *Le Diamant de l'herbe,* the portrait of a young woman waiting for her lover in a deserted pavilion. Xavier began with the folk belief in the ability of the glowworm to foretell events. "Par un soir où tout le souffle des anges volait sur la figure des hommes; par un de ces soirs où l'on voudrait avoir mille poumons pour leur donner à tous cet air qui semble venir des jardins du ciel." He set the scene: moon high, water rippling, and a glowworm predicting a beautiful morrow. Moving from the larger to the smaller, Xavier pictured the interior of the pavilion, the footprints of a man and a woman in the dust, a cleared area near a large armchair, faded flowers, and a coffer on the table. "L'eau coulait comme le temps passe,—toujours." Forneret sketched a young woman in love who came to her rendezvous breathlessly. "Je vais à mon rendez-vous d'amour,—dussé—je vais en passant vous laisser une partie de mon corps sur votre épée, . . . peu m'importe."

> Et elle allait, elle allait, la jeune femme caressant la terre de ses pieds, comme si elle l'eût baisée, parfumant, de son passage, les fleurs en l'air;—laissant partout un peu de ses yeux, un peu de son souffle, un peu de son âme.

In her mind she tasted forthcoming joys, yet was haunted by a sense of impending doom. When she entered the pavilion, the glowworm turned yellow, sign of "une étrange destinée." She knelt to pray and then, when nobody came, ran outside to stumble over her dead lover. The next day the glowworm turned yellow again and she died.

Forneret stripped his narrative of all irrelevancies as he built the tale in scenes, using description to imply much of the background. He called on nature for mood, on the glowworm for foreshadowing and closing the story. Once again he made his plot timeless and never named his characters. As before, he relied on rhythmic prose to increase the emotional impact. To be sure, the plot was a tired one, but his imaginative handling transformed it into one of romanticism's best contributions to short prose fiction.

However small his contribution to the short prose forms, Forneret stands as a landmark in the early development of the genre. By the time Xavier finished writing, the attitude of writers toward brief fiction had changed perceptibly. As is evident in Forneret's own work, the short story had by then earned artistic respectability. Increasingly, it had begun to attract serious writers willing to work at adapting old modes of expression to new needs. On the other hand, at about the same time, romantic experimentation in this medium had come to an end. For fifty years of seed time the romantics had struggled to shape an old structure to nineteenth-century attitudes. To be sure, the anecdote was still the most common form used, but Chateaubriand, Nodier, Mérimée, Gautier, Forneret, and perhaps others had helped rid the genre of its crippling burden of moralizing. They moved from without to within, showed others the possibilities inherent in the short tale for the creation of sketches, portraits, or symbolic comments on modern life. Their contribution was to build the story into an art form divorced from moralizing and from other fictional media. After them it became possible to experiment within the form, to soften and broaden it beyond the rigidity of a Mérimée. In this respect they stand as an esthetically radical wing of romanticism.

In the historical development of the French short narrative, the work of Xavier Forneret does not count heavily. Yet, unlike most of his colleagues in romanticism, he was one of the few in this age of the primacy of the poet who granted prose the right to artistic respectability. True, he used commonplaces—frustrated love, flaming passions—and, like the *bousingos*, he showed a predilection for portraying a world that contained little happiness for the young. But he did not flinch from the artistic heresy of trying to wed poetry to prose. From this marriage of the two media would come superb tales of atmosphere, rythmic and controlled, as Forneret overcame the disability of hackneyed prose by concentrating emotional effect to induce interesting and unified narratives. Moreover, his effective style raised this fiction well above the average of the age. For all this, Xavier Forneret deserves recognition.

VII

A Second Transition

Baudelaire

DURING the first five decades of the nineteenth century short fiction covered the spectrum of artistic achievement, from the very bad to the excellent, but with all their faults the romantics accomplished what their predecessors had never been able to do: they made the brief narrative an autonomous art form. Not all their efforts produced happy results. The bizarre tales of Borel, the sometimes complicated plots of Gautier, the anodyne moralizing of lesser writers had led the short narrative into many a blind alley. It would, in fact, take a Baudelaire, a Nerval, and a Flaubert to indicate both the lunacy of some of the romantic experimentation and those elements which constituted genuine contributions to literature. After them, writers could accept the genre without reservation, and the second half of the nineteenth century would witness the appearance of specialists in the short story like Maupassant. Even the poets made their peace with this medium, however reluctantly. The last to surrender were the purists, the *petits romantiques*, whose attitudes would culminate in Baudelaire's *La Fanfarlo* (1847). The only original bit of brief fiction he ever finished, it was not even considered important enough to be included in his *Oeuvres complètes*.

Not surprisingly, since in 1845-46 Baudelaire was dazzled by Balzac, the story parallels *Béatrix* exactly, although in this case it is Mme de Cromelly who, jilted by her husband for a dancer, begs Samuel Cramer to rescue her. He obliged by ridiculing La Fanfarlo until she became interested in him, and Mme de

Cromelly won back her husband because of his unorthodox methods of seduction.

Actually, Baudelaire was writing an epitaph for the *petits romantiques* and the frenetic fringe of romanticism in a tale that seemed to match Borel at his best. His hero recalls the *Jeunes-France,* particularly *Daniel Jovard* but, unlike Gautier, Baudelaire showed no fondness for writers of that stripe. In a manner similar to Stendhal's, he created his hero partly in his own image, then poked fun at himself in contempt for the kind of man he had become. Thus poor Samuel, or Manuela de Monteverde, as he signed his works, became a double butt, "l'homme des belles oeuvres ratées . . . le dieu de l'impuissance,—dieu moderne et hermaphrodite." After the artistically impotent Cramer read a fine book he could cry, "Voilà qui est assez beau pour être de moi!—et de là à penser: c'est donc de moi." Samuel lived in the world of his overactive imagination, as Mme de Cromelly sensed. Women like her formed the largest section of the nineteenth-century reading public, yet Samuel was surprised to find her intelligent enough to criticize his *Orfraies* as unrealistic, full of bizarre creatures, funereal thoughts, and unhealthy emotions. In him, Baudelaire was satirizing the writers for the little magazines who abused their access to the press by imitating the talent which they denigrated.

Samuel's personality is the major factor of the tale and, given his peculiar values, he can only agree to Mme de Cromelly's challenge. Baudelaire used her plight to fashion a story within a story, one determined by Samuel's eccentric course of action. Initially, he merely gave a flat characterization of the protagonist and furnished the transition that permitted Samuel to meet the lady in the park; then Madame took over to recount her marital woes in a banal story of an abandoned wife that sparked Samuel's frenetic romanticism. "Samuel était hardi comme les papillons, les hannetons et les poètes; il se jetait dans toutes les flammes et entrait par toutes les fenêtres." Simple country girl though she was, Madame de Cromelly maneuvered the pseudosophisticated poet into solving her dilemma by intimating he might expect ample reward. Samuel proclaimed at length "en patois séminariste de blessures à fermer ou à cautériser par l'ouverture de nouvelles plaies," but "plus nigaud qu'un savant," he fell into her trap.

The seduction of La Fanfarlo, in itself a small segment of the story, was the kind of narrative Borel specialized in, full of guile, energy, and the unusual. Samuel carried it off with aplomb, only to find that his reward was other than he had imagined. La Fanfarlo bitterly resented the casual explanation of why he had so ardently pursued her. He now knew passion and "toutes les horreurs de ce mariage vicieux qu'on nomme concubinage." The heartbreak of Baudelaire's affair with Jeanne crept into his world of fiction as Samuel tumbled into everyday life, the father of twins and the author of four pedestrian books, one of them on the synoptic gospels. La Fanfarlo was even plotting to get him the Legion of Honor, his consecration as a bourgeois. And here Baudelaire prophetically slipped into the future tense: "Samuel, mort à la peine, sera cloué *sous la lame*." He treated himself as harshly as Constant had done in *Adolphe*. His work, too, was a *roman de jeunesse*, full of the gall of unhappy autobiography.

Like a Balzac story, *La Fanfarlo* developed inexorably from a set of premises implicit in the lengthy portrait of Samuel. But Baudelaire did not believe in the fictional universe he was creating. Like Mérimée, he treated his characters and their values cavalierly, ever the poet, ill at ease in short fiction. He studded the transitions between episodes with comments on the action, ruined the economy of the tale with remarks on food, wine, architecture, and the dancer's room, or by posing rhetorical questions. And as he filled in an out-sized portrait of Samuel Cramer, he simultaneously inscribed the epitaph of the kind of short fiction so often practised by the *petits romantiques*.

By 1847, writers had become bored with the repetitive complaints of literary rebels and their latter-day lunatic progeny who cried in an ever expanding wilderness. It had become obvious that their cause was lost, and the next generation of writers, among them Baudelaire, did not wish to preside at the funeral. Since Baudelaire was interested primarily in extending the romantic revolution in poetry, *La Fanfarlo* represented for him the repudiation of the kind of writer he despised. The stereotype, the bleatings of unproved talent, and overworked formulae held little attraction for a real genius. He tolled the bell for a kind of short fiction that had come to the end of its road.

Gérard de Nerval

Gérard de Nerval, too, would go beyond the recipes of a Balzac or a Borel, and reject the rigid form in which Mérimée had encased the short narrative. Starting very young, Gérard had steadily added to his early distinction while most of his contemporaries were fading. His poetry echoed with a new sound that conveyed mysterious and seemingly hermetic thoughts. He was a poet's poet, yet the gentle Gérard would write his share of short narratives, some of them strange and wonderful, that would set new directions for brief fiction.

He began inauspiciously in 1832 with *La Main enchantée, histoire macaronique,* originally prepared for the *Contes du bousingo par une camaraderie.* Gérard wrote of Eustache Bouteroue, draper's apprentice during the reign of Henry the Great, who was told by a magician that he would die on the gallows. When the mild Eustache became involved in a duel with a braggart soldier, the terrified youngster begged the magician for a charm to aid him, for which he pledged his hand as bond. Miraculously, Eustache won the duel but when he neglected to pay, the charmed hand slapped a magistrate, for which the boy was sent to the gallows. After he died, the executioner cut off his hand, which dropped into the crowd and scrabbled sideways to the magician.

The story must have pleased Borel; it contained all the ingredients of his own narratives: a prophecy, magic, a duel in which a draper's assistant killed a professional swordsman, an execution described in loving detail, and an ending in the tradition of the *conte fantastique*. Gérard began in Balzacian manner with a long description of the Place Dauphine and the house of the *lieutenant civil du prévost de Paris*. He even commented on his own prolixity. "Je crois qu'il est l'heure de tirer la toile." Then he lavished the same care on the Pont Neuf, delighting in portraits of jugglers and magicians. The plot meandered as he chatted with the reader, "et maintenant, malgré notre respect, ou plutôt notre profond estime pour l'observation des unités dans le roman . . ." The magician read from Albertus Magnus on how to use the hand of a hanged man to rob houses. Nerval poked fun at obsequious Eustache selling pants to the magistrate, naïve Eustache having his fortune told, and terrified Eustache enmeshed in a duel. The middle class received cavalier treatment in a combination of horror tale and ironical portrait.

Thereafter Gérard neglected short fiction until 1839, when he published a war story, *Emilie*. The son of an army surgeon, Gérard was as fascinated by the Napoleonic epic as his contemporaries. He wrung all the pathos possible from the unfortunate marriage of a convalescent French officer to a conquered German. The officer, an orphan with no trade but war, was foredoomed to tragedy by circumstances. A lonely man, he had the promise of happiness snatched from him only because he had killed his bride's father while repulsing a surprise attack. He deliberately courted death and was slain at Hambergen. Gérard even used a dream to foreshadow the conclusion, and the tale ended sentimentally when the abbé who was telling the story asked his listener to accompany him to the convent where Emilie had gone to live.

Four years later, Gérard published *Jemmy*, "imité de l'allemand," the setting for which stands out as unusual in the romantic tradition. Jemmy O'Dougherty finally married the wealthy and ponderous Jacques Toffel but nagged her husband continually until, one day, a runaway horse carried her into the hands of Indian abductors. Five years later she escaped and trudged four hundred miles to find Jacques remarried. Unwanted, she returned to the Indians and became the wife of Chief Tomahawk, whom she immediately began to domesticate. *Jemmy* seems out of place in *Les Filles du feu*, where Gérard eventually placed it. Set in a valley less than two hundred miles from the confluence of the Allegheny and the Monongahela, full of raiding Indians and their tribal life, the narrative contained the proper exoticism for mid-century France. But Nerval chose to mock his characters. Jemmy had to maneuver Jacques, a stolid German, into noticing her. Gérard shrugged, "Que voulez-vous que je fasse d'un allemand." When Jemmy accepted his proposal, Jacques shook hands. And here, the author agreed, the story could have ended, "si l'on ne savait d'ailleurs que les mariages n'offrent pas moins de péripéties que les amours les plus traversés." Jemmy's compulsion to dominate led to her capture, but she quickly organized the poor red men, cooking appetizing meals, weaving a suit for Tomahawk, and showing great nursing skill. She thought nothing of a four-hundred-mile hike, but Nerval chose not to exploit the Enoch Arden theme and drove Jemmy back to the wilderness where she transformed the chief into the kind of man only fate had rescued Jacques from becoming.

Gérard considered *Jemmy* a chronicle, which meant only that the incidents were related chronologically. Thus, as a historian, Gérard could deal with Jacques as the major character, then shift to Jemmy after the marriage. As an omniscient author, Nerval intruded with comments on frontier posses, the German character, marriage, and the danger of traveling at night. He counted on the noble Indian to incite interest, even though Tom acted more like an African chieftain, with tenderer feelings toward his captive than a brave usually displayed. Since his readers knew even less than he about the frontier, Nerval felt no qualms about exploiting a tale of adventure for humorous purposes.

These first stories added little to his reputation, but when Gérard published *L'Histoire du Calife Hakem* in 1847, he began to move from recipe literature to a serious concern with religion and the occult. When the Caliph Hakem tried to alleviate the famine that gripped Cairo by seizing the grain hoards of the rich, he antagonized the Grand Vizier, who had him locked away in a madhouse. But Hakem roused the people and conquered the city. However, when he tried to found a super race by wedding his own sister, he was ambushed by three men, one of whom, his double, tried to protect him. No body was ever found and, according to legend, Hakem survived to flee to the desert, where his followers became the Druses.

In a tale supposedly told by a sheik, Nerval felt comfortable with a legend that demanded historical form and linear development. He disturbed the chronology only to have Hakem's young friend describe his narcotic-induced dreams. Gérard used the *petit romantique* experiments with drugs to emphasize the exalted character of the Caliph, reinforcing this with the theme of the *Doppelgänger*, a reminder that Gérard had recently begun to see his own double. When Hakem came to claim his sister as bride, he found her marrying his twin, Yousouf, who later reappeared as one of the assassins.

Nerval's troubled inner life seeped more and more into his prose as he began to confuse shadow with substance. He liked the chronicle form because his gentle, fey mind could not submit to the kind of discipline that would permit him to control his thoughts on religious history. He delighted in intellectual ramblings as much as he enjoyed wandering around the corners of Paris. And in this mood he recounted *L'Histoire de la reine du matin et de Soliman, prince des Génies* in *Le Voyage en Orient* (1851): Solomon in all his glory was planning to marry Balkis, Queen of Sheba, until she fell in love with Adoniram, the master builder who was beautifying Solomon's capital. The queen fled the city but Adoniram, unfortunately, was murdered as he prepared to join her.

This undistinguished plot offered Gérard a handy skeleton on which he tried unsuccessfully to drape three narratives: Solomon's attempt to marry Balkis, her affair with Adoniram, and the latter's mystic experiences. In the first, Nerval had fun at Solomon's expense as Balkis first praised his poetry, then criticized his contradictory ideas. The queen skilfully fended off the lovesick monarch until he tricked her and, when the persistent king arranged a quiet dinner for two, she drugged him and fled to her lover. Solomon consoled himself with five hundred wives and a plan to gain immortality through magic. But the lowly mite brought his palace tumbling down before the end of the 225 years necessary to complete the spell.

This section contained the elements of a fairy tale, but the second, the queen's affair with Adoniram, followed the old pattern of royal love for a talented commoner. Balkis, who admired the builder's artistry, pursued Adoniram as relentlessly as Solomon stalked her. They met secretly as talent won over birth, and only Solomon's fatuity kept them from being discovered by spies. As usual, a faithful old nurse showed the seemingly trapped lovers how to escape the king's wrath. Balkis fled ("J'emporte avec moi un gage précieux de notre hymen") and Adoniram perished at the hands of three traitorous workers.

Gérard's main concern lay in the portrait of the master creator, around whose adventures he elaborated a theory of art. Adoniram "enfantait des monstres sublimes," which brought him into incessant conflict with Solomon's middle-class tastes. In a continuation of the romantic debate, Balkis warned the king. "Redoutons . . . comme une négation dangereuse, l'idolâtrie de la routine." And a dejected Adoniram repeated to his disciple a cry uttered by most of the romantics. "Nous sommes nés trop tard; le monde est vieux, la vieillesse est débile. . . . Tu copies la nature avec froideur. . . . Enfant, l'art n'est point là; il consiste à créer . . . que ne cherches-tu de même des formes inconnues, des êtres innommés . . . le Dieu multiple de la nature vous a ployés sous le joug; la matière vous limite; votre génie dégénéré se plonge dans les vulgarités de la forme; l'art est perdu."

Adoniram's experiences came from Gérard's enormous readings in the occult. When three villains tried to ruin the castings of his statuary, a phantom whisked Adoniram to the center of the earth, where he heard Tubal-Cain, his ancestor and patron, defend himself against "ce Dieu jalous [qui] a toujours repoussé le génie inventif et fécond." Adoniram discovered that all artists descended from Cain, as his children would, "et leur grandeur fera leur supplice. . . . Ils seront le jouet de l'opulence et de la stupidité heureuse." Adoniram rescued his work with the help of his ancestors but he understood he was destined to receive sorrow in payment for the pleasure he gave. Gérard used the form of the Oriental tale as the vehicle for these ideas, lavishly scattering descriptions of an exotic and legendary world throughout, even invoking the magic of a ring and a fabulous hoopoe that could foretell the future. The fairy story atmosphere led him to associate Balkis with his beloved Isis as the priests and queen uttered prophecies that included even the Crucifixion.

In 1852, Nerval published some old legends of Valois, and repeated a *conte de la veillée* in *La Reine des poissons,* but a private demon was beginning to threaten his sanity. In 1851 he had been hospitalized for a mental disturbance, and his dream world, always on the edge of his consciousness, now became the only reality. He had been drifting toward this state for many years, and his handling of *Balkis* revealed how complex and insistent this inner life had become. In one respect he was following the romantic tradition of concern with mental states although, whereas writers like Nodier and Gautier had exploited hallucinations and emotional disturbances from a rational point of view, Gérard could speak from tragic experience. Not only did he represent the culmination of this trend but, of all the writers of the early nineteenth century, he alone had no need to use alcohol or hashish to free his unconscious.

He faced up to this central fact of his existence in *Sylvie* (1853) as he tried to adapt the irrational to the forms of fiction. "Le rêve est un habit tissé par les fées et d'une délicieuse odeur," he had written in *La Bohême galante.* He remembered "les chimères qui charment et qui égarent au matin de la vie," which he tried to fix with a sense of "l'amère tristesse que laisse un songe évanoui." Leaving the theater one night, he fell into "cet état où l'esprit résiste encore aux bizarres combinaisons du songe, permet souvent de voir se presser en quelques minutes les tableaux les plus saillants d'une longue période de vie." He dreamed he was meeting Adrienne and Sylvie in his beloved village, but his own *Voyage à Cythère* only revealed Adrienne in a convent and Sylvie completely modernized. The return home offered only disillusionment as the poet slid down the long back of time. He realized that Adrienne, Sylvie, Isis, Balkis, Jenny Colon, were aspects of a single strange love when Aurélie pointed out the bitter truth. "Vous cherchez un drame, voilà tout, et le dénoûment vous échappe."

The ending still escaped him in *La Pandore,* in which the dream world almost crowded out reality. Planned as the last of *Les Filles du feu,* an episode enlarged from *Les Amours de Vienne,* Part I had appeared in *Le Mousquetaire* on October 31, 1854; Part II remained unpublished until 1925. As the epigraph from *Faust* indicated, Gérard now felt himself to be two persons, one earthbound, the other ethereal. In Part I, the former courted Pandora in Vienna, an actress with the tastes of Baudelaire's Samuel Cramer, who made him dress only in black because her taste ran to men of ecclesiastical appearance. Nerval wandered over the city, out of funds and unable to satisfy the lady's caprices. But in Part II Gérard slipped into another world. He found Pandora dancing before him as Catherine of Russia. She flew off, and "mon esprit en vain voulut la suivre." While he munched pomegranate seeds, his head was lopped off, then a parrot flew him to Rome where he saw Imperia surrounded by cardinals. "Mon esprit perçait la terre," and he was cast upon the Ile des Amours where three young women revived him—and he awoke. The fragment ended with a tortured prayer. "Je sens encore à mon flanc le bec éternel du vautour dont Alcide m'a délivré. O Jupiter! quand finira mon supplice?"

Never, though he did not know it. *Aurélia ou le Rêve* (1855) was his descent into Hell, during which he finally discovered the sense of his dreams. "Le rêve est une seconde vie. Je n'ai pu percer sans frémir ces portes d'ivoire ou de corne qui nous sépare du monde invisible." Gérard stopped one night before a house the number of which equaled his age. When he met a pale, deep-eyed woman who resembled Aurélia, he recognized an omen of death. That night he wandered through a vast structure where he met a green-winged being dressed like Dürer's Angel of Despair. The next day he visited friends to say goodbye; he was on his way to the East.

"Ici a commencé pour moi ce que j'appellerai l'épanchement du songe dans la vie réelle." He walked toward a star singing; happily he shed his clothes and was waiting to ascend when the police picked him up. Transferred to a hospital, Gérard imagined himself across the Rhine in the home of a maternal uncle, dead for a century. Surrounded by long-deceased relatives, he attended a banquet at which all communicated silently; explanations and images came clearly to his eyes. "Le néant . . . n'existe pas dans le sens que l'on entend; mais la terre est elle-même un corps matériel dont la somme des esprits est l'âme. La matière ne peut pas plus périr que l'esprit, mais elle peut se modifier selon le bien et selon le mal. Notre passé et notre avenir sont solidaires. Nous vivons dans notre race et notre race vit en nous." Gérard watched the people in the room divide and combine until a woman guided him to a neglected garden that suddenly expanded to the sky and assumed feminine form. The garden metamorphosed into a cemetery and voices cried out, "L'univers est dans la nuit." Gradually Nerval calmed down, but when he tried to untangle the figments of his imagination, he sensed that he had "troublé l'harmonie de l'univers magique où mon âme puisait la certitude d'une existence immortelle." A convalescent Gérard cried out in anguish, "Mais le Christ n'est plus," when he heard children praying. He still kept seeing a goddess with the features of Mary, Isis, his mother, and all the women he had loved. He stumbled through a world of shadows, identifying himself with nature, talking to the stars, until one night he followed a spirit into the country, where the divinity of dreams announced that his test was over. Gérard returned to his family happy over his new illumination.

Ever since *René*, the romantics had been attracted to the description of inner states; since Nodier, they had concerned themselves with the relationship between the rational and the irrational, encouraged by contemporary scientific concern with the phenomenon of insanity. The vision, the dream, the hallucination born of stimulants, fascinated them because of the powerful imagery they induced. In a sense, the trend had come full circle; Nerval was following an accredited tradition but, unlike Nodier or Gautier, he did not have to invent. In *Balkis*, *Sylvie*, and *Aurélia*, he combined the quest for the composite woman he loved with his studies of the occult. He enriched *Aurélia* with a theory of art that had not been accepted by many of the romantics but which forms the basis of all great writing. As he came to consider his own life, to forget fiction as only make-believe, he could state in all sincerity that "la mission d'un écrivain est d'analyser sincérement ce qu'il éprouve dans les graves circonstances de la vie." Drawing on the turbulence of his inner anguish for material, he widened immeasurably the scope of the genre as he used content to shape form. A man's subconscious, seen intimately and portrayed with integrity, this would attract the Surrealists and the Freudians, even though Gérard's recollections still followed the structure of the chronicle form, with a beginning, a middle, and an end. Yet he carried concern for the subconscious to its ultimate, disregarding the limitations of time and space, which, for him, did not exist. Gérard transformed the conventions he had received in legacy into the possibility of a literary new vision. Baudelaire had killed off one form of the romantic brief narrative, but Nerval refined another. He fashioned the genre into an instrument fit for modern usage as he rejected the logic of the kind of tale at which Mérimée excelled. After him, after Gautier, Flaubert could come.

❖ ❖ ❖ ❖ ❖ ❖ *VIII* ❖ ❖ ❖ ❖ ❖

Synthesis

Flaubert

HOWEVER MOOT the question of the French romantics' success in brief fiction, it must be admitted that the tales they poured out to fill keepsakes, almanacs, collections, magazines, and newspapers constituted a mine of techniques and experiments from which a conscious artist could pluck all manner of information on the handling of the medium. Since most of the stories followed the anecdote or the chronicle form, many of them varied only in theme and episode. But in a half-century brief fiction had become an autonomous art form cleansed of moralizing, and the practice of a number of serious writers had produced promising new modes of approach. A vast pool of experience was thus accumulated on which men like Gustave Flaubert would draw as, during the second half of the century, they elevated the short narrative to even greater status.

Flaubert was one of the first to profit fully from the romantics' extensive, if chaotic, attempts to understand brief fiction. For years he paid little attention to the *conte*, but when he did, this polished artist demonstrated its enormous potential in three short stories which both summed up the past and foretold future developments. He began the *Trois Contes* in Brittany in the fall of 1875 with *La Légende de Saint Julien l'Hospitalier.* The next year, with a strong sense of imminent death, he started *Un Coeur simple.* (George Sand, for whom he was writing the tale, died in June, 1876, before she could read it.) In August, 1876, he turned to *Hérodias*, completing it in February, 1877. All three were then published in April of that year, though not in the order of their creation. They represent the finest art of a great writer, the superb refinement of the accumulated knowledge of a half-century.

Flaubert built *Un Coeur simple* from his own memories, a quiet tale of a simple peasant girl who served her mistress long and faithfully. The characters came from the accretions of his own past. Félicité, the heroine, was copied from Julie, an old family servant who would live to mourn Flaubert. The children of Félicité's mistress, Mme Aubain, seem to be the author himself and his sister Caroline, while the circumstances surrounding the sale of the widow Aubain's property recall that Flaubert had recently relinquished his own land at Deauville to raise money for his avaricious niece. Even Félicité's parrot, the ill-fated Loulou, was modeled on one belonging to a Trouville sea captain of Flaubert's acquaintance.

Fifty years of dedicated service, that was what Flaubert set out to chronicle. Although life was not kind, Félicité uncomplainingly did all the work at the Aubain household. An orphan, she had been thrown into an unpleasant world that seemed bent on conspiring against her. Her love affair with Théodore ended when he jilted her for a rich old lady. She left home to end up in Pont-l'Evêque as Mme Aubain's maid-of-all-work. Her life settled into the dull routine of a provincial town, where she obtained a meager measure of happiness. Félicité lived vicariously through the two children, Paul and Virginie, willing even to sacrifice her life for them. Quietly, with great compassion, Flaubert told how she lost Paul to school, then Virginie and nephew Victor to death. Despite all she did, nobody showed any gratitude; on the contrary, even her sister's family took advantage of her. Uneducated, she knew the world only through a picture book, religion from Virginie's catechism lessons, yet "toutes ces choses familières dont parle l'Evangile se trouvaient dans sa vie." Félicité suffered through Victor's death, herself wrapped Virginie in a shroud, "et les anciennes connaissances peu à peu s'en allèrent... ," leaving the maid with only a motley collection of other people's cast-offs. She cared for the filthy old

Père Colmiche, and had a mass said for his soul when he died. Her only possession was the parrot, Loulou, given her by Mme Aubain, on which she lavished all the loving kindness with which she had been endowed. When she lost her hearing, her narrow world shut down to the voice of the parrot; she could rescue from life only his stuffed body, which she came to confuse with a cheap lithograph of the Holy Ghost. After the death of her mistress, Félicité "la pleura, comme on ne pleure pas les maîtres." She gave everything she had to the world, Loulou's wormy, broken body to the Corpus Christi altar of repose, but the simple heart died in an abandoned farm as the procession mounted toward her. "Et, quand elle exhala son dernier souffle, elle crut voir, dans les cieux entr'ouverts, un perroquet gigantesque, planant audessus de sa tête."

La Légende de Saint Julien l'Hospitalier moved back into the medieval period as Flaubert drew on a story fixed in a stained glass window. Julien was born under the double prophecy that he would become a saint and, after much slaughter, a member of an emporer's family. As a child, blood lust had driven him to the indiscriminate hunting of game until a stag cursed him: "Un jour, coeur féroce, tu assassineras ton père et ta mère!" When a hastily thrown javelin just missed his mother, Julien became a mercenary, successful enough for the Emperor of Occitania to give him his daughter. He fought down the blood lust until one evening he killed his parents by mistake, and fled from home to do penance. Shunned by mankind, he sought out the lonely places, even tried suicide before "l'idée lui vint d'employer son existence au service des autres." He ran a ferry for a long time until he rowed across a hideous leper, fed him, and warmed him with his own body. As the leper clasped him tight, Julien ascended to heaven in the arms of Christ.

Hérodias took Flaubert farther into the past as he retold the story of Salome and the beheading of John the Baptist. Using the evocative skill developed in *Salammbô*, he reconstructed the day of John's execution, skilfully indicating the political, religious, and personal issues involved. Herod Antipas and Herodias filled the story, she with her driving ambition and hatred for the man who humiliated her, he with his lust. John died not only for insulting her but also because the Romans misunderstood his prophecy of the coming of a new king. As Phanuel and his two friends carried the head away, one of them remarked, "Il est descendu chez les morts annoncer le Christ."

> L'Essénien comprenait maintenant ces paroles: "Pour qu'il croisse, il faut que je diminue."
> Et tous les trois, ayant pris la tête de Iaokanann, s'en allèrent du côté de la Galilée.
> Comme elle était très lourde, ils la portaient alternativement.

From the moment of their publication, the *Trois Contes* received high critical acclaim as tales that showed masterly control of short fiction. In *Un Coeur simple*, Flaubert had taken a common, romantic variation on the chronicle structure and produced a moving story of selflessness. With the exception of a flashback to sketch Félicité's life before her arrival at Pont-l'Evêque, the narrative follows a straight chronological order. *Saint Julien* seems cut from the same pattern, but here Flaubert showed his familiarity with the fairy tale tradition, and the romantic interest in exploring the workings of the human mind. Julien's birth was accompanied by prophecies, one by a monk who rose into the air along a moonbeam, another by a gypsy who vanished in the grass; the required third augury was uttered by a dying stag.

> Solennel comme un patriarche et comme un justicier, pendant qu'une cloche au loin tintait, il répéta trois fois:
> "Maudit, maudit, maudit! Un jour, coeur féroce, tu assassineras ton père et ta mère!"

Flaubert moved in and out of time, in and out of Julien's consciousness, so smoothly that the transitions are scarcely noticeable. Time and the timeless are used polyphonically. Time

vanished as, against a black sky, Julien knew only that "il était
en chasse dans un pays quelconque, depuis un temps indéter-
miné par le fait seul de sa propre existence, tout s'accomplissant
avec la facilité que l'on éprouve dans les rêves." On the day of
his parricide, he slipped back into the dream world, where he
butchered the animals, but now his skill had gone. The dead
creatures silently gathered in a pack around the terrified hunter.
"Une ironie perçait dans leurs allures sournoises. . . . Ils sem-
blaient méditer un plan de vengeance." He stumbled home
deranged, murdered his parents, "et il reconnut terrifié, le
bramement du grand cerf noir." Even when Julien fled, the sun
splashed blood on the clouds, his dreams swelled with nightmares. Only service to mankind saved him, and he underwent
the supreme test when, summoned thrice by the leper, he did
as asked, even warming flesh "colder than a snake and as rough
as a file" with his own naked body.

Hérodias, however, was articulated more like a play by
Racine, with the tragic explosion about to take place as the
story opened. After an introduction that set the scene and detailed the background, the Romans appeared as John was revealed in prison, heaping the curses of the ancient prophets
upon Herodias. Flaubert made John's death inevitable by
building on the queen's ambition, Herod's quick eye for a young
girl, Roman suspicion of a new "king," and priestly rivalries.
Over the whole story hung Phanuel's prophecy: the death of a
man of importance that very night in Machaerus. Except for
the short epilogue, the narrative ended with the presentation
of the head.

Trois Contes historically has been considered a collection of
independent tales, but the epilogue suggests that Flaubert had
something else in mind. "Pour qu'il croisse, il faut que je di-
minue." Viewed in this light, the separate narratives become a
tryptich and a clever use of disparate elements to form a whole.
Short fiction though the components may be, Flaubert intended
to produce a longer work, for which reason he rearranged the
stories in an order other than that of their creation.

In all three the major theme involves Phanuel's statement. Félicité was a maidservant beyond compare; she served Mme Aubain faithfully, dedicating her life to Paul, Virginie, and her nephew. When a bull threatened the children, she was prepared to die for them. In her simple way she is a saint who went out into the world to serve others, that they might increase. Julien also sallied forth, though for purposes of atonement. A nobleman, he debased himself more than the pure Félicité, serving all men humbly, willing to satisfy even the needs of the loathsome leper. And John came out of the wilderness to work for all mankind as the herald of a new religion. He, too, served, at the cost of his life.

All three inhabit merciless worlds. Félicité never expected, and never received, any thanks from those who fed parasitically on her affections. Throughout the narrative, Flaubert ran the theme of the Holy Ghost, theologically the living spirit of God, constantly associating it with Loulou and making it a central part of Félicité's thoughts. Julien, of course, saw Christ and attained recognized sanctity as a result of his self-abasing dedication to others, while John the Baptist became the servant of the savior of mankind. Like Félicité, neither Julien nor John expected any reward; even Julien, though he was atoning for his crimes, decided to consecrate himself to humanity without any assurance of redemption. His world, too, had been a harsh one of humiliation and starvation in which all men turned away from him. John had fled man, like Julien, but returned to face torture and death to accomplish his mission.

A whole series of thematic progressions binds together the three narratives. The sacrifice and service of the characters increase quantitatively, from the unlettered peasant to the noble, to the prophet. Flaubert shifted from Félicité's unthinking devotion to Julien's more complicated motives and the martyrdom of John, as each attained the highest fulfillment of self by the very renunciation of that self. And *Hérodias* ended with the prophecy of the greatest sacrifice. From service to family and travelers, service to an essential belief encompassing all mankind, Flaubert implicitly moved from the three tales to a fourth that is a fundamental part of the culture of western civilization.

Each, then, becomes a parable over which hovers the odor of death. "For greater love hath no man . . ." The major characters set out to accomplish a mission in which they thought only of others. This, according to Flaubert, constituted the highest good attainable by humanity. Although the *Trois Contes* began with Félicité's odyssey, *Saint Julien* was the first written. Therefore, for him, the order established for publication was necessary for the progression of the meaning. But, if that order is reversed, it is apparent that Flaubert had a sense of epic thrust as powerful as that of the medieval cycles; like Hugo in the first series of the *Légende des siècles* (1859) he grouped the smallest genres to produce the largest. The time sequence, in reverse, runs from the ancient to the medieval to the modern, a sweeping span during which only a few lived up to the highest ideals. In this manner, Flaubert set down his final comment on civilization and reached a solution to the doubts raised in *La Tentation de Saint Antoine*.

It would be easy to read into the stories an indication that Flaubert had finally come to a belief in the Christian God, since all three *contes* treat Christian themes sympathetically. But the third version of *La Tentation de Saint Antoine* (1874), in which Flaubert decided that he could not justify Christianity more than any other religion, precludes such a statement. The meaning of the tales rises, rather, from Flaubert's life. A nonbeliever, he had recently had to sell his patrimony and turn the money over to his niece; each year he consumed more of his inheritance to keep Caroline and her husband from bankruptcy. Moreover, he sensed that he, too, was near death as he saw old friends vanishing. He envied Félicité, Julien, and John their solid faith; in their actions he found the greatest good, one he hoped he was approximating in his treatment of the avaricious Caroline. *Trois Contes,* then, is Flaubert's tribute to a nonintellectual code.

The romantic experiments with short fiction came to their full flowering in *Trois Contes*. Baudelaire had laughed to death the frenetic plots of the *petits romantiques,* but from the more solid tradition established over fifty years, Flaubert drew the experience that permitted him to write his masterpiece. The moralizing, the effectism, the uncomplicated chronological structure of the anecdote, even the different but equally rigid conception of Mérimée gave way to a softer, more malleable form that passed beyond fact and event into suggestion. The time-bound form of the past was freed from age-old restrictions and shown to be capable of even the most sophisticated statement. The short narrative had finally come into its own.

IX

Conclusion

DURING some fifty years of anguished travail, French short fiction slowly groped its way to mature respectability. In that relatively short time it managed to overcome the taint of plebeian origins which for centuries had kept the brief narrative in literary limbo. Long-deferred change overtook time-honored but limited forms when the coincidence of a technological revolution with major political and social disruptions forced early nineteenth-century writers to transform the *conte* into a more supple instrument for artistic communication.

When the age of romanticism opened, French writers firmly held to a premise established by classical theorists, namely, that form somehow preceded content, from which it could exist separately. As a result, critics had established almost sacrosanct categories and hierarchies for poetry and the drama. Prose had received only cursory attention, principally because of the seventeenth century's determined orientation toward verse. Even during the Enlightenment, after the surprising success of *Manon Lescaut*, when men like Voltaire honed the *conte philosophique* to razor edge for social satire, the short narrative gained no greater measure of prestige. It smacked too much of the people and for the people in a nation whose literary tastes were set by an aristocracy.

The short tales this elite scorned were all constructed along the same lines: histories or anecdotes in which one event marched after another in strict chronological order. Authors firmly controlled their universe as they told stories they felt impelled to interpret for their readers. They interposed themselves between their audience and an action which was heavily encumbered with moral commentary. Since the chronicle had served for centuries as a vehicle for social commentary, no one, prior to the Revolution, had compelling reasons to modify a structure which satisfied the small demands made on it. As long as the social organization remained relatively unchanged, as long as the literary pundits continued to look askance at prose, long or short, the traditional brief narrative persisted.

However, by the end of the eighteenth century this kind of short fiction had been fully exploited. It was used variously for exempla, moral apologues, fairy tales, love stories, anecdotes about the never-ending war between the classes and the professions, and had been converted into the *conte philosophique*. But when the aftermath of the Revolution produced a new mind-set and situations hitherto unsuspected, writers found themselves unable to make the old forms of short fiction fit their needs. Chénier to the contrary, new wine could not always be funneled into old bottles. Consequently, when technological advances encouraged a vast increase in brief narratives for an expanding reader market, the more conscious artists began groping their way out of the restrictions of the simple anecdote.

Not all writers, by any means, felt constrained by the chronicle form. After all, old shoes fit most comfortably. Xavier de Maistre, for instance, perpetuated a variation in the *conte philosophique* or fashioned rambling, sentimental tales of adventure; Mme de Staël gladly accepted the eighteenth-century tradition of the recital of frustrated love. For almost three decades after the Revolution most of the brief fiction that poured off the presses, even after 1828, steadfastly held to the old formulae. During the Empire and the Restoration, reaction to the traumatic experiences of the fall of the Ancien Régime and the Napoleonic epic had been carefully controlled as successive governments labored long and diligently to suppress evidence of an age a-borning.

Even so, strange new attitudes toward short tales glimmered through the dull gray uniformity of the usual productions as a more modern vision of the world came into being along with the special problems of an industrial era. Nodier contentedly used tried and true recipes until he came to write of his own preoccupations. Then, in *Smarra* and *La Fée aux miettes,* he found it necessary to modify the ancient format in order to be able to discuss his concern with the irrational and the world of nightmares. Similarly, although Benjamin Constant acknowledged *Adolphe* to be an anecdote, with it he began to reverse the contemporary penchant for burying plots under an overlay of moralizing, lavishly applied from without. Preach he did, but he permitted the plot itself to yield a meaning more powerful than any interjected commentary.

These men represented those few sensitively attuned writers who were striving to communicate within the terms of a rapidly changing society. They received little aid or comfort until the beginning of the real popularity of short fiction at the end of the Restoration when they were joined by Stendhal, Balzac, and Mérimée. The talents of this trio helped considerably to increase the genre's literary respectability. In so doing, Balzac paradoxically arrived at a recipe that would congeal brief fiction into a shape that later generations would find hard to modify. At the turn of the century writers were in the process of shifting the focus of interest from classical psychology to a new vision of human nature. Previous literature had been based on the notion of man always and everywhere the same. Consequently, authors had dealt in what they imagined to be universals, in terms of the code of the seventeenth century. By the end of the eighteenth century most of their observations had degenerated into well polished clichés that had been repeated *ad nauseam.* After the Revolution, interest moved naturally from the general to the particular. What differentiated men became more important than what joined them. The personal, the subjective, the mysterious inner world of the mind and the emotions offered enticingly fresh subject matter, particularly since the early nineteenth century was reacting violently to the confusion and hypertensions of the aftermath of revolt. The problems of man's fate, of his relationship both to himself and to his fellows obviously needed reappraisal. The whole puzzling world of the subconscious, of obscure but powerful motive, led to a universe of discourse in which the illogical became logical, where the unfathomable and the fleeting needed to be fixed and clarified. Chateaubriand's *René* and Constant's *Adolphe* opened vistas of possibilities for the interpretation of hidden personality that dazzled their contemporaries.

Their very success, however, worked to slow the development of brief fiction. The delineation of a strong or peculiarly different character became the hallmark of what the romantics recognized as superior short fiction. Thus, Balzac's first essays into social caricature and Stendhal's *Chroniques* both originated from a desire to unveil full-length portraits of exceptional, strong-willed personages or contemporary stereotypes.

The brief narrative, in fact, lent itself particularly well to the bold sketching of unusual figures, since the elements of a tale necessarily had to be concentrated. This possibility was emphasized by the writing of contemporary historians, many of whom conceived of events as personified by men like Louis XIV, Louis XVI, or Napoleon. Modern history had come into being during the romantic era when Frenchmen began to wonder about the origins of the cataclysmic events that had rudely precipitated them into an uncomfortably alien world. Men of all political faiths sought to reconstruct a system of cause to effect that would illuminate the present, either for solace, for defense, or as a political weapon. The subsequent debates not only entranced the public but ultimately influenced the writing of fiction.

Between 1830 and 1850 the study of history was transformed into an academic discipline as the learned and the curious struggled to resolve the riddle of 1789. As long as historians clung to the chronicle form, an easy and time-sanctioned mode of relating events in sequence, they had no difficulty expressing themselves. But inevitably they ran into the same problems that plagued fiction writers of the time when they attempted to impose meaning on the facts, to interpret data, or to impute a specific direction to history itself. How to express the simultaneity of episodes, how to indicate the manner in which events from different times coincided at a single moment, how to grasp the essence of a personality, became crucial problems of exposition. Already in 1830, Carlyle had noted this in his essay, "On History."

> The most gifted man can observe, still more can record, only the *series* of his own impressions; his observation, therefore, to say nothing of its other imperfections, must be *successive,* while the things done were often *simultaneous;* the things done were not a series, but a group. It is not in acted, as it is in written History. . . . So all Narrative is, by its nature, of only one dimension; only travels forward towards one, or towards successive points: Narrative is *linear,* Action is *solid.*

The historians busily theorized on the proper method of describing the flow of events, or of indicating patterns of action and their relationship to character. How lively the discussions, how diverse and fruitful the inquiry, can be grasped from the multitude of answers and the asperity with which the historians approached their task. A sharp debate raged all over Europe as preface countered preface, essay answered academic lecture: Ranke believed that he could resuscitate the past *wie es eigentlich gewesen;* Carlyle understood history as biography. Like many others, Michelet fell back on philosophy, on Vico, to find a mechanism built into society that explained all change and, to some extent, forecast the future. The positivistically inclined Englishman, Buckle, looked to history for the general laws of human development, while Marx and Engels emphasized the materialistic basis of events. All these conceptions of how to grasp the patterns of the past, how to tell a story, offered writers new approaches to the modes of narration, the vivid depiction of places, the recreation of character in the process of developing. Interested as the romantics were in history, they learned lessons from the academicians that enlarged their art. The modern short story would be enriched as a result of all this hard-won experience.

Concerned as they were with the various aspects of the past, the historians and fiction writers both had to face the problem of handling time sequences. A modest little philosopher, Pierre-Simon Ballanche, had revealed time to the French romantics as a function of life. Following his lead, they constructed a series of major themes around the subject of time as the corrosive of personality, time as an irretrievable element, the nostalgia of the elusive past, and time as the river of life. In due course the romantics came to recognize psychological time as distinct from clock time, and their interest in dreams, hallucinations, and drug-induced states led them to consider timelessness within time. Some of their characters, then, became conglomerations of these various aspects of time, and the story of a major personality, as in several of Gautier's tales, Nerval's personal revelations, or Flaubert's *Saint-Julien,* could be related on various time planes. The romantics learned slowly and clumsily, but they did pass on to later generations the secret of the destruction and mastery of time. And in passing beyond the limits of chronology, of history as sequence, they added a major dimension to the short narrative.

Not surprisingly, therefore, the first man to cut through the welter of custom to produce the most distinguished short fiction of the first half of the century possessed a sharp sense of history. Prosper Mérimée did not consider himself a professional writer, but he had the talent and quality of imagination that enabled him to jolt the brief narrative from the rut of tradition. Never a theorist, he still succeeded in transforming the anecdote and the *histoire* into what later critics would laboriously categorize as sketches, tales, ghost stories, formal short stories, chronicles, and *nouvelles.* Like Constant, he preferred to let the contours of the plot reveal the statement he was making and the obvious polish and power of his work contributed to give the genre a shape which later writers could accept as viable. For Mérimée was a modern man, concerned, however ironically, with contemporary matters. His mind functioned neatly and precisely along the lines of selection required of a master of brief fiction. The result was a production of the first order, surprising in that it came during the infancy of the modern short story, when he could not benefit from previous experimentation.

Mérimée, however, was to remain almost isolated as other forces conspired to frustrate any consistent attempt to fashion the brief tale into a major literary instrument. Most of the romantics accepted without challenge the ancient dictum that poetry represented the highest form of literary endeavor. Their revolution was fashioned around the proposition that verse forms freed of old taboos could best serve to mirror the nascent post-revolutionary world. Even though they wrote novels or occasionally dabbled in the shorter forms, they never warmed to prose. Many of them were controlled by imaginations tinged with Titanism because of which they found it difficult to narrow their field of vision, a fact which Hugo soon proved to his own satisfaction. Of them all, only Musset managed to intrigue a small, select audience with frothy, sentimentally gay stories directed at a special audience.

Moreover, just when the short narrative appeared to promise a retarded emergence from adolescence, it ran headlong into its giant cousin, the novel. The longer prose forms had come into the nineteenth century under the prestigious aegis of Sir Walter Scott, a recommendation which helped counterbalance the adverse opinions of seventeenth- and eighteenth-century critics. Romantics like Hugo and Vigny gravitated toward it because of its possibilities for large-scale murals and for the representation of elaborate theses on the meaning of contemporary civilization. With Stendhal and Balzac, among many, the novel rapidly became the proletarian form of literature, one that could claim a far larger audience than either poetry or the theater. Thus, at the very moment circumstances seemed auspicious for the blossoming of the genre, the spectacular development of the novel worked to stunt its growth. When writers like Stendhal and Balzac turned to short fiction, they did so as novelists, both concerned only with manipulating prose to create life-sized portraits. As a result, Stendhal treated plot cavalierly, though chronologically, indulging a ripe taste for the bizarre in order to underline those facets of his strong-willed creations that he wished to emphasize. For his part, Balzac quickly elaborated a structural recipe which was also intended to delineate the main features of a character. Each worked as a novelist too, and brought his conception of the longer forms to the shorter. The result was a treatment of the genre as the miniature of a larger work. Occasionally the method succeeded—in the *Curé de Tours,* for example—but, in the main, this approach did little to advance the cause of brief fiction.

Despite these handicaps, between 1830 and approximately 1850 a few conscious artists wrestled manfully with the problem of adapting the short tale to their needs. As long as authors were content to make the anecdote fit their needs, they failed to produce any works of distinction. But when, like Mérimée, they learned to let new content shape new form, they began to create the varieties of modern short fiction. In his unhurried moments Gautier incised formal short stories in Poe's manner while Forneret exploited the enormous possibilities of the tale for atmosphere and suggestion.

Of course the old notions of the anecdote and the chronicle were never destroyed; they continued to provide the principal source of tales for the hungry periodical press. Most of the short narratives revolved around boy-girl situations, preached a staunch middle-class morality, or led the reader into the vicarious pleasures of high adventure. But changes inevitably were made, even by the most conservative, because only then could writers use short fiction as a vehicle for their metaphysical ideas, their political views, and their radical notions of human psychology, all of which overflowed the limits of the chronicle or the anecdote. Though their philosophies of history tended toward the doctrine of optimism, the romantics viewed life as a bitter conflict carried on in a hostile world, as witness the astounding number of stories of frustration, murder, suicide, and dismal failure. To explain this paradox, most of the romantics jettisoned the Catholicism into which they had been born to develop personal beliefs, many of which leaned heavily on the old Chain of Being. But they knew that the short narrative did not offer sufficient leeway for philosophical explanations of a post-Newtonian universe; hence, like Gautier and Nerval, they favored themes that originated in their notions of a man's relationship to the world beyond. To be sure, tales of the supernatural formed part of every author's stock in trade but, for men like Gautier, the supernatural lay close at hand, the vampires were as real as the capacity to communicate with the dead. In the realm of the political, a vigilant censor and stern judges restricted the political hostility of a Gautier or a Nerval to the more subtle forms of objection. Consequently, dislike of the regime in power appeared in satirical portraits of the middle class, irony directed at its cultural values, or unflattering sketches of the ruling cliques. But in the domain of the new psychology, the romantics made a major contribution as, from Chateaubriand on, they investigated a new vision of man. Their theory of genius rested on the uniqueness of the artist; the greater the genius, the greater his variation from the norm, a concept which inevitably led them to the neurotic and the eccentric. All the romantics held dearly to this notion as they constructed public personalities for their readers and for themselves. The younger generation in particular fell into this trap, since the theory stressed the exaggerated and the unusual in its unequal conflict with conformists and literary reactionaries. As the romantics moved from exterior to interior portraiture, they became concerned with inner states, the mind and imagination. Consequently, their plots shifted from the sequential relation of incidents to the depiction of a reaction to events, and their writing changed from expository to revelatory. How the characters felt became more important than what they did, a trend that would culminate in Gérard de Nerval's writings. This was the seed time of the genre. Time has proved unkind to many of the tales that delighted readers of the first half of the nineteenth century. To moderns they seem unsophisticated, often blatantly sentimental or naive, insufficiently ambiguous and ambivalent for an age nursed on popularizations of Freud. But it must be realized that this profusion of tales was necessary for later writers to learn their trade. The various shapes of modern brief fiction grew not a priori but from the realization that certain forms communicated contemporary ideas, attitudes, and reactions more successfully than others. Out of the mass of short fiction printed between 1800 and 1850 came a number of exceptional narratives which critics would later decide to distinguish as the sketch, the tale, the formal short story, or the portrait. Meanwhile, the word *conte* was assuming a meaning that differentiated it from *nouvelle,* the former accepted as more concentrated, with one major episode, the latter more complex and consisting of several scenes. But the problem of definition would not attract attention until after 1850, when, with the main lines of brief fiction more discernible, critics would endeavor to impose distinctions after the fact on the basis of past practice. In a sense, their efforts threatened to congeal the form.

At any rate, by mid-century French writers had learned to recognize the limitations as well as the potentialities of short prose during the accretion of a huge pool of experience. Baudelaire did later writers a great service by indicating, in his satire of an overworked tradition, how much one branch of the short narrative had degenerated into commonplaces and boring repetitions. Like him, Nerval and Flaubert not only had the fulsome advantage of hindsight but were able to work with the new conception of the role of the imagination in literature which the poets had developed. The romantics had made emotion felt and emotion expressed central to their work, thus encouraging effectism. Through works like *Les Orientales* and Gautier's prose and poetry, writers began an association with the plastic arts that made literature highly pictorial. But by 1850 the conception of the function of the imagination had shifted from the romantic doctrine of *vérité,* from a picture-making faculty so handy for the chronicler, to that of the creation of poetic imagery and suggestion. Thus the work of Nerval and Flaubert profited not only from new concepts of form, but from broader use of the visionary, a perception of the world totally unlike that of Chateaubriand and Nodier. Form came to be conceived as a function of content and at that point the men of the age of romanticism could boast that they had created a new genre for a new world.

Index

❦   *Index*   **245**